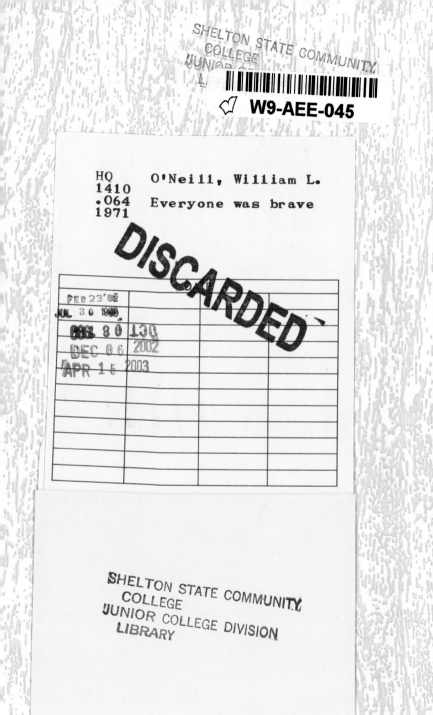

everyone was brave

· ·

. . . .

*"Everybody was brave from the moment
she came into the room."*
—Newton D. Baker of Florence Kelley

WILLIAM L. O'NEILL

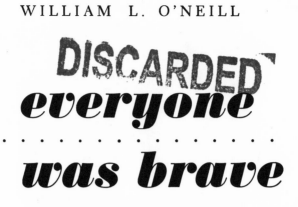

everyone

was brave

a history of feminism in America

With a New Afterword by the Author

Quadrangle / The New York Times Book Co.

Library of Congress Catalog Card Number: 71-78313
International Standard Book Number: 0-8129-6192-7

Typography by Joan Stoliar

Third paperback printing, April 1976

· · · · · · · · · · · · · ·
for Carol

preface

. . . .

it took seventy-two years for women to get the vote. Generations wore out their lives in pursuit of it. Some women went to jail, many picketed, marched, and protested their deprived state in other ways. In the last stages of the fight for equal suffrage, literally millions of women contributed something to the cause. Yet when the vote was gained it made little difference to the feminine condition. A few women were elected to office, political campaigning became more refined, and the sex lives of candidates were more rigorously policed. The ballot did not materially help women to advance their most urgent causes; even worse, it did not help women to better themselves or improve their status. The struggle for women's rights ended during the 1920's, leaving men in clear possession of the commanding places in American life. For nearly a century women had demanded access to college and the professions, and had insisted on their right to work at whichever jobs they pleased. They did make progress on the economic front, but when the feminist movement ended they were still discriminated against in many ways. They found employment on the lowest rungs of the occupational ladder; few made much money or rose very high no matter what their field of enterprise. The position of women did improve over time, yet this seems mainly to have been the result of broad socio-economic changes which affected the entire population. No one has been able to demonstrate that feminism was directly responsible for the tangible gains that were secured.

Was it all in vain then? Does it matter now that there ever was such a thing as the woman movement? This is not the sort of question historians like to ask. Generally they feel it their duty to examine the past, not to sit in judgment on it. This is a sound principle, but where matters of great moment are concerned it cannot, and probably should not, be construed too literally. People rightly expect that the histories of contemporary problems will in some way illuminate those problems. The woman question has been reopened in our time, and so I have tried to make this study bear on some of the issues troubling us today. The first step in this direction, it seems to me, is to determine the comparative success or failure of feminism. When I began studying the history of women it was with the usual assumption that the feminist movement had been at least moderately successful. I now think otherwise, for reasons that will become clearer as we go along. This book, then, is first of all an inquiry into the failure of feminism.

I have made several other decisions which the reader will want to know about. To begin with, I have avoided the question of whether or not women *ought* to have full parity with men. Such a state of affairs obtains nowhere in the modern world, and so, since we do not know what genuine equality would mean in practice, its desirability cannot fairly be assessed. What I have tried to do is indicate the ways in which feminists struggled for equality and the extent to which their ideas and activities were functionally related to their goals. It is possible, I think, to evaluate the relevance of a given strategy, and its strengths and weaknesses, without committing oneself to the cause it was meant to advance. Thus, for example, I argue that it was a mistake (though probably an unavoidable one) for Victorian feminists to abandon their critique of marriage, not because I am in favor of free love but because it seems evident that the institutions of marriage and the family, as presently conceived, are among the chief obstacles to feminine equality.

A further caveat concerns the scope of this book. I have made what is essentially an internal study of the woman movement. I assume that the choices women made or failed to make were important and deserving of analysis. It should be obvious, however, that the struggle for feminine equality was conditioned by the direction American society as a whole took. Even if feminists had never made a mistake of any kind, it does not follow that their movement would have prevailed. Their ability to control events and shape their environment was always very limited. In retrospect, perhaps the best course for feminists would have been to join the Socialist party, which alone promised to change the American social order enough so that women could exercise in practice those rights they were increasingly accorded in principle. The greatest weakness of the feminist movement was precisely this inability to appreciate the limits that the organization of society placed upon its larger aspirations. What I have tried to do here is show why the feminists' analysis of their position was generally shallow and inadequate; to illustrate the variety of events and circumstances that prevented them from coming to grips with their greatest needs; and to demonstrate how they contributed to their own downfall. This is not the whole story of women in America, but it is, I hope, that part of their story which most needs telling.

A word on terms. The feminist vocabulary was never standardized in this country, and there were further variations in usage here and abroad. Americans generally preferred singular terms (the woman movement, woman's suffrage), the English favored the plural (the women's movement, women's suffrage). The English made a distinction between the orderly suffrage workers who were called "suffragists" (or sometimes "constitutionalists"), and the extremists in Mrs. Pankhurst's Women's Social and Political Union who were called, even by themselves, "suffragettes." In America, suffragette was hardly ever used except invidiously. Militancy in both countries referred to direct-action techniques—picketing, demonstrating, and the like —and those who employed them were therefore called "militants." Most American militants belonged to the Woman's party rather than its much larger counterpart, the National American Woman's Suffrage Association. These definitions did not become settled until the last stages of the suffrage struggle. A further distinction is that "woman suffrage" in America was interchangeable with the term "equal suffrage." In England, however, where universal manhood suffrage did not exist, equal suffrage and woman suffrage were quite distinct causes. The exact conditions for the enfranchisement of English women were negotiable.

"Feminism" is an older term and was always used to describe the woman's rights movement as such. I have found it useful to distinguish between those who were chiefly interested in women's rights (whom I call hard-core or extreme feminists), and the social feminists who, while believing in women's rights, generally subordinated them to broad social reforms they thought more urgent. The term woman movement appears in the late nineteenth century to describe all the public activities of women, whether directly related to feminist goals or not. The woman movement, in fact, included anti-suffragists and anti-feminists (often simply called "antis") as well as the partisans of feminine emancipation. In practice, "woman movement" was used interchangeably to mean either women's rights as such, or the entire complex of feminine activities. But in context the exact meaning is usually clear enough. I have tried to adhere to the original usages, except for the term social feminism, which is my own.

acknowledgments

. . . .

i am much obliged to the following organizations for access to their archives: the American Association of University Women, the National Woman's party, and especially the General Federation of Women's Clubs, whose historian, Mrs. Mildred White Wells, gave me every possible assistance. Also helpful were the staffs of the Swarthmore College Peace Collection and the Social Welfare History Archives Center at the University of Minnesota.

Many thanks to Eleanor Flexner of Northampton, Massachusetts, for advice and counsel, and to Professors Dorothy E. Johnson of the Old Dominion College and Louis Lee Athey of Franklin and Marshall College for reading all or part of my first draft. I am much in debt to Professor Laurence R. Veysey of the University of California, Santa Cruz, for a brilliant critique of my manuscript. Some of the ideas in this book first appeared in my essay "Feminism as a Radical Ideology" in *Dissent: Explorations in the History of American Radicalism*, edited by Alfred Young and published by Northern Illinois University Press, 1968.

A special word of appreciation to the Council on Creative Research of the University of Colorado for financial assistance, and particularly to the Graduate School of the University of Wisconsin which generously supported me at several crucial points.

To Ivan Dee of Quadrangle Books, my friend and editor whose sustaining confidence has meant so much to me, my heartfelt thanks. My wife Carol did not help me write this book. Instead she gave me love, happiness, and two beautiful daughters, for all of which I am grateful beyond words.

contents

. . . .

everyone was brave

. . . .

1

the origins of American feminism

$\mathcal{W}$e know very little about the causes of social change, a process always easier to describe than explain, and this is especially true where our domestic institutions are concerned. For a long time scholars believed that the Victorian family (always known to its critics as the patriarchal family) was of ancient lineage predating the Christian era. But now, thanks especially to Philippe Ariès' pioneering work *Centuries of Childhood*, it appears that the modern conjugal family emerged quite recently. If so, the origins of feminism are easier to understand.[1] When it was thought that the conjugal family, with its emphasis on privacy and domesticity, and its preoccupation with the training of children, went far back in time, it was difficult to explain why women suddenly began to press against its limitations in the 1830's. If in truth women had been abused for centuries, why did they wait so long before rebelling? Generally, Americans advanced two arguments in explanation—one economic and the other ideological. The economic argument was most concisely expressed by Walter Lippmann who observed in 1914 that "the mere withdrawal of industries from the home has drawn millions of women out

1. Philippe Ariès, *Centuries of Childhood: A Social History of Family Life* (New York, 1962).

of the home, and left millions idle within it." [2] The industrial revolution forced women to alter their styles of life and inevitably brought them into conflict with customs and institutions based on obsolete economic factors. Alternatively, it was often argued that women were belatedly responding to the libertarian ideologies fostered by the French and American revolutions, that they were demanding equal rights denied them by prejudices, superstitions, and tyrannies incompatible with the enlightened social and political ideals of the nineteenth century.

There is something to be said for both these contentions, but they leave much untold. The industrial revolution is a catchall often used to explain everything for which we do not have a better answer. The sociologist William J. Goode points out that there is nothing in the industrial process itself which determines how families will be organized, and that industrialism has shown itself compatible with a variety of family systems.[3] Similarly, knowing that libertarianism is infectious does not help us appreciate why specific groups make certain responses at particular times. Why, for example, did women wait for more than half a century after the American Revolution before asking that the Declaration of Independence be applied to them as well as to men?

If we assume, however, that the conjugal family system with its great demands upon women was a fairly recent development and became general only in the nineteenth century, then the feminist response becomes explicable. In completing the transformation of the family from a loosely organized, if indispensable, adjunct of Western society into a strictly defined nuclear unit at the very center of social life, the Victorians laid a burden on women which many of them could or would not bear. The Victorians had attempted, moreover, to compensate women for their increased domestic and pedagogic

2. Walter Lippmann, *Drift and Mastery* (New York, 1914), p. 214.
3. See especially his *World Revolution and Family Patterns* (Glencoe, Ill., 1963).

responsibilities by enveloping them in a mystique which asserted their higher status while at the same time guaranteeing their actual inferiority. Hence the endless polemics on the moral purity and spiritual genius of woman which found their highest expression in the home, but which had to be safeguarded at all costs from the corrupting effects of the man-made world beyond the domestic circle. Unfortunately for the Victorians, this rationale was ultimately self-defeating, as William R. Taylor and Christopher Lasch have suggested.

> The cult of women and the Home contained contradictions that tended to undermine the very things they were supposed to safeguard. Implicit in the myth was a repudiation not only of heterosexuality but of domesticity itself. It was her purity, contrasted with the coarseness of men, that made woman the head of the Home (though not of the family) and the guardian of public morality. But the same purity made intercourse between men and women at last almost literally impossible and drove women to retreat almost exclusively into the society of their own sex, to abandon the very Home which it was their appointed mission to preserve.[4]

The libertarian rhetoric of the early feminists masked, therefore, separatist and sororital impulses which affected vast numbers. Discontented women first expressed themselves, as Taylor and Lasch point out, in literary pursuits and church work. By the end of the nineteenth century these small shoots had flowered into great national organizations like the National American Woman Suffrage Association (NAWSA), the Woman's Christian Temperance Union (WCTU), and the General Federation of Women's Clubs (GFWC), which took millions of women outside the home.

Feminism is, then, perhaps best understood as one reaction to the great pressures that accompanied the emergence of the nuclear family. It was not a rebellion born of ancient slavery but part of a collective response to the sexual awareness de-

4. William R. Taylor and Christopher Lasch, "Two 'Kindred Spirits': Sorority and Family in New England, 1839–1846," *New England Quarterly*, XXXVI (March 1963), 35.

liberately inspired by Victorian society in an attempt to foster what the twentieth century would consider an oppressive domesticity. The Victorians taught women to think of themselves as a special class. Having become conscious of their unique sexual identity, however—a consciousness heightened by the common experiences forced upon them by the cult of purity—they could no longer accept uncritically those role definitions drawn up for them by the alien male. Victorian society created The Woman, where before there had been only women. Yet the alternatives were even less agreeable. The worst thing about the situation of women in the nineteenth century was, as Ronald V. Sampson has pointed out, that because they were denied liberty they sought power, and, especially, power over their children.

> The Victorian family as depicted by [Samuel] Butler is essentially an unholy alliance between an overbearing but petty patriarch and a vain adulatory consort for the purpose of deceiving their offspring as to the real nature of their parents and of a society composed of them and their like.[5]

Every society learns to endure a certain discrepancy between its professed aims and its real ones—ideology and actuality never correspond exactly. But every so often, for reasons no one really knows, the gap becomes too great to be papered over with pious assurances. If the chasm is wide enough it may lead to rebellion or civil war, as was the case when slavery could no longer be reconciled with republican principles; if the distance is not so great, less drastic responses become possible. Feminism exploited one such weak point. It was disquieting because its very existence was a contradiction in terms for the Victorians, who believed they had accorded women a higher and more honorable estate than had any previous generation. That so many women failed to agree with them called into question the whole system of values which revolved around the home and the chaste Mother-Priestess who made

5. Ronald V. Sampson, *The Psychology of Power* (New York, 1966), p. 104.

it possible. In this very special sense, therefore, feminism was a radical movement. On the face of it, equal rights for women was not a demand likely to compromise the essential Victorian institutions. In fact, it threatened to do so because the Victorians had given the nuclear family a transcendent significance all out of proportion to its functional value. In the process they created a social problem which threatened to undo a patiently constructed domestic system and, what was worse, by its very existence undermined the animating principles of the Victorian ethos.

It is hard for us now to appreciate the strength and courage of the early feminists who set themselves against the network of ideas, prejudices, and almost religious emotionalism that simultaneously degraded and elevated women—"the cult of true womanhood," as one historian calls it, which made central virtues of piety, purity, submissiveness, and domesticity. Almost the only form of activity permitted women was religious work, because it did not take them away from their true "sphere." "From her home woman performed her great task of bringing men back to God." [6] Woman, it was believed, was morally and spiritually superior to man because of her highly developed intuition, refined sensibilities, and especially because of her life-giving maternal powers which defied man's comprehension. But woman was also physically weaker than man, inferior to him in cognitive ability, and wholly unsuited to the rough world outside the home. This was just as well, because women were largely responsible for The Family—the principal adornment of Christian civilization and the bedrock upon which society rested.[7]

While the Victorian conception of women as wan, ethereal, spiritualized creatures bore little relation to the real world where women operated machines, worked the fields, hand-

6. Barbara Welter, "The Cult of True Womanhood: 1820–1860," *American Quarterly*, XVIII (Summer 1966), 162.
7. For a more elaborate survey of these ideas, see William L. O'Neill, *Divorce in the Progressive Era* (New Haven, 1967), Ch. 3.

washed clothing, and toiled over great kitchen stoves, it was endorsed by both science and religion. Physicians, clergymen, and journalists churned out a stream of polemical literature in support of this thesis. Even fashion conspired to the same end, for the bustles and hoops, the corsets and trailing skirts in which women were encased throughout much of the nineteenth century seemed designed to prevent all but the desperate from entering the vigorous world of men. The weight of metal, cloth, and bone which women were expected to bear as a matter of course should itself have disproved the notion that they were peculiarly delicate creatures, but, of course, it did not. Feminine delicacy was considered visible evidence of their superior sensibilities, the "finer clay" of which they were made. Women who were not delicate by nature became so by design. In the end, the fashion was self-defeating, for it aroused fears that women would become incapable of discharging their essential functions. The Civil War helped wake middle-class women from "their dream of a lady-like uselessness," and when Vassar College was founded its trustees put physical education at the head of their list of objectives.[8]

The cult of delicacy was an extreme and transient expression of an enduring conviction that feminists had to deal with if they were to win equality. They could not admit that the differences between the sexes were so marked as to make women inherently and eternally inferior; neither could they escape the fact that women everywhere were subordinate to men. Moreover, the weight of opinion against them was so great that it was hard for even the most talented women to free themselves of the invidious assumptions that kept them in their place. Margaret Fuller, who pressed with exceptional vigor against the binding conventions of her day, consistently fell back on transcendental clichés like "the especial genius of Woman I believe to be electrical in movement, intuitive in function, spiritual in tendency," thereby denigrating her own

8. Amy Louise Reed, "Female Delicacy in the Sixties," *Century*, LXVIII (October 1915), 863.

intellectual capacities while struggling for recognition as a social philosopher.[9] Of course, her career belied her words, for throughout her life she attacked (with little apparent success) a whole range of important topics. At bottom she must have felt that intuition was not entirely a substitute for reason. Although Miss Fuller was the most intellectually ambitious American woman of her generation, she was certainly not alone, for the acute Englishwoman Harriet Martineau observed at the end of the 1830's that "in my progress through the country I met with a greater variety and extent of female pedantry than the experience of a lifetime in Europe would afford." But, she hastened to add, pedantry was not to be despised in an oppressed class, as it "indicates the first struggle of intellect with its restraints; and it is therefore a hopeful symptom." [1]

. . . .

Underneath the cheerful cant (which was to grow rather than diminish with time) about women's superior morality and intuitive genius, we can sense the first uncertain efforts of intelligent American women to find their true selves. The most alert feminists did not accept the prevailing sentiments as final, or worry about their inherent nature. They took the inferiority of women as an existential reality and concerned themselves with bringing women to an awareness of it. The great suffragist Elizabeth Cady Stanton, in a characteristic letter to her colleague Lucy Stone in 1856, asked why woman put up with her degraded state, and answered herself by saying:

> She patiently bears all this because in her blindness she sees no way of escape. Her bondage, though it differs from that of the negro slave, frets and chafes her just the same. She too sighs and groans in her chains; and lives but in the

9. Sarah Margaret Fuller Ossoli, *Woman in the Nineteenth Century* (Boston, 1855), p. 115.
1. Harriet Martineau, *Society in America*, III (London, 1837), 107.

hope of better things to come. She looks to heaven; whilst the more philosophical slave sets out for Canada.[2]

Feminists were willing to concede that social disabilities had produced an inferior woman, but they did not see this as a good reason for perpetuating the order responsible for her condition. In 1878 Joslyn Gage, corresponding secretary of the National Woman's Suffrage Association, told a committee of the New York Senate that the argument that women should not be given their freedom until they had become fit for it reminded her of Macauley's statement that "if men [or women] are to wait for liberty till they have become good and wise in slavery, they may indeed wait forever." [3]

The parallel with slavery which the early feminists drew again and again was, on the face of it, strained and unreal. Yet, even though *feeling* enslaved is clearly not the same as *being* enslaved, there were real similarities between the women's rights and anti-slavery movements. Not only were women, and usually the same women, active in both causes, but the causes themselves were in many respects alike. Both aimed at removing unconscionable handicaps imposed by law and custom on specific groups in American society. Harriet Martineau summed up the whole case for woman suffrage in these words: "One of the fundamental principles announced in the Declaration of Independence is, that governments derive their just powers from the consent of the governed. How can the political condition of women be reconciled with this?" [4]

2. Elizabeth Cady Stanton, Susan B. Anthony, and Matilda Joslyn Gage, eds., *History of Woman Suffrage, 1848–61* (New York, 1881), p. 860. This rich collection of letters, speeches, newspaper cuttings, and the like extended into six volumes as follows: Volumes II, *1861–76* (New York, 1882) and III, *1876–85* (Rochester, 1887) were edited as above. Volume IV, *1885–1900* (Rochester, 1902) was edited by Susan B. Anthony (who also published Volumes III and IV) and Ida Husted Harper. Volumes V and VI, *1900–1920* (New York, 1922) were edited by Ida Husted Harper and published by the National American Woman Suffrage Association.

3. *Ibid.*, III, 94.

4. Martineau, *Society in America*, I, 199.

But while efforts to extend the rights and opportunities already enjoyed by white males to the rest of society were consistent with the essential premises of the American system, and therefore conservative, such attempts violated conventions and beliefs which, however much they compromised the spirit of the Constitution, were venerated equally with it. Thus, both abolitionists and feminists found themselves in the ironic but characteristically American position of those who put themselves outside the national consensus by a too literal rendering of its sacred texts.

If women were not slaves, to be at once patronized and discriminated against was bad enough. "While woman's intellect is confined, her morals crushed, her health ruined, her weaknesses encouraged, and her strength punished, she is told that her lot is cast in the paradise of women: and there is no country in the world where there is so much boasting of the 'chivalrous' treatment she enjoys." In brief, "indulgence is given her as a substitute for justice." [5] Since most Americans seemed ignorant of womankind's degraded state, the first tasks confronting feminists were relatively uncomplicated. They had, on the one hand, to agitate and propagandize against the prevailing system of ideas, and on the other to seize whatever private advantages they could for themselves. Religion formed the cornerstone of the case against feminine equality, and consequently the first major work by an American feminist, Sarah Grimké's *Letters on the Equality of the Sexes and the Condition of Women* (1838), was directed against those clergymen who believed God had ordained women's inferior state. Miss Grimké took the offensive because she and her sister Angelina had come under fire for their anti-slavery lectures. In a pastoral letter, the General Association of Congregational Ministers of Massachusetts denounced such activities and urged women to refrain from any public works save only leading souls to pastors for instruction. This was bad advice indeed, according to Miss Grimké. "I have suffered too keenly from the teaching of man

5. *Ibid.*, III, 105–106.

to lead any one to him for instruction. More souls have probably been lost . . . by trusting in man in the early stages of religious experience, than by any other error." [6]

Miss Grimké made no concessions whatever to masculine complacency. Man "has done all he could to debase and enslave her mind; and now he looks triumphantly on the ruin he has wrought and says, the being he has thus deeply injured is his inferior." [7] The burden of Miss Grimké's arguments was, however, scriptural. She insisted that false translations and perverse interpretations of the sacred writings had obscured God's true intent. It was perfectly clear to her that "whatsoever it is morally right for a man to do, it is morally right for a woman to do." This forceful, dignified, and lucid exposition did not immediately lay waste the enemy clerics. Nonetheless, Miss Grimké deserves some credit for the changes that finally made the Protestant clergy more sympathetic to woman's emancipation than any other professional group.

Less successful was the direct assault on Christian doctrine launched by Elizabeth Cady Stanton. Ardently skeptical from the time when as a girl she had suffered a nervous collapse on hearing the great revivalist Charles G. Finney preach, Mrs. Stanton missed no opportunities to slam the churches. She was responsible for the anti-clerical resolutions passed by the National Woman Suffrage Association, which described woman as the victim of "priestcraft and superstition." Mrs. Stanton capped her long campaign with the *Woman's Bible*, a two-volume reinterpretation so embarrassing to orthodox feminists that it was officially disowned by her own suffrage association. One of her last communications to the association was a defiant letter indicting the canon law as "more responsible for woman's slavery today than the civil code."

While bold women were calling attention to the human record as a "history of repeated injuries and usurpations on the

6. Sarah M. Grimké, *Letters on the Equality of the Sexes and the Condition of Women* (Boston, 1838), p. 17.
7. *Ibid.*, p. 11.

part of man toward woman, having in direct object the establishment of an absolute tyranny over her," and demanding for women "immediate admission to all the rights and privileges which belong to them as citizens of the United States," more were finding self-help and self-culture useful to their private emancipation.[8] Gradually their thirst for knowledge found expression in female seminaries and colleges (beginning with Emma Willard's Troy Female Seminary in 1821), in the admission of women to regular colleges and universities, and in the opening of professional training on a limited scale. Few women secured a good education before the Civil War, but by 1870 eleven thousand women were enrolled in some 582 institutions of higher learning, while many more had obtained enough formal schooling to become teachers themselves. Equally if not more important was the growth of women's clubs and societies which gave married women in particular outlets for their frustrated energies and sororital aspirations.[9]

By 1860 the emancipation of women was proceeding apace on two distinct levels. Privately, as students, teachers, and in a few cases professionals, and as members of small, often informal societies, middle-class women were enlarging their "sphere" and reaching out for wider opportunities beyond the domestic circle. Publicly, in their still-limited women's rights movement, in temperance work, and most strikingly of all as abolitionists, they were challenging Victorian stereotypes and laying the groundwork for that empire of women's organizations soon to be born. Although the fortitude required for these novel efforts ought not to be minimized, neither level demanded complex intellectual rationales. Self-culture and education were hard to fault in an age of progress and enlightenment. Moreover, the pioneers of female education were

8. From the "Declaration of Sentiments" adopted by the first Woman's Rights Convention at Seneca Falls, New York, in 1848. *History of Woman Suffrage*, I, 70–71.

9. Mildred White Wells, *Unity in Diversity* (Washington, D.C., 1953), pp. 9–17. Some of these still exist, e.g., the Ladies Association for Educating Females of Jacksonville, Illinois, founded in 1833.

principally concerned with making women better wives, mothers, and teachers of the young. Catherine Beecher, the most prolific advocate of educated women, saw education as the cure for every social ill, but she was specifically concerned with training women in "domestic economy" for their true profession as housewives, and providing spinsters like herself with useful employment. She flatly disagreed with the feminist demand for equality in all things. The bible clearly stipulated that man was to be the "chief magistrate" of the home, and she believed this was in no way demeaning to woman who acquired certain compensations in the process.[1]

The case for women's rights, although far more offensive to Victorian sensibilities, was equally simple. It was based largely on the Declaration of Independence and the republican and egalitarian principles advanced since 1776. The force of an argument so framed could hardly be denied in America, and Victorians were forced to combat its lucid precepts with biblical citations of decreasing weight, and confused references to psychological, physiological, and anthropological principles of uncertain value. Democratic Americans did concede much of the feminist case in fact, however much they resisted it in principle, as the substantial number of legal reforms enacted from the 1830's on showed. The country held firm on woman suffrage, but otherwise reformers found it possible to improve property and marriage laws in state after state. The early feminists were thus encouraged to believe that equality could be won in their lifetimes.

. . . .

The Civil War had a powerful effect on the fortunes of women. Having acquired some practical experience and some education outside the home, they were able for the first time

1. Catherine Beecher, *Woman's Profession as Mother and Educator* (Philadelphia, 1872). See also her *The True Remedy for the Wrongs of Woman* (Boston, 1851), and *The Duty of American Women to Their Country* (New York, 1845).

to participate actively in a national enterprise. The Union's Sanitary Commission and other relief agencies, although controlled largely by men, gave vast numbers of women public work to do. Thousands served as nurses, and daring individuals such as Clara Barton, Mary Livermore, and Louisa May Alcott, not to mention the eccentric few who became spies, soldiers, and the like, distinguished themselves.[2] On the ideological front, Elizabeth Cady Stanton and Susan B. Anthony formed the National Woman's Loyal League to inspire patriotism, support the Thirteenth Amendment, and secure for women an honorable role in the war effort. Most importantly, perhaps, the war gave Union women a heroic myth which echoed down the generations. Their considerable services lost nothing in the retelling. It quickly became a fixed principle that when the war ended "woman was at least fifty years in advance of the normal position which continued peace would have assigned her." [3] Women understandably needed to believe that large benefits had flowed from their large contribution to a long and horrid war, but in reality they had gained little of permanent use from it. The improvement in their educational opportunities was well under way by 1860, and the war only slightly increased the demand for women teachers and, in a few cases, women undergraduates in colleges depleted by the Army.[4] A few women became government clerks, and after the war some hung on to their ill-paying jobs, but government

2. The range of feminine activities is described in Mary Elizabeth Massey, *Bonnet Brigades: American Women and the Civil War* (New York, 1966).

3. *Ibid.*, p. 339. A statement made by Clara Barton in 1888. Confederate women performed more traditional services during the war, and suffered in ways that Union women did not, but in time they also idealized these experiences. By the end of the century their shared memories were an important unifying force making it possible for Northern and Southern women to work together in organizations like the General Federation of Women's Clubs.

4. Coeducation came into being at the University of Wisconsin, for example, largely because there were not enough male students left to assure its continuation during the war. See the unpublished master's thesis by Jean Rasmusen Droste, "Women at Wisconsin" (University of Wisconsin, 1967), p. 28.

service did not become an attractive or important occupation for women until the next century. Perhaps an additional hundred thousand women found jobs in industry after 1861, but an army of overworked and underpaid female operatives already existed, and the war had little effect on industry's long-range employment patterns. The war enhanced women's self-confidence, and to some extent it stimulated them organizationally, but the mobilization of women on a national scale did not begin until the 1880's.

For women the most important consequence of the war was not masculine recognition of their services, or (mostly) the lack of it. Rather, it was the passage of the 13th Amendment which crowned the labors of female abolitionists and at the same time touched off a crisis in the women's rights movement with far-reaching consequences. Quickened by their fruitful labors during the war, and certain that the Negro's hour must be theirs also, suffragists assumed in the flush of Union victory that they would soon win the vote. At the first postwar women's rights convention, Theodore Tilton, a liberal journalist, spoke for many when he asked, "Are we only a handful? We are more than formed the Anti-slavery Society . . . which grew into a force that shook the nation. Who knows but that tonight we are laying the cornerstone of an equally grand movement." The aged Sojourner Truth, ex-slave and a beloved figure in the movement, called for woman's immediate enfranchisement. "I want it done very quick. It can be done in a few years." The youthful Frances Gage assured her listeners that in speaking for temperance around the country she had found her audiences alive to the need for women's votes. "They are ready for this work." [5]

But if the cry of votes for women no longer seemed as bizarre in 1866 as it had in 1848, suffragists were still badly out of step with the rest of America. It soon became apparent that the 14th Amendment would apply to men only, and in 1867, despite great efforts, a woman suffrage referendum was

5. *History of Woman Suffrage*, II, 177–198.

overwhelmingly defeated in Kansas. These two setbacks embittered the more extreme feminists, who concluded after Kansas that men could not be trusted. Years later the authors of *The History of Woman Suffrage* recalled that after their humiliation, "we repudiated man's counsels forevermore; and solemnly vowed that there should never be another season of silence until woman had the same rights everywhere on this green earth, as man." Man could be of little help in the great work, because while he regarded woman as "his subject, his inferior, his slave, their interests must be antagonistic." Also in 1867 feminists attempted to have the word "male" struck from the New York State constitution, like the word "white," over the objections of Horace Greeley who felt with most reformers that it was the Negro's hour and that feminists should wait to press their claims until black suffrage was secured. To which Mrs. Stanton and her friends replied:

> No, no, this is the hour to press woman's claims; we have stood with the black man in the Constitution over half a century, and it is fitting now that the constitutional door is open that we should enter with him into the political kingdom of equality. Through all these years he has been the only decent compeer we have had. Enfranchise him, and we are left outside with lunatics, idiots and criminals for another twenty years.[6]

Their shocked disbelief that men would so humiliate them by supporting votes for Negroes but not for women demonstrated the limits of their sympathy for black men, even as it drove these former allies further apart. Early in 1869 Elizabeth Cady Stanton observed that at a recent suffrage convention in Washington several Negroes had said men should always dominate women, and that white women were the Negro's worst enemy. Mrs. Stanton complained that this "republican cry of 'manhood suffrage' creates an antagonism between black men and all women . . ." This trend, she warned, in language as ominous as it was unfortunate, "will culminate in fearful out-

6. *Ibid.,* II, 267–270.

rages on womanhood, especially in the southern states." [7] Additional evidence of the suffragists' hardening attitudes came when Mrs. Stanton and Miss Anthony aligned themselves with a notorious speculator and bigot, George F. Train, who campaigned with them for woman suffrage and provided financing for their weekly journal, *Revolution*. With his usual delicacy, Garrison described Train as a "crack-brained harlequin and semi-lunatic," a "ranting egotist and low blackguard," and a "nigger-baiter." [8] Train may not have been all that bad, but he was bad enough to antagonize those friends of woman suffrage who had not already been put off by the women's fight against the 14th Amendment. The Stantonites candidly admitted to judging every man solely on his views toward immediate woman suffrage, and Train was the only man they knew who did not worry about the effects of equal suffrage on the Negro's chances. All he asked in return was that *Revolution* carry news of his financial schemes. Not even Wendell Phillips, a good friend of the suffragists' cause, was pardoned for thinking that black men needed the vote more than white women. "Mr. Phillips, with his cry, 'this is the negro's hour,' has done more to delay justice for woman, and to paralyze her efforts for her own enfranchisement, than any man in the Nation," Mrs. Stanton declared.[9]

By 1869 the Stanton-Anthony forces had worked themselves into an untenable position. Their policies of simultaneously advancing a wide range of reforms while taking a hard and narrow line on woman suffrage exerted unbearable strain on the suffrage movement as a whole. Feminists divided, therefore, into two groups, with the radical New Yorkers becoming the National Woman Suffrage Association, and the more conservative Bostonians, led by Henry B. Blackwell,

7. Elizabeth Cady Stanton, "Women and Black Men," *Revolution*, February 4, 1869, p. 88.

8. William Lloyd Garrison, "Letter to Editor," *Revolution*, January 20, 1868, p. 149.

9. Elizabeth Cady Stanton, "A Pronunciamento," *Revolution*, July 15, 1869, p. 24.

Lucy Stone, Julia Ward Howe, and T. W. Higginson, among others, forming the rival American Woman Suffrage Association. The AWSA conceded that this was indeed "the Negro's hour," but mainly it confined itself to the woman question. Its position on black suffrage notwithstanding, the National has generally been admired by historians for the large, generous approach it took to contemporary social questions. *Revolution* did have a good word to say about every good cause, but its general strategy remained hopelessly confused and obscure. The journal's first issue announced modestly that "we shall show that the ballot will secure for woman equal place and equal wages in the world of work; that it will open to her the schools, colleges, professions and all the opportunities and advantages of life; that in her hand it will be a moral power to stay the tide of crime and misery on every side." [1]

Obviously, if the vote would do all this the Stantonites had good reason to go as far as they did in pursuit of it. But, of course, it would not, and there were those in the group who understood the suffrage's limitations and the importance of advancing other reforms as well. When Boston suffragists (in their own organ, the *Woman's Journal*) attacked *Revolution's* policy of backing every worthy cause, the radicals pointed out that they wanted to vote:

> But we are not dreamers or fanatics; and we know that the ballot when we get it, will achieve for woman no more than it has achieved for man. And to drop all other demands for the sake of uniting to demand the ballot only, may seem the whole duty of the *Woman's Journal*, but is only a very small part of the mission of the REVOLUTION. The ballot is not even half the loaf; it is only a crust—a crumb. The ballot touches only those interests, either of women or men, which take their root in political questions. But woman's chief discontent is not with her political, but with her social, and particularly her marital bondage. The solemn and profound question of marriage . . . is of more vital conse-

1. "The Ballot-Bread, Virtue, Power," *Revolution*, January 8, 1868, p. 1 .

quence to woman's welfare, reaches down to a deeper depth in woman's heart, and more thoroughly constitutes the core of the woman's movement, than any such superficial and fragmentary question as woman's suffrage.[2]

How splendidly put, how true—how confusing to loyal readers whom *Revolution* had previously urged to labor for a right which would of itself secure their emancipation.

Suffragists could not have it both ways. Either the vote was central to woman's freedom, in which case the American was pursuing a proper course, or it was but one of many necessary items, and the National was fully justified in casting a broad net. Time was to show that the Stantonites had reached, however imperfectly, the appropriate conclusions. But their diagnosis was obscured by a habit of using every available argument for woman suffrage, even when they contradicted one another, and by the organization's congenital inability to make those compromises essential to a struggling movement which could ill afford to alienate its friends. Having already lost their allies in the old anti-slavery camp, the radicals quickly proceeded to offend the nascent labor movement. Susan B. Anthony encouraged working women to form trade unions and was a delegate to one of the early National Labor Congresses. Meanwhile, *Revolution* was being printed in a "rat office" (one paying less than the union scale), and Miss Anthony was urging women to better themselves by acting as strikebreakers. Still, when the National Labor Congress refused to readmit Miss Anthony as a delegate in 1869, the radical feminists could see this only as another example of male chauvinism. Elizabeth Cady Stanton concluded that the incident "proved what THE REVOLUTION has said again and again, that the worst enemies of Woman's Suffrage will ever be the laboring classes of men." [3] Having previously consigned Negroes and reformers to that

2. Laura Bullard, "What Flag Shall We Fly?," *Revolution*, October 27, 1870, p. 264.
3. Elizabeth Cady Stanton, "National Labor Congress," *Revolution*, August 26, 1869, p. 120.

same category, *Revolution* by its own admission had no friends at all and no reason for believing that women would ever get the vote.

. . . .

All this having been said, it remains true that the National possessed something of value, the loss of which was greatly to affect the future of American women. Alone of the major women's groups in this period, the NWSA admitted, however fitfully, that the heart of the woman question was domestic and not legal or political; that woman's place in the family system was the source from which her other inequities derived. Marriage, its members believed, was organized exclusively to gratify man's selfish needs and wants, and consequently was "opposed to all God's laws." Mrs. Stanton declared:

> For what man can honestly deny that he has not a secret feeling that where his pleasure and woman's seem to conflict, the woman must be sacrificed; and what is worse, woman herself has come to think so too.[4]

Mrs. Stanton insisted that she and her friends were not against marriage as such, "only against the present form that makes man master, woman slave. The only revolution that we would inaugurate is to make woman a self-supporting, dignified, independent, equal partner with man in the state, the church, the home."[5] Of course, this is so far from being the case even today that Victorians had reason to think her proposals quite revolutionary enough. Apart from easy divorce, the radical feminists had few other specific proposals to offer. Sex education for boys appealed to some women as one way of insuring a more tender regard for wives, as well as a deter-

4. Elizabeth Cady Stanton to Lucy Stone, November 24, 1856, *History of Woman Suffrage*, I, 860.
5. Elizabeth Cady Stanton, "Anniversary of the National Woman Suffrage Association," *Revolution*, May 19, 1870, p. 306.

rent to "solitary vice." [6] But these suggestions were bound to seem feeble, perhaps even disingenuous, in view of the impassioned language used to denounce the prevailing sexual norms. Rape appeared to Mrs. Stanton as merely another expression of the general malaise. Citing a recent case, she explained in 1869 that the statutes which "make woman man's chattel slave; theologies that make her his subject, owing obedience; customs that make her his toy and drudge, his inferior and dependent, will ever be expressed by the lower orders of men in such disgusting outrages." [7]

These repeated charges amply warrant our belief that Victorian women generally entertained a low opinion of the sexual act. Yet clearly it does not follow from this that marriage in the nineteenth century was considered a satisfactory expression of sexual refinement, or an adequate defense of female gentility. By today's standards marital sex was perhaps infrequent and decorous, but the double standard of morality and the cult of true womanhood had the curious effect of making such high demands on male continence that few normal men could exhibit the self-control women demanded of them. When the dangers of childbirth were added to the horrors of "conjugal commerce," we ought not to be surprised that sex was something a great many women could readily do without, and that they viewed as loathsome and perverse a system which forced it on them. This was especially true of advanced women, and while most suffragists were married, they tended to marry later, have fewer children, and to be much more divorce-prone than the average woman. Mrs. Stanton did not conform to this pattern. She had five children and only one husband. But in her memoirs she tells us that her life began at fifty when her children could take care of themselves.

6. Mrs. L. B. Chandler, "Motherhood," *Woodhull and Claflin's Weekly*, April 29, 1871, p. 6. Isabella Beecher Hooker expressed the same thoughts in a more unbalanced way. See Robert E. Riegel, *American Feminists* (Lawrence, Kans., 1963), pp. 142–143.

7. Elizabeth Cady Stanton, "Woman's Protectors," *Revolution*, January 21, 1869, p. 40.

It would be wrong to think that Mrs. Stanton was prudish or unreasonable on sexual matters. She was, in fact, one of the very few women reformers who thought that women's willingness to identify chastity with moral worth was a sign of their slave mentality. She never believed, as most other women did, that purity was essential to greatness in either men or women. When in the 1890's the brilliant Irish leader Charles Parnell was driven out of British politics for living in sin with a married woman, she remarked dryly that "if the women of England take up the position there can be no true patriotism without chastity, they will rob some of the most illustrious rulers of their own sex of any reputation for ability in public affairs." [8] She ardently championed the brightest female spirits of her own day, who often led unconventional sex lives. Most American women were scandalized by George Sand; even those like Margaret Fuller who admired her were forced to lament that "a woman of Sand's genius—as free, as bold, and pure from even the suspicion of error might have filled an apostolic station among her people." [9] Others like Harriet Beecher Stowe were less charitable, inspiring Mrs. Stanton on one occasion to declare flatly that "George Sand has done a grander work for women in her pure life and bold utterances of truth, than any woman of her day and generation; while Mrs. Stowe has been vacillating over every demand for her sex, timidly watching the weathercock of public sentiment and ridiculing the advance guard." [1] But few women agreed with Mrs. Stanton. Frances Willard surely represented the great majority when she said, rightly no doubt, that Parnell's disgrace showed the growth of women's influence. With a characteristic disregard for the facts of the case, she cried out, "God be thanked that we live in an age when men as a class have risen to such an appreciation of women as a class, that the mighty tide of their

8. Elizabeth Cady Stanton, "Patriotism and Chastity," *Westminster Review*, CXXXV (January 1891), 2.

9. Fuller, *Woman in the Nineteenth Century*, p. 233.

1. Elizabeth Cady Stanton, "A Word About George Sand," *Revolution*, September 15, 1870, p. 169.

public sentiment will drown out any man's reputation who is false to woman and the home." [2]

Thus, while the Stanton group's position on marriage was not really very radical, and reflected much the same fear and suspicion of sex which animated most feminists, the fact that it recognized the existence of a marriage question was itself enough to put it beyond the pale. The last serious effort to reunite the suffrage movement failed in 1870, despite the best efforts of Theodore Tilton, when Mrs. Stanton's views on marriage and divorce were strongly condemned at the American Woman Suffrage Association's convention. The split which was originally caused by the Stantonites' refusal to accept Negro suffrage, was now being sustained, personalities apart, by their critique of Victorian marriage. While the National's position on marriage was not especially daring, except by comparison with the prevailing norms exemplified by the American, it was further compromised through the National's association with the fantastic Victoria Woodhull.

Mrs. Woodhull had arrived in New York in 1868 with her sister Tennessee Celeste Claflin, after divorcing her first husband, Dr. Channing Woodhull, a luckless fortune teller and quack nostrums peddler. With the support of Commodore Vanderbilt the sisters entered the brokerage business, but they were most attentive to their periodical *Woodhull and Claflin's Weekly*, a lively magazine devoted to the promotion of feminism, suffrage, spiritualism, and the doctrines of Stephen Pearl Andrews, an eccentric philosopher who had discovered Universology, the key to all knowledge, and had devised Alwato, the scientific universal language. The beautiful and eloquent Victoria rose rapidly to a commanding position in the suffrage movement and scored what was considered a great coup in 1871 when she persuaded the House Judiciary Committee to hold hearings on a proposed constitutional amendment to give women the vote. She testified before the committee to good

2. In Rachel Foster Avery, ed., *Transactions of the National Council of Women of the United States* (Philadelphia, 1891), p. 38.

effect and was subsequently inspired to run for President on her own Cosmo-Political party's ticket. Both Susan B. Anthony and Elizabeth Cady Stanton thought highly of her. Mrs. Stanton wrote her a letter of encouragement from the territory of Wyoming, where women had just been given the vote, which began, "To you, the last victim sacrificed on the altar of woman's suffrage, I send my first word from the land of freedom." [3] Miss Anthony had been roused to a considerable pitch of enthusiasm by the favorable minority report of the House Judiciary Committee on woman suffrage, and wrote Mrs. Woodhull that "I have never in the whole twenty years' good fight felt so full of life and hope. I know now that Mr. Train's prophesy—nay, assertion—three years ago in the Kansas campaign, that 'the women would vote for the next President,' is to be realized. I am sure you and I and all women who shall wish to will vote for somebody, if not for George F. Train or Victoria Woodhull." [4]

Unhappily for the Stantonites, Mrs. Woodhull was an incredibly dangerous woman by virtue of her peculiar temperament and bizarre views. She not only supported every drastic prescription for society's ills, from spiritualism to Marxism, but represented another outcropping of that vein of free love which underlay Victorian monogamy. Free love, or any variant of it, was always a dangerous cause in the nineteenth century. It destroyed Frances Wright's Nashoba community and forced John Humphrey Noyes to move his utopian colony from Vermont to the wilds of western New York. But until the 1870's the relative openness and dispersed character of American society enabled sexual radicals to stay in business. After the Civil War there was a noticeable hardening in American attitudes and institutions, symbolized by the emergence of Anthony Comstock, secretary of the New York Society for the

3. Elizabeth Cady Stanton to Victoria Woodhull, *Woodhull and Claflin's Weekly*, July 15, 1871, p. 9.
4. Susan B. Anthony to Victoria Woodhull, *Woodhull and Claflin's Weekly*, February 25, 1871, p. 5.

Suppression of Vice, who led a nationwide campaign for moral censorship that became known as Comstockery. The Comstock Act itself, which empowered the Post Office to deny mailing privileges to morally offensive works, put a mighty weapon in the hands of censorious Americans and made the transmission of unconventional sexual ideas all but impossible. Opinion was so tense and easily inflamed that even the popular Harriet Beecher Stowe suffered after revealing, for entirely proper reasons, certain colorful facts about Lord Byron's sex life. A poorer time to make a fresh assault on monogamy could hardly be imagined.

Moreover, Victoria Woodhull's intense partisanship and unrestrained invective had given many people good reason to hate her. When Horace Greeley explained that he was against woman suffrage because of its ties with free love, Mrs. Woodhull accused him of wrecking the health and happiness of his wife and causing the deaths of five of his seven children. Although specifically exempting Greeley, she went on to observe that moralizing editors in general were lecherous monsters who, because she was known to favor "social freedom," had made "disgusting revelations of their own natures" to her.[5] Of Catherine Beecher, who had recently been speaking against woman suffrage, Mrs. Woodhull said at the outset of a five-hundred-word sentence:

> If the Catherine Beechers who now clog the wheels of progress, and stand forth as the enemies of their sex, and therefore of the human race, doing their utmost to cement the chains of their degradation, giving to man the same power over them as he possesses over his horses and dogs, and other chattel property, if we say they consider this to be their mission, and they are satisfied to be the puppets of man's caprice—the playthings of his passion—the wretched serfs of his supreme power and authority, and prefer to be voted for in the simplest concerns of life, and dandled upon his knees after the manner of courtesans . . . ,"

5. Victoria Woodhull, "To Horace Greeley," *Woodhull and Claflin's Weekly*, August 26, 1871, pp. 8–9.

let them do so, but not at the expense of other women.[6]

Thus, despite her generous opinions (in an anti-Catholic age she was not afraid to praise religious orders), patriotism (she enthusiastically supported President Grant's attempt to steal Santo Domingo), and many talents, Mrs. Woodhull had no reason to expect much help should she ever get into serious trouble. Indeed, at first she exercised what was for her a degree of caution. She favored licensed prostitution—anathema to virtually all women but not without support in official quarters—in rational and persuasive terms. Noting the efforts of Boston women to redeem and reform prostitutes, she pointed out that of the two approaches used to combat prostitution, rehabilitation and suppression, neither had worked well. Once prostitutes were made they could not easily be rehabilitated, she thought, while making prostitution a crime led only to blackmail and official corruption.

> The only repressive agency admissible is a system of police licensing and rigorous visitation. This is not authorizing sin by statute, simply recognizing social and physiological facts. In this way, and in this way alone, until a wholesome moral sentiment can be induced can legislation deal with the subject.[7]

For the customary police tactics the sisters had nothing but contempt. After a mass arrest of prostitutes in Greenwich Street, the *Weekly* noted with heavy irony that "when they come out from their purification, the ninety-four will have been reformed by good teaching; work will be provided for them; and having been washed and regenerated by the humanizing influence of Blackwell's Island, they will not go back to Greenwich street. Oh, no." [8]

These comments were dangerous enough, but even more

6. Victoria Woodhull, "Editorial," *Woodhull and Claflin's Weekly*, January 14, 1871, p. 10.

7. "The Social Evil," *Woodhull and Claflin's Weekly*, July 2, 1870, p. 8.

8. "Policemen and Prostitutes," *Woodhull and Claflin's Weekly*, April 29, 1871, p. 10.

hazardous was the manner in which the sisters edged closer and closer to openly advocating free love. Their early essays on marriage were suitably obscure and characterized by the usual —among radical feminists—calls for "perfect equality" between the sexes. They also ran occasional pieces by Sarah F. Norton who, according to another contributor, had been expelled from the New York suffrage movement because of her attempts to link equal suffrage with free love. Whether this was literally true or not hardly mattered, for what Miss Norton had to say was serious enough. In a typical effusion she accused *Revolution* of having retreated from its earlier stand on marriage and of being an "orthodox truckler of the weakest type," while announcing that "woman suffrage really means the abolishment of this vile system of marriage." [9]

Apparently tiring of these veiled locutions, Mrs. Woodhull decided to disclose publicly her belief in free love and did so from the stage of Steinway Hall in New York on November 20, 1871. It is difficult to imagine why she expected what was left of her reputation to survive this event. When her intentions became clear, Theodore Tilton, an extraordinarily open-minded person, the author of a flattering biographical pamphlet about her, and perhaps one of her lovers, was the only man of standing in New York willing to preside at the meeting. Nonetheless, Mrs. Woodhull was stunned by the ferocious response to her appeal for a sexual revolution, and when the press and public assailed and harassed her she seemed to lose her reason. After threatening to retaliate against her critics by "carrying the war into Africa," she went on to tell all she knew of the Beecher-Tilton affair. In the November 2, 1872, issue of the *Weekly* she revealed that Henry Ward Beecher, the most famous preacher of his day and a friend of woman suffrage, had for years maintained an affair with Elizabeth Tilton, the wife of her principal champion. Professing to admire Beecher's potent charms, she claimed that her only reason for publiciz-

9. Sarah F. Norton, "The True Issue of the Woman's Rights Question," *Woodhull and Claflin's Weekly*, September 3, 1870, p. 7.

ing the affair was to call attention to Beecher's hypocrisy in not admitting his conversion to the higher sexual morality. Whatever her motives—and they seem to have been remarkably complicated—the result of her outburst was predictable. Tilton sued Beecher, Beecher denied everything, and, although probably guilty, was essentially sustained by both the courts and public opinion. Tilton fled the country a broken man and was soon followed by the Claflin sisters, whose magazine was put out of business by the Post Office Department and whose lives were made unbearable by an indignant populace.

. . . .

While the affair had its ludicrous aspects—Beecher's pomposities, Anthony Comstock's efforts to suppress the *Weekly*—it was the greatest scandal of the day, involving as it did America's most popular minister, a well-known editor, and some of the country's more prominent women. And it had the immediate effect of stifling all further discussion of the marriage question. Mrs. Stanton continued to defend free divorce, but otherwise the outburst of public feeling drove radical feminists back from their advanced position and forced them to concentrate more narrowly than before on law and politics. Since the American was already committed to a policy of expedience and compromise as a result of the controversy over black suffrage, the differences between it and the National rapidly diminished. Before long only personal dislikes stood in the way of a reunion which was finally effected in 1890, years after both groups had come to stand for essentially the same things. Nor was this lesson lost on the next generation of suffragists, who were not "distinguished by the breadth of their social views" to begin with.[1] Although sympathetic with the respectable goals of social feminism, the new leaders were determined to avoid complicating the suffrage question by associating it

1. Eleanor Flexner, *Century of Struggle* (Cambridge, Mass., 1959), p. 219.

with daring or unconventional speculations, no matter how important. In this manner a vital part of the woman question simply disappeared. Having already taken the economic context of American life as essentially given, feminists went on to do the same thing for the marital and domestic system, accepting, for the most part, Victorian marriage as a desirable necessity. In so doing they assured the success of woman suffrage while guaranteeing that when women did get the vote and enter the labor market in large numbers, the results would be bitterly disappointing.

Neither the Woodhull debacle nor the general climate of Victorian opinion fully explain the feminist position on sex in the late nineteenth century. Also important was the social purity crusade which played a prominent role in the woman movement. Of course, campaigns against prostitution in a century as sexually obsessed as the nineteenth were inevitable, but social purity meant much more than the suppression of vice. Its origins lay in the mothers' associations which began as early as 1815 and, especially during the 1830's and 1840's, developed a considerable interest in suppressing vice and "uplifting" fallen women. Thereafter, maternal societies seem to have lost interest in these matters. It was not until the 1870's that social purity became a coherent and persistent movement, in reaction to the growth of regulated prostitution in both England and the United States. In the 1860's the British Army tried to license prostitution in the continental manner, inspiring a counterattack which spilled over into the United States once regulation had been turned back in England.

The scattered efforts of American vice reformers were crystalized in 1877 when a delegation of English anti-regulationists visited this country. Vigilance committees were formed in New York and elsewhere, and the movement swelled until it reached a peak in 1895 with the formation of the American Purity Alliance. Like all such reforms, social purity progressed erratically. In the early 1880's it languished, but was revived in 1885 by W. T. Stead's exposures of the vice industry, which occasioned almost as great a scandal here as in Britain. Mothers' meetings were held around the country, the WCTU's Social Purity Department was energized, and another department for the suppression of obscene literature added. By the 1890's social purists had not done much to eliminate prostitution, but they had destroyed any chance of regulating it. The physicians, military men, and public health officers who supported regulation had either been persuaded or intimidated, and with this threat removed social purity lost its separate identity.[2]

Social purity was by no means an entirely feminine affair, but its ranks were largely filled with women, and it represented in an especially intense and emotional way the woman movement's characteristic attitudes on sexual questions. It stood for the abolition by law of impure practices, and the censorship for moral reasons of all forms of expression. Famous censors like Anthony Comstock and Josiah W. Leeds of Philadelphia were highly regarded by moral reformers. Female moralists were, however, by no means unsympathetic to the prostitute herself, whom they tended to see as an innocent victim of economic want and masculine lust—as against the still popular view of the inherently depraved harlot.

Less durable than these convictions, which continued to be widely held in the twentieth century, was the Victorian feminists' opposition to birth control. Because the public fight for birth control was won in the United States by a coalition which included emancipated women, it is sometimes assumed that feminists always favored contraception. In the Victorian age, however, organized women invariably opposed it. English feminists consistently preferred continence to contraception and saw birth control as merely another way of encouraging mascu-

2. See the unpublished doctoral dissertation by David Jay Pivar, "The New Abolitionism: The Quest for Social Purity, 1876–1900" (University of Pennsylvania, 1965), p. 304.

line lust. Hence the militants' slogan in 1913, "Votes for Women and Purity for Men." American social purity forces took much the same line, not only out of their fear and hatred of sexual intercourse but because they believed in the conservation of energy. Since they visualized the body as an energy system that was running down, they were eager to avoid the physically depleting effects of coitus.

Social purity, with the Victorian woman's anti-eroticism, completed the work of reorienting feminism away from a serious consideration of sexual issues. Especially after the Woodhull affair it was almost impossible for suffragists to see sexual irregularities as anything but immoral, and immorality as something that could not be suppressed by votes for women. As one suffragist put it while discussing Stead's exposures of the London vice scene, "One thing is evident, without the votes of women no vice that appeals peculiarly to the appetites of man can ever be suppressed or the laws enacted for the suppression of such vice be properly enforced." [3] While there were feminists, particularly after the turn of the century, who did not share these prejudices, the leadership of the woman movement united under the banner of absolute purity. Two important consequences flowed from this. By closing their eyes to the sexual elements regulating the life of women, feminists prevented themselves from developing a satisfactory analysis of the female dilemma. And, as we shall see, when the great changes in female sexual behavior became visible in the 1920's, feminists were unable to react to it in such a way as to command the respect of emancipated young women. It was their sexual views more than anything else that dated the older feminists after World War I, and made it difficult for them either to understand or to speak to a generation moved by quite different ambitions.

This blind spot was true even of a woman like Charlotte

3. Elizabeth Boynton Harbert, "Mothers to the Rescue," *New Era*, I (September 1885), 282.

Perkins Gilman, almost the only major second-generation feminist to continue attacking the cult of domesticity.[4] The original suffragists were fully aware that "concentrating all woman's thoughts and interests on home life intensifies her selfishness and narrows her ideas in every direction, hence she is arbitrary in her views of government, bigoted in religion and exclusive in society."[5] They also understood that if woman were to be man's equal she would have to occupy the same positions and do the same work. Susan B. Anthony persistently reminded the social purity movement that "whoever controls work and wages, controls morals. Therefore we must have women employers, superintendents, committees, legislators; wherever girls go to seek the means of subsistence, there must be some woman."[6] Although never very precise about the means by which woman's liberation would be effected, the founders always insisted that it meant "emancipation from all political, industrial, social and religious subjection."[7] But while feminism was born out of a revolt against stifling domesticity, and nurtured in the understanding that for women to be really free the entire fabric of

4. Generation is not a very exact term, but when speaking of the suffrage movement it seems fair to say that there were three distinct waves of women involved over time. The founders surfaced in the 1830's and 1840's and dominated the movement until the seventies and eighties. These included Mrs. Stanton, Miss Anthony, Lucy Stone, Amelia Bloomer, and many others, some of whom retained authority to the century's end. The second generation developed in the 1880's and 1890's. It included women like Carrie Chapman Catt, Anna Howard Shaw, and Harriot Stanton Blatch, who led the movement to final victory. A third generation consists of the younger women who emerged in the twentieth century, were active in the last years of the struggle, but for reasons discussed later never enjoyed the cohesion or prestige of earlier generations.

5. Elizabeth Cady Stanton, "Stand By Your Guns Mr. Julian," *Revolution*, January 14, 1869, p. 25.

6. "Social Purity," an address first given by Miss Anthony in 1875, in Ida H. Harper, *Life and Work of Susan B. Anthony* (Indianapolis, 1898–1908), II, p. 1008.

7. *Ibid.*, p. 1011.

their lives had to be rewoven, by the end of the century most feminists had succumbed to what Charlotte Perkins Gilman called the "domestic mythology." Home and family were so revered in the Victorian age that the temptation to exploit rather than resist the current of opinion was irresistible. The original feminists had demanded freedom in the name of humanity; the second generation asked for it in the name of maternity. What bound women into a selfless sisterhood, it was now maintained, was their reproductive capacity. Over and over again feminists asserted that "women stand relatively for the same thing everywhere and their first care is naturally and inevitably for the child." [8]

Maternity was not only a unifying force but the enabling principle which made the entrance of women into public life imperative. As another suffragist put it in 1878, "The new truth, electrifying, glorifying American womanhood today, is the discovery that the State is but the larger family, the nation the old homestead, and that in this national home there is a room and a corner and a duty for 'mother.'" [9] Not only was the nation a larger home in need of mothering, but by impinging upon the domestic circle it made motherhood a public role. Jane Addams was a persistent advocate of this doctrine:

> Many women today are failing properly to discharge their duties to their own families and households simply because they fail to see that as society grows more complicated it is necessary that woman shall extend her sense of responsibility to many things outside of her own home, if only in order to preserve the home in its entirety.[1]

So the effort to escape domesticity was accompanied by an

8. Mrs. Ellis Meredith at the 1904 convention of the NAWSA, *History of Woman Suffrage*, V, 101.

9. Elizabeth Boynton Harbert in *History of Woman Suffrage*, III, 78–79.

1. Jane Addams, "Woman's Conscience and Social Amelioration," in C. Stelzle, ed., *Social Applications of Religion* (Cincinnati, 1908), p. 41.

invocation of the domestic ideal—woman's freedom road circled back to the home from which feminism was supposed to liberate her. In this manner feminism was made respectable by accommodating it to the Victorian ethos which had originally forced it into being.

Given the plausibility and elasticity of this contention, women were, inevitably perhaps, lured into using it to secure their immediate aims. Yet in retrospect it does not seem to have been a completely successful ploy. One historian has recently hailed Frances Willard's "supreme cleverness" in using the WCTU "to advocate woman suffrage and child labor laws and other progressive legislation always in the name of purity and the home." [2] But the history of the WCTU illustrates the weakness of an argument that begins by accepting the opposition's premise. In conceding that better homes were of equal importance to anti-feminists and feminists alike, these women reduced their case from one of principle to a mere quarrel over tactics. To redeem itself the opposition had only to prove that its tactics were superior. This is apparently what happened to the Temperance Union afer the death of Frances Willard (which coincided with a significant change in its social composition), when new leaders came to believe that temperance was more crucial to the home than suffrage, child welfare, and other progressive causes.[3] Perhaps this new orientation would have come about in any event, but the suffragists in the WCTU made it all the easier by their willingness to use the cult of domesticity in pursuit of quite separate and distinctively feminist objectives.

The truth was that while feminists resented the demands made upon them in their roles as wives and mothers, they were

2. Andrew Sinclair, *The Better Half* (New York, 1965), p. 223.

3. On the Union's changing character, see the unpublished doctoral dissertation by Janet Z. Giele, "Social Change in the Feminine Role: A Comparison of Woman's Suffrage and Woman's Temperance, 1870–1920" (Radcliffe College, 1961).

not alert to the danger of even a partial accommodation to the maternal mystique. They gravely underestimated the tremendous force generated by the sentimental veneration of motherhood, and assumed they could manipulate the emotions responsible for the condition of women without challenging the principles on which they rested. Moreover, while denying that under present circumstances mothers could be held accountable for the failings of their children, they implied that once emancipated, women could properly be indicted for the shortcomings of their progeny. In 1901 Susan B. Anthony herself went so far as to say that:

> Responsibilities grow out of rights and powers. Therefore before mothers can rightfully be held responsible for the vices and crimes, for the general demoralization of society, they must possess all possible rights and powers to control the conditions and circumstances of their own and their children's lives.[4]

Her remark would seem to mean that once granted political equality, mothers would have to answer for all the ills of society—a great weight to lay on posterity. Such statements contributed to the unhealthy and unrealizable expectations which feminism encouraged.

A further hazard stemming from the feminist emphasis on motherhood was the support it gave to the notion that women were not only different from men, but superior to them. Julia Ward Howe, a moderate and greatly admired feminist, persistently reminded women that emancipation was intended to make them better mothers as well as freer persons.

> Woman is the mother of the race, the guardian of its helpless infancy, its earliest teacher, its most zealous champion. Woman is also the home-maker; upon her devolve the details which bless and beautify family life. In all true civilization she wins man out of his natural savagery to share

4. *History of Woman Suffrage,* V, 5-6.

with her the love of off-spring, the enjoyment of true and loyal companionship.[5]

Definitions like this left men with few virtues anyone was bound to admire, and inspired women to think of themselves as a kind of super race condemned by historical accident and otiose convention to serve their natural inferiors. Such indeed was the case with some women who, encouraged by the new social sciences—especially anthropology, which demonstrated that matriarchies did exist and may in prehistory have been common if not universal—were moved to take themselves with a seriousness few men could share. Elizabeth Cady Stanton elaborated this hypothesis in 1891 in an impressive paper that she called "The Matriarchate, or Mother-Age." [6] She argued that in prehistoric times women had been superior, or at least equal, to men, but that Christianity and especially Protestantism drove the feminine element out of religion and subordinated women to the rule of men. Society, therefore, lost the beneficent moral and conservative forces of the female intellect and the mother instinct.

With this line of argument Walter Rauschenbusch, no enemy of women's rights, was compelled to take issue. He must have disapproved of the anti-clerical flavor of much feminist thought, but he was specifically motivated by the feminists' moral pretensions.

> Many men feel that women are morally better than men. Perhaps it is right that men should instinctively feel so. But it is a different matter when women think so too. They are not better. They are only good in different ways than men.[7]

5. Florence Howe Hall, ed., *Julia Ward Howe and the Woman Suffrage Movement* (Boston, 1913), p. 158.

6. Published in Avery, ed., *Transactions of the National Council*, pp. 218–227. For an illuminating discussion of this feminist *Herrenvolk* thesis, see Sinclair, *Better Half*, pp. 234–237.

7. Walter Rauschenbusch, "Moral Aspects of the Woman Movement," *Biblical World*, XLII (October 1913), 197.

Rauschenbusch believed in the emancipation of women, but he reminded his readers that the feminine virtues could easily be exaggerated. In recent times, he pointed out, both Christian Science and Theosophy had demonstrated a particular appeal to women, even though both stressed authority and unexamined belief. As Rauschenbusch's observation suggests, the attempt to demonstrate woman's superior nature led only to a dead end. It was really just one more variation of the Victorian mystique, another way of exploiting the belief that women's unique power was rooted in the mystery of her life-giving capacities. Taken one way it led back to a preoccupation with motherhood. Read differently it supported a rejection of men so complete that women could retain their integrity and spirituality only in spinsterhood. Or by subscribing to the principles of Ellen Key, who elevated motherhood even above marriage and made the right to have illegitimate children the central aspect of feminism, women could have their cake and eat it, too. They could realize their generative and instinctual potential without an unseemly dependence on the contaminating male. Having a child in this way meant, of course, a degree of masculine cooperation, but in a delicious reversal of ancient custom man became a passive instrument of woman's purpose and his ungoverned passions the means to her full emancipation. This was radicalism with a vengeance, but a radicalism that had little to do with the normal objects of revolutionary ardor.

. . . . . .

Seen against this background, Mrs. Gilman's scorching attack on the maternal pieties is all the more impressive. She had suffered as a young wife from the conflict between ambition and motherhood, but she ultimately resolved her problem by divorcing an entirely satisfactory husband and giving up an agreeable child. Having thus cleared her decks she went on to enjoy a successful career as a writer and feminist theoretician

—about the only one, in fact, the American movement ever produced. She was able not only to work her way out of the domestic trap, something other women have also done—less brutally one hopes—but to take the next step by confronting intellectually the system that had forced her to take such heroic steps, something no other American woman had managed to do. In bringing her strong and original mind to bear on the large problem of woman's social role she produced, most notably in *Women and Economics*, the best contemporary analysis of it.[8]

Women and Economics, her first book, was written like all her many works—at top speed, sloppily edited, and rushed to print in 1898.[9] Despite its many imperfections the book's arguments were so lucid, its suggestions so original, and its phrases so often brilliant and arresting that Mrs. Gilman became famous almost overnight. She believed that all women needed to work, both for their own sake and for society's, and that the domestic system needed drastic reorganizing to permit this. She advanced her argument on several fronts, claiming that it was both morally necessary and economically desirable that women work in the same way as men. It was morally necessary because while women depended on their husbands for support, they were forced to develop an exaggerated sexuality. The most desirable women got the best husbands and thus, through a process of natural selection, women's sexual attributes became overdeveloped at the expense of other, more important, characteristics. Only when they earned their own living could women form with men those equal partnerships that alone would guarantee marriage's survival. After they married women still needed work in order to continue growing. "Science, art, government, education, industry—the home is

8. For more on this remarkable woman, see Carl N. Degler, "Charlotte Perkins Gilman on the Theory and Practice of Feminism," *American Quarterly*, VIII (Spring 1956), 21–39, and her autobiography, *The Living of Charlotte Perkins Gilman* (New York, 1935).

9. *Women and Economics* (Boston, 1898).

the cradle of them all, and the grave if they stay in it. Only as we live, think, feel and work outside the home, do we become humanly developed, civilized, socialized." [1] Apart from developing a finer womanhood, society stood to gain economically from the employment of women who would increase the national output of goods and services.

Mrs. Gilman had a low opinion of housework, and it was at this point that most suffragists began to disagree with her. Since middle-class women did not work and apparently did not want to work, feminists generally claimed that inequality in the home derived from society's failure to value properly the contribution housewives made to the domestic economy. Mrs. Gilman easily disposed of the inflated claims for domestic work by pointing out that no matter how good a housekeeper a woman was, her standard of living was unrelated to her performance. "What she gets out of life is not proportioned to her labors, but to his." Over and over again Mrs. Gilman called on women to distinguish between the essential and non-essential aspects of their social role. "When women are wise enough to be free, and free enough to be wise, they will learn to dissociate the joys of love, the status of marriage, the blessings and cares of motherhood, from the plain trade of cooking, and the labors of personal service." [2]

What made Mrs. Gilman's failure to win many converts to her position so important for the future of women was, as Aileen Kraditor has pointed out, that if the work they did at home was as valuable as the work men did outside it, then "no fundamental economic change would be necessary in home relationships for women to achieve equality." [3] While suffragists wanted every woman to have the same vocational opportunities as men, they expected most women to stay at home most of the time. Since they accepted the domestic

1. *Ibid.*, p. 222.
2. "Does a Man Support His Wife?" (New York, 1911), pp. 10–20.
3. Aileen S. Kraditor, *The Ideas of the Woman Suffrage Movement, 1890–1920* (New York, 1965), p. 121.

system as unalterable, this meant that, in effect, they thought women's domestic inequities could be remedied by changed attitudes and symbolic reorientations. Hence the vote, while it would not affect family life in any direct way, would improve women's domestic status by raising their self-esteem. Similarly, some feminists thought husbands should pay their wives a salary in recognition of their contributions to the familial economy. It was natural for suffragists to think this way because they venerated motherhood and, for the most part, subscribed to the prevailing domestic pieties. When they did not, they had to appear to in order not to offend people who did. Moreover, to admit that women's dilemma was institutional and not simply a matter of bad habits and poor attitudes, was to admit the need for a domestic revolution—something few suffragists wanted.

It was Mrs. Gilman's principal virtue that she accepted the logic of her own position. If domesticity crushed woman's spirit and weakened her morals, then the home would have to be replaced by something better. Nor was Mrs. Gilman afraid to suggest what that better something might be. She envisioned large housing units which would provide nurseries, central kitchens, maid service, and the like, thereby freeing wives and mothers for productive work. By putting cooking, cleaning, and child care on a professional basis they would be done better than by a horde of amateur housewives, the scale of operation would create economies, and, of course, to meet the added expenses each family would have the wife's salary. The concept was not unique to Mrs. Gilman (indeed, *Woodhull and Claflin's Weekly* once predicted that urban families would some day live in residential hotels which would free women from housework), but she became its most forceful proponent and the idea was always associated with her.[4] From

4. "Sixteenth Amendment. Independence vs. Dependence: Which?," *Woodhull and Claflin's Weekly*, June 25, 1870, p. 5. For an elaborate and cumbersome plan aiming in the same direction, see the articles by Mrs. C. F. Peirce from November 1868 to March 1869 in the *Atlantic Monthly*.

Walter Lippmann's point of view, Mrs. Gilman's plan made simple good sense. While it was no more than the domestic counterpart of the rationalization and reorganization transforming the national economy, it would also assist those processes which Lippmann was eager to see consummated. By enabling women to specialize, either outside the cooperatives or as cooks or housekeepers within them, it would break down the narrowness and individualism through which women clogged the wheels of progress. "One of the supreme values of feminism is that it will have to socialize the home," Lippmann wrote in 1914. "When women seek a career they have to specialize. When they specialize they have to cooperate. They have to abandon more and more the self-sufficient individualism of the older family." [5]

Lippmann's enthusiasm for cooperative housekeeping in this sense derived, of course, from his hopes for the nationalization of American life rather than from any special desire to emancipate women. But he was probably right in thinking that it would advance both causes. Mrs. Gilman was herself a socialist, eager to reduce women's parochialism, but the immediate virtue of her plan was that it could be put into effect immediately, at least on a small scale, and need not await the social revolution. Yet it took little time for her to recognize that the traditional family and the myths on which it rested were much stronger than most people realized. Even though the falling birthrate, the increased number of working women, and the decline of the family as a unit of production, among other things, were popularly supposed to be destroying the family, domestic life seemed little changed. Accordingly, Mrs. Gilman delivered an even mightier blow against the system in a devastating book entitled simply *The Home* (1903).

This witty and savage attack on the cult of domesticity included some of her best writing. "The home," she conceded, "is the cradle of all the virtues, but we are in a stage of social

5. Lippmann, *Drift and Mastery*, p. 232.

development where we need virtues beyond the cradle size." One by one she destroyed the clichés that supported domesticity. Was the home not sacred? On the contrary, the home was devoted principally to eating, sleeping, resting, and other such elemental processes. They were necessary functions, of course, "but are they more hallowed than the others?" By this token, were not learning, working, and the like equally sacred, was not, in fact, the school more sacred than the home because more valuable to civilization? What about the privacy of the home? But who, Mrs. Gilman asked, has any real privacy in the home? Not the children,

> under the close, hot focus of loving eyes, every act magnified out of all natural proportion by the close range, the child soul begins to grow. Noticed, studied, commented on, and incessantly interfered with; forced into miserable self-consciousness by this unremitting glare; our little ones grow permanently injured in character by this lack of one of humanity's most precious rights—privacy.

Nor was privacy possible to the wife who must supervise her children, deal with tradesmen and callers, and entertain her friends. Perhaps the husband, if he had a den or study of his own, could gain some privacy, but as a rule the best way to gain peace was to have your servants tell everyone you were not at home. Thus, "to be in private, you must claim to be out of it."

The worship of motherhood did not escape Mrs. Gilman's withering pen. "Matriolatry" seemed to her one of the most dangerous of all social myths because it encouraged women to think that their reproductive capacities alone assured their success as mothers. The care of children required reason, not instinct, and clearly this was in short supply. Who but mothers "raised our huge and growing crop of idiots, imbeciles, cripples, defectives, and degenerates, the vicious and the criminal; as well as all the vast mass of slow-minded, prejudiced, ordinary people who clog the wheels of progress?"

The temptation is to go on quoting from this remarkable book for, although its theme is much like the attack on domestic myths and realities in *Women and Economics*, Mrs. Gilman rang as many changes on it as wit and invention could devise. Persistently, ingeniously, sometimes elegantly, she hunted down every loose thought, wrung the truth from every careless phrase, and exploded the pretensions of every piece of nonsense anyone had ever uttered about domestic life. *The Home* was a *tour de force*, in its own way more impressive than *Women and Economics*, yet it had no discernible effects. This was not because of any flaws in Mrs. Gilman's reasoning. The cult of domesticity and the inefficiencies of private housing certainly inhibited the development of women and perpetuated their inferiority. Self-culture and improved educational opportunities did not cancel out the narrowing influences of home life because "it is use, large, free, sufficient use that the mind requires, not mere information." [6] It followed logically from this that to free woman, particularly during the middle years when they had large families to manage, more was required than the simple elimination of discriminatory laws and customs which, when swept away, would still leave women in a state of *de facto* inferiority by reason of their domestic entrapment.

.   .   .   .

Broadly speaking, the emancipation of women in this sense could be accomplished in only two ways. One method would be to erect a welfare state, as Sweden was to do, which through a system of nurseries, paid maternity leaves, and similar benefits would ease the burdens of motherhood and make women genuinely competitive with men in the job mar-

6. Charlotte Perkins Gilman, *The Home: Its Work and Influence* (New York, 1903), pp. 40–261.

ket. The other, and by no means antagonistic, way was to reorganize domestic customs and institutions to achieve the same end. These were not mutually exclusive alternatives, but they demanded quite different strategies. Building the welfare state called for political action, while reforming the domestic system involved social action, propaganda, experimentation, persuasion, and the other techniques by which individuals are induced to change their behavior. It would appear that Mrs. Gilman took this latter course because there were no true welfare states in existence yet to show how the thing was done. Moreover, the utopian socialist tradition was still strong in America, not only on account of the many communitarian societies which had flourished here, but because the whole idea of effecting social change by example rather than by edict was congenial to the American temperament.

Our experience in this century suggests that the advantages of Mrs. Gilman's strategy were less clear-cut than they seemed at the time. The welfare state has contributed, in Europe at least, to the emancipation of women, while nowhere in the West has the effort to change the basic patterns of domestic life met with much success. It is true that the development of a welfare state has proceeded much more slowly in the United States than in any other developed Western nation, and in this sense Mrs. Gilman was not wrong to think that the prospects for effective action on a national scale to emancipate married women were poor. What she could not have guessed in 1898 was the extraordinary affection Americans would demonstrate for the detached, self-contained, single family dwelling. The retreat to suburbia had already begun, thanks to the streetcar, but in the twentieth century it became a rout. After World War II the G.I. Bill, the Federal Housing Administration, and similar developments made it possible not only for the middle but for the regularly employed working classes to enjoy the benefits of suburbia. Housing projects snaked out from and around every major city, laying waste the countryside and erecting in place of meadow and woodland acres of identical domestic boxes and forests of utility poles and TV antennas. The cities which, for all their problems, had seemed at the turn of the century to be alive with possibilities for new and better ways of living, were abandoned to the very rich and the very poor.

The crucial point about the suburban explosion is not that tract housing is inferior; indeed, for most people such a home, no matter how drab, monotonous, or aridly situated, represents an improvement over their previous quarters. What is important about these sprawling new developments is that they freeze the domestic pattern. To the wife's other roles is now added that of chauffeur, because the automobile, while it made tract housing feasible for the masses, corroded the system of public transportation. In cities the proximity of schools, nurseries, jobs, shops, and the like, and the transit facilities which service them, make it possible, if not easy, for wives to stretch themselves beyond the home. But in suburbs housewifery is itself a full-time job. Thus the laws which make it easy to build and sell houses on a massive scale, the business customs and institutions that are geared to this type of residential construction and none other, and the durability of Victorian domestic concepts have conspired to frustrate the hopes of visionaries and perpetuate woman's functional inferiority in the great world.

There remained a further alternative which Mrs. Gilman did not explore. She attacked the home because it seemed to her the weakest point in the domestic system. In effect she accepted marriage and the family while proposing to change the physical shell enclosing them. It remained theoretically possible, however, to do just the opposite: to take the home as given and instead to redefine marriage and the family. This was the direction radical feminists were taking before the Woodhull affair, and while their nerve was shattered by it, the stream of criticism directed against Victorian marital and familial patterns lasted well into the twentieth century. The decline of communitarianism and the suppression of Mormon bigamy may have reduced the visible alternatives to monogamy, but radical sexual ideas continued to be advanced. Ellen Key's advocacy of motherhood without marriage involved quite a different sense of what constituted a family. Similarly, Judge Ben Lindsey's appeal for "companionate marriages" broke sharply with the conventional notion of marriage as a lifelong sexual union. Mrs. Havelock Ellis' suggestions for a "novitiate for marriage" (trial marriage) and "semi-detached marriage" (separate domiciles for each spouse) had the same effect.[7] But Mrs. Gilman was unable to speculate on these matters, not only because of her own rigidly conventional views on sex but because the entire area was out of bounds to serious feminists. The movement was just large enough to contain her socialism and her critique of domesticity and motherhood, even while rejecting it. No one could go any further and keep the confidence of organized American womanhood.

From this survey it should be clear that well before 1917 the woman movement, while not altogether bankrupt intellectually, had lost its original verve and openness to new ideas. It had, moreover, embraced a code of sexual morality that precluded serious attention to the social context of emancipation and would cost it the full attention and respect of the generation that came of age in the 1920's. But what would in the long run be fatal to the movement was not so much prudery as its inability to ask fundamental questions about itself. Hard-core feminists, having firmly rejected their own radical origins, were, by the turn of the century, too respectable and too certain that women's rights was a simple political matter to learn much from Mrs. Gilman—who was unique

7. For a lengthy discussion of the radical attack on marriage, see my chapters on The New Morality in *Divorce in the Progressive Era*, and Sidney Ditzion, *Marriage, Morals and Sex in America* (New York, 1953).

in any event. Woman suffrage thus became a substitute for all the things feminists were unwilling to do or consider. As their vision narrowed, the emotional weight they invested in the ballot became all the greater, and their need to exaggerate its value all the more urgent. After the 1890's, therefore, ardent feminists became increasingly obsessed with the suffrage question, and to understand the dead end into which this led them we must examine in more detail what they expected from the vote.

2

. . . .
the demand for equal suffrage

*t*he soundest reason for woman suffrage was that in a free country to deny women the vote solely because of their sex was unjust, undemocratic, and ought properly to have been unconstitutional. There were, however, only so many ways to state this elementary proposition, and having said them suffragists had to seek other arguments which would keep the public's interest and advance their cause. Hence, from the first, suffragists attributed functional values to the ballot as evidence of the good it would do women to have it. Inevitably, such an emotional issue led to exaggerated claims. At an equal-rights convention held in Rochester, New York, only two weeks after the pioneering one at Seneca Falls in 1848, a young newly-wed leaped to her feet with an appeal for equality that held the audience "spellbound." She predicted that when women had the vote:

> The heterogeneous triflings which now, I am very sorry to say, occupy so much of our time, will be neglected; fashion's votaries will silently fall off; dishonest exertions for rank in society will be scorned; extravagance in toilet will be detested; that meager worthless pride of station will be forgotten; the honest earnings of dependents will be paid; popular demagogues crushed; imposters unpatronized; true genius

sincerely encouraged; and above all, pawned integrity redeemed! [1]

Such apocalyptic claims for the ballot were made throughout the long struggle for woman suffrage. Nearly forty years after the Rochester convention, Rosa Miller Avery, a second-generation suffragist, declared:/"The men and women of to-day who are in earnest for woman's political emancipation stand on Mt. Sinai and make covenant with heaven for the speedy union of spiritual or woman's kingdom to man's or the material world." [2] But by this time crucial shifts had already occurred, and the ideology of woman suffrage was assuming its final form. As Aileen Kraditor has pointed out, "The new era saw a change from the emphasis by suffragists on the ways in which women were the same as men and therefore had the right to vote, to a stress on the ways in which they differed from men, and therefore had the duty to contribute their special skills and experience to government." [3] At first, feminists had keenly resented the assumption that their sexual characteristics were physical and emotional while the higher, more civilized faculties were reserved for men. Sarah Grimké complained that nothing "has tended more to destroy the true dignity of woman than the fact that she is approached by man in the character of a female," and insisted that "man has inflicted an unspeakable injury upon woman, by holding up to view her animal nature, and placing in the background her moral and intellectual being." [4] But in time most feminists gave up the effort to maintain their likeness with men and accommodated themselves to the Victorian definition of womanhood while attempting to turn it to their own purpose. Thus, as early as 1874 Isabella Hooker was saying that the chief effect of woman suf-

1. *History of Woman Suffrage*, I, 77.
2. Rosa Miller Avery, "Interior View of the Suffrage Question," *New Era*, I (June 1885), 177.
3. Aileen S. Kraditor, *The Ideas of the Woman Suffrage Movement* (New York, 1965), p. 66.
4. Sarah M. Grimké, *Letters on the Equality of the Sexes and the Condition of Women* (Boston, 1838), pp. 23–24.

frage upon politics would be moral. Because women would not tolerate immorality in political figures, higher standards would be forced upon them; while the entrance of women into government service would infuse it with a finer sensibility. "Women will work so gradually into the machinery of government that their distinctive influence will not be felt consciously but atmospherically." [5]

If this was in part a surrender to the Victorian mystique, it was also necessary if suffragists were to link up with the vastly larger number of social feminists who by the end of the century dominated the woman movement. While many organized women did believe the ballot was essential, many did not, and to bring them into the suffrage camp it was necessary to show them that their ends could not be realized without equal suffrage. Social feminists were chiefly concerned with problems like child labor and the exploitation of working mothers. This clashed with the formal ideology of nineteenth-century capitalism, but it did not unduly strain the feminine image of middle-class women. In time, the conviction that women had a right and duty to intervene in those affairs which affected domestic life—or elicited the philanthropic and benevolent impulses thought peculiar to them—hardened into dogma. Having accepted this rationale, suffragists perpetuated it in the League of Women Voters, which justified its existence in much the same terms. "Women unite on a humanitarian basis. There is a kinship of motherhood that binds together all women of all classes. So where the home and children are concerned, women will stand side by side in spite of creed or caste. We have also learned that home does not mean house, nor children . . . it includes world-wide welfare." [6]

5. Mrs. J. B. Hooker, "A Consideration of Certain Effects upon Politics and Jurisprudence of the Enfranchisement of Women," *Papers and Letters Presented at the First Woman's Congress of the Association for the Advancement of Women* (New York, 1874), p. 127.

6. Grace Clendenning, "The Opportunity of the League of Women Voters," *Woman Citizen*, June 5, 1920, p. 15.

Although by 1920 feminine unity could no longer be assumed, during the Progressive era there was substantial agreement among organized women on these questions. The socially conservative *Outlook*, which opposed equal suffrage and worried a good deal about the woman movement, was forced to conclude after an extensive survey of the feminine scene in 1904 that the old parochial divisions among women had been pretty well abolished. Middle-class women everywhere had come to resemble one another.

> Their philanthropic enterprises differ very little, their educational theories are almost exactly identical; even their conceptions of civic responsibility are intrinsically the same. And in more personal matters—things connected with the home—they are almost exactly alike in their ideals.[7]

The explosive growth of the General Federation of Women's Clubs during these same years was, of course, even more impressive testimony to the broad consensus that had been reached on the many causes it espoused.

The conservative spirit which dominated suffragists after the 1870's was, therefore, of a very special kind. It accepted certain Victorian stereotypes, rejected radical ideas about the condition of women, and gave priority to the vote. It did not mean an end to reformism within the movement, but rather focused on those essentially conservative social issues that moved organized women. The difference between hard-core feminists and social feminists was chiefly that the latter either could wait for the ballot, or did not think it necessary for their purposes, while the former believed with Susan B. Anthony that woman suffrage was essential to the success of all other reforms. Miss Anthony laid down the basic line on peace, for example, when at the turn of the century she reproached a group of DAR ladies—in those halcyon days more interested in peace than war—for failing to put first things first.

7. Elizabeth McCracken, "The Social Ideals of American Women," *Outlook*, October 1, 1904, p. 325.

It does seem very strange to me that you should be more interested in peace and arbitration between nations than in the enfranchisement of the women of this so-called republic. It is evident that if the women of our nation had been counted among the constituencies of every State Legislature and of the Congress of the United States, the butchery of the Spanish-American War would never have been perpetrated.

In words identical to those later used by the Woman's party in 1917, she continued: "There is no possible hope of justice among the nations of the world while there is such gross injustice inside of the highest and best Government of them all." [8] Maude Nathan of the Consumer's League assured women that they needed the vote to insure their right to buy pure, honest goods "purchased under clean, wholesome and humane conditions. For this right the Consumers' League persistently contends, but it can be only partially successful . . . so long as it depends entirely upon moral suasion, while manufacturers and merchants have the voting power to hold in terror over its administration." [9]

In 1885 Florence Kelley had complained that suffragists were preoccupied with the problems of middle-class women—education, property acts, and the like.[1] But the wctu had already begun to take a broad view of social questions, and before long Mrs. Kelley, though never fully satisfied, had reason to think better of the woman movement. The relationship between woman suffrage and protective legislation for women and children was especially obvious and frequently invoked. Mrs. Kelley often addressed the nawsa on this point, and in 1910 she told a congressional committee of her failure to get the city of New York to appropriate money for factory inspectors. "One candid friend, Mayor Van Wyck, in listening to our

8. Ida H. Harper, *The Life and Work of Susan B. Anthony* (Indianapolis, 1898–1908), III, 1199.

9. *History of Woman Suffrage*, V, 97.

1. Florence (Wischenwetzkey) Kelley, letter to editor, *New Era*, I (May 1885), 150.

pleas, told us the whole trouble. Said he: 'Ladies, why do you waste your time year after year in coming before us and asking for this appropriation? You have not a voter in your constituency and you know it, and we know it and you know we know it,' and they never did give it to us." [2] Owen Lovejoy was but one of many child-labor reformers who believed that for the protection of working children "the participation of women in the law-making of the State is vital." [3]

If middle-class women needed the vote for benevolent purposes, working women needed it to protect themselves and their families. Mrs. Kelley repeatedly told the NAWSA that until working women could vote, the places where they lived and worked would never be well served by municipal agencies. Such elemental needs as pure water and regular garbage collection went unmet in the slums because those who cared most about them could not vote. Margaret Dreier Robins of the National Women's Trade Union League believed the suffrage would help working women organize, because when they did form unions or go on strike "the power of the police and of the courts is against them in many instances, and whenever they try to meet that expression of political power, they are handicapped because there is no force in their hands to help change it." [4] The NWTUL rejected the advice of the mine workers' Mother Jones that "you don't need a vote to raise hell," and her view that woman suffrage was a plutocratic trick to divert women from the real issues and keep them busy with "suffrage, prohibition, and charity." [5] Mrs. Robins' argument had its merits, especially by comparison with the misguided attempt of some suffragists to demonstrate a direct connection between votes and wages. In a speech she gave frequently in the 1870's,

2. *History of Woman Suffrage*, V, 307.

3. *Ibid.*, p. 500.

4. *Ibid.*, p. 303.

5. Mary Field Parton, ed., *The Autobiography of Mother Jones* (Chicago, 1925), pp. 203–204.

Miss Anthony insisted that economic power followed political power. "The disfranchised must always do the work, accept the wages, occupy the position the enfranchised assign them." [6] In 1887 the National Woman Suffrage Association "Resolved, That we call the attention of the working women of the country to the fact that a disfranchised class is always an oppressed class and that only through the protection of the ballot can they secure equal pay for equal work." [7]

. . . .

Few of these propositions were as self-evident as most suffragists and social feminists thought. Because the sharpest criticism of their position came from anti-suffragists whom feminists despised, they were inclined to ignore it. Much "anti" propaganda was, to be sure, vicious or ignorant. The typical male anti-suffragist seems to have been either passionately dedicated to the cult of domesticity which feminism was thought to weaken, or so personally insecure that his own status was threatened by every change in the position of women. Grover Cleveland was the most prominent defender of women's traditional and inferior place, and he was but one of many who called theology, psychology, anthropology, history, and physiology to the aid of beleaguered mankind. Floyd Dell, a radical journalist and poet, caught the flavor of this rhetoric when he reported back to *The Masses* after a fact-finding mission to anti-suffragist headquarters in 1915, where he had purchased a quantity of pamphlets. "I learned about women from them. There is that master psychologist, the Hon. Elihu Root, and Mr. Henry L. Stimson, former Secretary of War, who has searched out the deepest secrets of Woman's heart." A careful reading of this material disclosed all manner of shocking truths about the nature of women. "They show not merely that

6. Harper, *Susan B. Anthony*, II, 996.
7. *History of Woman Suffrage*, IV, 122.

woman isn't fit to vote, they give good reasons for believing that she isn't fit to live.[8]

Such arguments reached a peak of sorts during the First World War when the president of the Aero Club of America, Henry A. Wise Wood, testified before a congressional committee on the enfeebling effects of woman suffrage. Votes for women meant "the dilution with the qualities of the cow, of the qualities of the bull upon which all the herd's safety must depend." He then cried out, "It is a damnable thing that we should weaken ourselves by bringing into the war the woman, who has never been permitted in the war tents of any strong, virile dominating nation." [9]

There were obvious drawbacks to a line of attack that appealed chiefly to masculine chauvinism and female timidity. It offended women of spirit and men of sense, and ran against the mainstream of Progressive social thought. Accordingly, the shrewdest anti-suffragists, most of them women, gradually developed a more subtle strategy. Catherine Beecher, who opposed equal suffrage for fear that women would misuse the ballot, made the strongest possible case against it when she pointed out that women could get what they wanted without the franchise. "Any man who would grant the ballot would grant all for which the ballot is sought." [1] Antis generally were more addicted to Victorian formulas than feminists. The Illinois Association Opposed to the Extension of Suffrage to Women began its declaration of principles:

8. "Adventures in Anti-Land," reprinted in William L. O'Neill, ed., *Echoes of Revolt: The Masses, 1911–1917* (Chicago, 1966), pp. 199–201.

9. Remarks before the House Committee on Woman Suffrage, *History of Woman Suffrage*, V, 585. This vituperative tradition continued long after the question was settled. See, for example, Anthony M. Ludovici, "Woman's Encroachment on Man's Domain," *Current History*, XXVII (October 1927), 21–25, which blames feminism for, among other things, poor cooking and cancer.

1. Catherine Esther Beecher, *Woman's Profession as Mother and Educator* (Philadelphia, 1872), p. 18.

> We are unalterably opposed to Woman Suffrage because . . .
> we believe that above all the materialistic activities of life
> lies the realm of love and faith, that spiritual world in which
> the higher interests of humanity center, and that it is in
> this domain of domestic affections, of ethics and of religion,
> that the development of the highest womanly capacities is
> to be found.[2]

Unhappily, in combating feminism antis were forced to violate their own notions of proper feminine conduct in order to sustain them. Such a contradiction was not easily overcome.

The first important anti-feminist gesture was made in 1870 when a group of distinguished women led by Mrs. Madeline V. Dahlgren (the wife of the Admiral), Mrs. William T. Sherman, and Mrs. Almira Lincoln Phelps, the sister of Emma Willard, collected fifteen thousand signatures for a petition urging Congress not to enfranchise women. The effort was accompanied by many blushing apologies for their unwomanly behavior, and so unnerved the participants that it was never repeated.[3] In the 1890's anti-suffragists gained a better grip on themselves, and in that decade a number of Associations Opposed to the Extension of Suffrage to Women were founded. By this time woman suffrage had become so respectable that a counteroffensive was essential. Even more important, it would seem, was the fact that many antis had been caught up in the burgeoning woman movement themselves. Most of the organized anti-suffragists were clubwomen. More conservative than the General Federation's leaders, they were like them in enough other respects so that all could live under the same roof. Many antis were earnest social reformers. In 1912, for example, the officers of the Massachusetts Association Opposed to the Further Extension of Suffrage to Women (MAOFESW) had as presi-

2. "Declaration of Principles," in *Why Women Do Not Want the Ballot*, published by the Illinois Association Opposed to the Extension of Suffrage to Women (n.p., n.d.).

3. "The Woman Movement in America," *ibid.* Eleanor Flexner corrects the date to 1872 and the number of signatures to one thousand in *Century of Struggle* (Cambridge, Mass., 1959), p. 295.

dent a woman who was also president of the Woman's Municipal League and an officer of numerous philanthropic and educational societies; a treasurer who had served for twenty-five years on the State Board of Charity and Lunacy and was one of the first two women Overseers of the Poor elected in Massachusetts (the other being a former president of the MAOFESW); an officer who served on the Massachusetts Prison Commission; and another who belonged to the Massachusetts Consumers' League.[4]

Since organized antis were so much like suffragists, it was natural for them to argue that the vote would not help advance those interests they held in common. Although less pacific than most suffragists, antis pointed out that there was no historical evidence to show that women would cast their votes against war. On the contrary, the great women rulers had fought wars just like men, and, most strikingly of all, both Northern and Southern women had ardently supported the Civil War.[5] The suffragist argument that votes for women would mean higher wages was as easily disposed of.

> If the ballot had raised men's wages there might be some justification for the belief that it would do the same for working women, but we all know that if a man could control his wages by means of a vote on election day, or determine in the same manner how many hours should constitute a working day, he would never have felt the necessity of organizing or joining trade unions or participating in strikes. It is the unions organized in nearly every trade which has raised men's wages, not the ballot.[6]

4. "Organization and Leaders Who Yearly Defeat Suffrage Bill," *Boston Sunday Herald,* April 28, 1912.

5. George Harvey, "War and the Woman," *North American Review,* CCI (March 1915), 344–347; Annie Nathan Meyer, "Woman's Assumption of Sex Superiority," *North American Review,* CLXXVIII (January 1904), 103–109.

6. Alice Hill Chittenden in "Annual Meeting of the Association," *Remonstrance* (July 1909), p. 2.

Even if the ballot did matter, the same critic pointed out, the median age of working women was under twenty-one and therefore most would not be able to vote. The friends of working women would do better by assisting trade unions and cultivating public opinion.

By conceding that women were so different from men as to require special protective laws, social feminists also laid themselves open to the charge that they were trying to have their cake and eat it, too. They wanted equality in politics and preferential treatment in industry. In the 1920's hard-core feminists used this contradiction to argue for industrial equality. Before the suffrage era it was more usual to take the opposite line. In a reasonable essay, Mrs. Arthur M. Dodge, founder and first president of the National Association Opposed to Woman Suffrage, pointed out that

> because of her lowered physical and nervous vitality the
> woman worker has had to be protected in her industrial
> life in order that the state might conserve her value as the
> woman citizen. Women cannot be treated exactly as men are,
> and motherhood, potential or actual, does determine woman's
> efficiency in industrial and social undertakings.[7]

By the end of the nineteenth century anti-suffragists had created a substantial body of argument. Mary A. J. M'Intire summed it up neatly in a lucid article for the *Boston Sunday Herald*, which was distributed as a pamphlet by the Massachusetts AOFESW.[8] The case for woman suffrage, she said, fell into two parts, one based on justice and the other on expediency. Miss M'Intire had trouble showing that it was just to deny women the vote on account of their sex, but she effectively attacked the operational claims made for woman suffrage. Women voters would not reform politics because the bad

7. Mrs. Arthur M. Dodge, "Woman Suffrage Opposed to Woman's Rights," *Annals* LVI (November 1914), 101.
8. Mary A. J. M'Intire, "Of What Benefit to Woman?: She Is a Far Greater Power Without Suffrage" (Boston, n.d.).

women would be enfranchised along with the good, leaving political morality about where it had been. Temperance would not be furthered because the votes of dry women would be canceled out by those of foreign women accustomed to the use of alcohol. Peace would not be assured because the Civil War had shown women to be no more pacific than men. Wages would not increase because working women needed unions, not votes. The only point on which she really faltered was the right of a majority of anti-suffragists who did not want the vote to keep it from the minority of suffragists who did.

The most valuable weapon in the anti-suffragist arsenal was not rhetorical, however. It was the evidence accumulated in those states and territories where women did vote. Few of the early examples proved much one way or another. They were all in underpopulated Western areas with atypical problems. Women were enfranchised in Wyoming partly by accident and partly because the authorities hoped thereby to encourage women to settle in a territory where men outnumbered them seven to one. In Utah the Mormons adopted equal suffrage in order to retain their advantage over a growing Gentile minority. Colorado, on the other hand, was a reasonably good demonstration of what woman suffrage would mean in practice. It had at least one real urban center, and was more highly developed than the other mountain states. Although antis had naturally opposed woman suffrage in Colorado—which passed in part because the Populists in 1893 hoped (wrongly as it turned out) to attract grateful women to their cause—it proved in many ways a blessing to them. Almost immediately they began pointing out that Colorado did nothing to advance the case for woman suffrage. "Equal Suffrage has not raised the pay of women workers in Colorado, during its three years of trial there, nor in Wyoming where it has been in force for a quarter of a century; a fact which its advocates agree to ignore, but which is convincing to any intelligent mind." [9] Federal Judge

9. Priscella Leonard, "A Help or a Hindrance" (New York, n.d.), p. 6.

Moses Hallett summed up the feelings of most Colorado citizens when he remarked that "the presence of women at the polls has only augmented the total votes; it has worked no radical changes. It has produced no special reforms, and it has had no particularly purifying effect upon politics." [1] In 1911 the Colorado state legislature legalized racetrack gambling with the four women members voting in favor.[2] All this only confirmed the judgment of thoughtful Coloradans, articulated by the *Fort Collins Express* after an election in which Denver voted down prohibition by a margin of two to one.

> If Colorado as a result of woman suffrage had laws above
> the average, especially on moral questions and where the
> rights of women are affected, if it was a state that could
> be pointed to with pride in regard to its laws and their
> enforcement, if the City of Denver as a result of their ballot
> could be changed from the worst city, morally, in the land,
> to one of even average decency, then the suffragettes could
> give a reason for asking for the franchise in other states,
> aside from the bare statement that the right is theirs, and
> that no one denies.[3]

Of course, many did deny them that right, which was why there was a suffrage movement in the first place, but otherwise this editorial fairly stated the case. In view of these facts, probably the most realistic position on woman suffrage was the one taken by Theodore Roosevelt.

> Personally I believe in woman's suffrage, but I am not an
> enthusiastic advocate of it, because I do not regard it as a
> very important matter. I am unable to see that there has
> been any special improvement in the position of women in
> those states in the West that have adopted it. I do not think
> that giving the women suffrage will produce any marked
> improvement in the condition of women. I do not believe

1. Quoted in Frank Foxcroft, "The Check to Woman Suffrage in the United States" (Boston, n.d.), p. 4.
2. "The Proof of the Pudding," *Remonstrance* (October 1911), pp. 1–2.
3. Quoted in "By Its Fruits," *Remonstrance* (July 1910), p. 10.

that it will produce any of the evils feared, and I am very
certain that when women as a whole take any special
interest in the matter they will have suffrage if they desire it.[4]

As was so often the case when his emotions were not involved,
TR aptly summed up the situation. In practical terms, equal
suffrage would have few effects, either positive or negative,
and since few women seemed to want it there was no reason to
take an active hand in the matter. When they wanted it they
would get it, and in a few years this was exactly what happened.
By 1917 the NAWSA may have had as many as two million
members, and in New York City alone it was able to secure
500,000 female signatures to a petition demanding the ballot.
Thereafter no one could say that the women who wanted to
vote were only a small minority. This is not to minimize the
effort involved in the suffragists' final drive to victory, but
rather further proof of Roosevelt's perspicacity in realizing that
a demonstrably powerful demand for the vote was an essential
precondition for securing it.

Nor is this meant to imply that anti-suffragists were all
models of sweet reason and suffragists entirely hysterical or
flabby-minded. A thousand examples of anti-suffragist venom
could be cited, and the evidence suggests that secret combina-
tions of businessmen (mainly in the liquor industry) conspired to keep women from voting.[5] But it was absurd to say
that the many anti-suffrage organizations were mere fronts for
the liquor interests, as suffragists often charged, and most
unwise to ignore that part of the anti-suffrage case that was
rational and well founded. Historians usually sympathize with
the suffragists, so their conviction that they enjoyed a monopoly
of intelligence has gone largely unchallenged. One has only to
read *Remonstrance*, published by the Massachusetts AOFESW

4. From a letter to Lyman Abbott, November 10, 1908, read by him
at an anti-suffrage rally. "An Anti-Suffrage Meeting in New York,"
Remonstrance (January 1909), p. 3.
5. See Flexner, *Century of Struggle*, pp. 294–305.

and a paper that compared favorably with most suffrage journals, to appreciate that this was not so. *Remonstrance* was a dignified, sensible organ full of material supporting its basic charge that the vote would not do for women what suffragists claimed for it. The association's eminent and wealthy members obviously did not need the brewers' tainted gold to support their paper, and could not understand why suffragists made such allegations.[6] What the suffragists in turn could not understand, and what in retrospect remains obscure, is why the antis made such great efforts to resist something which by their own admission would make little difference if accomplished. Suffragists did not, of course, agree, but they had to assume that the antis believed their own charges, a faith which rendered their activities all the more baffling.

Although the anti-suffragists have received so little attention that generalizations about them are hard to make, a clue to their puzzling behavior lies in the intensely emotional character of the whole suffrage question. The public controversy over woman suffrage was, at bottom, almost entirely irrational. The notion that suffragists had all the good arguments and their opponents only a network of prejudices and archaic convictions does not, as we have seen, hold water. The antis had many faults, but they were quite right in contending that suffrage would make little difference to the feminine condition. Suffragists, on the other hand, had countless plausible expectations about the good work women could do if only they had the vote. Most of these were either false or so overstated that they might as well have been false. Suffragist emotionality is easily explained. It took millions of dollars and an incalculable number of hours to win the vote, and there was little point

6. This does not apply to the last stages of the anti-suffrage campaign. Once it became clear (around 1917) that woman suffrage was going to prevail, many antis either converted or gave up the fight. The remaining hard core became progressively more bitter and bigoted, as the *Woman Patriot* of the 1920's demonstrated.

to this colossal expenditure unless the vote would make an important difference. Then, too, for the many reasons already discussed, suffrage became a focal point for the feminist revolution of rising expectations which had been diverted from more radical and far-reaching enterprises in the nineteenth century. Anti-suffrage emotionality is less easily understood, particularly among the considerable body of antis who were themselves a part of the woman movement and subscribed in a general way to the benevolent goals of social feminism. Perhaps they suffered from deep personality disorders or status conflicts, but until we know more about them little can be added to what has already been said.

.   .   .   .

If the suffragists' inability to recognize the holes in their argument is explicable, the fact remains that their failure to work out an ideology based on a realistic appraisal of the evidence was ultimately fatal to the feminist movement. Their peculiar shortsightedness in this regard deserves, therefore, further attention. The place Colorado enjoyed in their calculations is the most striking demonstration of the casual way in which they constructed the case for equal suffrage. If today Washington, D.C., with its Negro majority, was suddenly given home rule, we may be sure that a legion of investigators, reporters, and propagandists would descend on the city. By comparison, when Colorado became the first representative state to enfranchise its women, the public response could not have been more negligible. Of course, every good thing in the state was thereafter attributed by feminists to woman suffrage, but they ignored the state's unimpressive record of social legislation during the Progressive era and thus missed a valuable opportunity to think more deeply about why they wanted the vote and what they thought it should accomplish.

The principal exception to this rule occurred when the

New York Collegiate Equal Suffrage League sponsored the only serious inquiry into the effects of woman suffrage in Colorado. The assignment was given to Helen L. Sumner, a University of Wisconsin Ph.D., who during 1906–1907 carefully studied the problem. Her findings were published in 1909 under the title *Equal Suffrage*. She discovered that few women held public office because few women ran for office, and those who did were "handicapped by the discovery that other women in voting cling much closer to party than to sex lines." [7] There was, in fact, no woman's vote as such in Colorado except on a very few issues, and the party structure had been undisturbed by equal suffrage. Because the caucus and primary system was rigged in favor of "the machine," women had no more incentive than men to attend meetings whose outcome was foreordained. "It is no reflection, then, on equal suffrage to show women's incapacity to cope with the existing machinery of nominations. Equal suffrage, indeed, serves to show, in the most striking way, the essential rottenness and degrading character of the existing system." [8] In the legislative field, "though it is impossible to prove beyond the possibility of a doubt that the woman's club movement alone would not have brought about the passage of the same laws, it seems probable that the votes of women have effected the desired end with less effort and in less time than would have been required in nonsuffrage states." [9] Miss Sumner was able to say more definitely that the effect of equal suffrage on the position of working women had been slight. Regardless of how women voted, they earned good wages only in those trades where unions were strong, and where women workers did not compete with men.

There were, however, some advantages resulting from woman suffrage. A study of urban voting patterns showed that middle-class women voted more regularly than lower-class

7. Helen L. Sumner, *Equal Suffrage* (New York, 1909), p. 148.
8. *Ibid.*, pp. 95–96.
9. *Ibid.*, p. 211.

women. Apparently, instead of increasing the "ignorant vote" as was often feared, equal suffrage reduced it. On the whole, then, "the Colorado experiment certainly indicates that equal suffrage is a step in the direction of a better citizenship, a more effective use of the ability of women as an integral part of the race, and a closer understanding and comradeship between men and women." [1]

Helen Thomas Flexner of the sponsoring organization was, however, more cautious in her introduction to *Equal Suffrage*. It demonstrated to her satisfaction that women were slightly more independent than male voters, and more inclined to split their ticket, making it possible to keep in office men like Judge Lindsey, who would long since have been turned out or silenced if the major parties had had their way. The study also failed to support many reservations about woman suffrage. The ignorant vote was not increased, the pace of reform not slowed, and so forth. But Miss Flexner noted that, judging by Miss Sumner's questionnaires, while male acceptance of woman suffrage had grown since 1893, it had not grown as much as one might think, given the experiment's clear success. This seemed to her a direct result of the inflated claims made for equal suffrage before it went into effect. She warned prophetically that "every reform suffers from the fundamental psychological tendency of its advocates to claim too much for it, and from the consequent inevitable reaction against it after it has been carried through." [2] Precisely! And, if this were not enough, the following year Judge Lindsey, who owed his post to women voters, pointed out again that while equal suffrage was a good thing it made little practical difference because, for the most part, women voters were subject to the same influences and given to the same responses as men voters.[3]

1. *Ibid.*, p. 260.
2. *Ibid.*, p. xix.
3. Ben B. Lindsey, "The Beast and the Jungle," *Everybody's*, XXII (May 1910), 632–634.

Other friendly voices cautioned suffragists not to expect that voting of itself would promote great social changes. The leader of Iowa's suffragists told them that the chief benefits would be psychological. "The granting of the ballot, in each state . . . marks one of the greatest changes in the history of the world in the mental attitude of men, and women themselves, toward women." [4] The distinguished social worker Julia Lathrop put the vote in perspective at the 1912 NAWSA convention when she said, "Suffrage for women is not the final word in human freedom, but it is the next step in the onward march, because it is the next step in equalizing the rights and balancing the duties of the two types of individuals who make up the human race." [5] Agnes Repplier, who scoffed at the assertions that enfranchised women would end war, that the mother instinct would triumph over all, and the like, told her fellow suffragists near the struggle's end that victory would bring its troubles, too. "Emancipation implies the sacrifice of immunity, the acceptance of obligation. It heralds the reign of sober and disillusioning experience." [6] Floyd Dell suggested, half seriously, that the muffling effects of democratic procedures ought to console men like Rudyard Kipling who had written political verses to the effect that the female was deadlier than the male.

> Republican government . . . is an expensive, cumbrous, and highly inefficient method of carrying out the popular will; and casting a vote is like nothing so much as casting bread upon the waters. It shall return—after many days. By voting, by exercising an infinitesimal pressure on our complex, slow-moving political mechanism, one cannot—it is a sad fact —do much good; but one cannot—and it should encourage the pessimistic Mr. Kipling—one cannot, even though a woman, do much harm.[7]

4. Miss Flora Dunlap, quoted in "A 'Mental Change,'" *Remonstrance* (January 1916), p. 6.

5. *History of Woman Suffrage*, V, 344.

6. Agnes Repplier, "Woman Enthroned," *Atlantic Monthly*, CXXI (March 1918), 308.

7. Floyd Dell, *Women as World Builders* (Chicago, 1913), p. 31.

Mary Putnam Jacobi, the foremost woman physician of the nineteenth century, in her aptly named little book *Common Sense*, wrote that no one expected the vote to raise women's wages or drastically reform the social order. "But what is imagined, claimed, and very seriously demanded, is that women be recognized as human beings, with a range of faculties and activities co-extensive with that of men, whatever may be the difference in the powers within this range." [8] Since the vote would clearly not do this of itself, its value would seem to lie in the symbolic affirmation of women's changed status that voting would confer. This was the point of many essays in the *New Republic's* special supplement on woman suffrage in 1915. Under the heading "The Vote as a Symbol," Walter Lippmann suggested once more that the ballot was desirable not for the slight consequences it might bring but as a sign that women had come of age.

Inevitably, an exception to this line of reasoning was the belief that voting would nonetheless make women better women, which was to say better mothers. Speaking to the 1910 NAWSA convention in his capacity as secretary of the New York Men's League for Woman Suffrage, Max Eastman declared that "the great thing to my mind is not that women will improve politics but that politics will develop women." [9] And this was especially true of those women who did not want to vote, but would be led through possession of the franchise to exercise it and thereby broaden their outlooks, if only a little. At the 1905 NAWSA convention Anna Howard Shaw wrapped up both these themes, the limitation of the vote and its relation to motherhood. When the Oregon humorist C. E. S. Wood asserted that enfranchised women would doubtless only join the line of "little stuffed men going to a little stuffed ballot box," Dr. Shaw tartly replied:

8. Mary Putnam Jacobi, *"Common Sense" Applied to Woman Suffrage* (New York, 1894), p. 100.
9. *History of Woman Suffrage*, V, 285.

"I would rather be a little stuffed woman having my own say than to be ruled by a little stuffed man without my consent, and the only way we will cease to have little stuffed men is for them to be born of free mothers." [1]

When Dr. Shaw died, the *Woman Citizen* made the usual observation that "the winning of the franchise was never to her the end, it was but the means." [2] Yet this was said of every suffragist, even though for many the vote had become an end in itself. In the face of every warning that the cause was being oversold, that suffragists were running up a moral bill they would be unable to pay, they nonetheless pressed forward, made the most extreme claims, ignored every criticism no matter how genial or cogent, and made every other cause, however worthy or beloved of social feminists, a distant second to equal suffrage. The effect of generations of concentration on this one issue, the narrowing of feminism itself from the wide-open early days, the compromises made, opportunities exploited, and sacrifices endured all in the name of votes for women, destroyed the balance and perspective of hard-core suffragists. They came to desire the vote not for what it actually was or for what it could do but for its own sweet sake.

. . . .

Nowhere were the unfortunate consequences of this devolution more apparent before 1920 than in the movement's attitude toward immigration and race. Many of the early suffragists never recovered from their humiliating discovery that Negro men were considered better qualified to vote than they. In consequence, it became customary for them to exploit racial prejudices to their own advantage, as Mary A.

1. *History of Woman Suffrage*, V, 135.
2. "Anna Howard Shaw," *Woman Citizen*, July 2, 1919, p. 137.

Stewart did in opening her testimony before the Senate Judiciary Committee in 1880 by saying, "The negroes are a race inferior, you must admit, to your daughters, and yet that race has the ballot." [3] As memories of the great struggle for abolition faded, it became easier for Northern suffragists to adopt this line. By the 1890's the growth of racist feelings throughout the country and the emergence of a Southern suffrage movement combined to make, as Aileen Kraditor puts it, a "pact between woman suffrage and white supremacy" both natural and expedient.[4] It was sealed at the NAWSA convention in New Orleans in 1903. On that occasion Anna Howard Shaw advised that it was wrong to think woman suffrage would pave the way for social equality between the women of both races, for they already were equal in their votelessness. "But you have done more than that. You have put the ballot into the hands of your black men, thus making them the political superiors of your white women. Never before in the history of the world have men made former slaves the political superiors of their former mistresses." Warming to her task she concluded, "There is not a color from white to black, from red to yellow, there is not a nation from pole to pole, that does not send its contingent to govern American women. If American men are willing to leave their women in a position as degrading as this they need not be surprised when American women resolve to lift themselves out of it." [5] When Dr. Shaw, who grew up in Michigan, took so crude a line, no one would expect Southern women to be less candid. Miss Belle Kearney of Mississippi assured her auditors that woman suffrage with an educational or property requirement would insure white supremacy forever since ten out

3. *History of Woman Suffrage*, III, 158.

4. Kraditor, *Ideas of the Woman Suffrage Movement*, p. 200. Her chapter on "The Southern Question" documents this point fully.

5. Anna Howard Shaw, *The Story of a Pioneer* (New York, 1915), pp. 312–313.

of eleven literate Southern women were Caucasian. The NAWSA, like most other national organizations, was faithful to its prejudices. Negro women were usually segregated in suffrage parades, and they were discouraged from joining the association.

When people talked about the race issue at the end of the nineteenth century they more often meant immigrants than Negroes. The new immigration from Southern and Eastern Europe which hit its stride in the 1880's profoundly unsettled native-born middle-class Americans and gave rise to strong fears that woman suffrage would mean a further great expansion of the "ignorant vote." There were really only two ways suffragists could ease these anxieties, apart from denying there was any such thing as an ignorant vote. The first suffragists, as Professor Kraditor has pointed out, often put themselves in the awkward position of saying that women had been degraded and enslaved for centuries, but that they were as well qualified to vote as men nonetheless. Their later shift in favor of expediency undermined the argument from justice, but by proposing various sorts of qualifications it also made their case more coherent and enabled them to admit that some women were unfit to vote. They could then draw attention to the fact that native-born women outnumbered alien men and would tip the balance in favor of American values. They could also advocate a restrictive suffrage that would enfranchise middle-class women while disfranchising most foreigners. In practice they did both, but their rejection of universal suffrage was more consequential.

Politically there was very little chance, of course, that immigrants would be denied the ballot. Still, in calling for such drastic action suffragists demonstrated not only how far they had moved from the free-wheeling democracy of their early days but how seriously the whole middle class viewed the alien threat. Again and again suffragists were told in so many words that the new immigration made it too dangerous to admit an untried new category of voters. In the 1880's and early 1890's *Harper's Weekly* had supported equal suffrage, but in 1894, after H. L. Nelson replaced Carl Schurz as editor, it went over to the antis because "the introduction of woman suffrage means . . . the enfranchisement of those classes of women who correspond in character and education to the plantation negro and the ignorant immigrant." [6] When William Howard Taft became the first President to address a NAWSA convention, he bluntly told it that although as a young man he had been led by his father and John Stuart Mill to support equal suffrage, he now feared that "if the power is conferred, that it may be exercised by that part of the class least desirable as political constituents and be neglected by many of those who are intelligent and patriotic and would be most desirable as members of the electorate." [7]

To meet these fears, which they often shared, suffragists largely abandoned the argument that voting was an intrinsic human right and advanced their case by appealing to the lowest instincts of native Americans. Thus, at the 1889 National WSA convention the Reverend Olympia Brown of Wisconsin observed that in a recent election immigrant voters outnumbered the natives by a margin of two to one. She called upon American men to save themselves from alien domination by enfranchising their own women who were well born, well educated, capable, and yet "the political inferiors of all the riff-raff of Europe that is poured upon our shores." [8] Even Mrs. Stanton called for a literacy test that would "abolish the ignorant vote." [9] Although Mrs. Catt believed in universal suffrage—she defended it at the 1908 conference of the International Woman Suffrage Alliance, where some women charged that universal manhood suffrage

6. "Woman Suffrage," *Harper's Weekly*, June 16, 1894, p. 554.
7. *History of Woman Suffrage*, V, 270.
8. *Ibid.*, IV, 149.
9. *Ibid.*, IV, 317.

had failed in the United States—in 1920 she too called for an educational qualification.[1] Nor was Mrs. Catt the only great figure in the movement to falter. In a single month Florence Kelley of the Consumers' League testified before Congress that it was unfair to force women to work for state suffrage amendments because it forced them into humiliating contacts with foreign-born voters, and then berated delegates to the annual NAWSA convention for their contemptuous attitude toward immigrants.[2]

The argument for some kind of limited suffrage had, however, the defects of its virtues. Apart from its inherently undemocratic character and the moral confusion it engendered, in moving from the high ground of principle to the low ground of expediency suffragists still had to prove the functional value of votes for women and this, as we have already seen, was not nearly as easy to do as it appeared. Moreover, doing so narrowed the distance between suffragists and antis by a considerable margin. The best anti-suffragists shared many of the same values and wanted the same things as their suffragist counterparts in the NAWSA, and it was not hard for them to concede that a limited suffrage raised few of the problems that votes for all women did, especially as it guaranteed that equal suffrage thus construed would be innocuous. Grace Goodwin Duffield believed with many antis that it was woman's duty not to add to the burdens of an unfinished experiment in democratic government. A limited suffrage, on the other hand, would not strain the political fabric unduly, even though "in this day of frenzied democracy limited suffrage is not popular with men, much less with women." [3] Her remarks demonstrated how perilous the call for voter qualifications was, in that it very nearly destroyed

1. Carrie Chapman Catt, "What We Need," *Woman Citizen*, March 6, 1920, p. 943.

2. Quoted in Kraditor, *Ideas of the Woman Suffrage Movement*, p. 139.

3. Grace Goodwin Duffield, *Anti-Suffrage: Ten Good Reasons* (New York, 1912), p. 5.

both the popular and democratic rationales of the woman suffrage movement. Finally, of course, anti-alien harangues simply confirmed foreign-born voters in their belief that woman suffrage was dangerous to them, and accelerated the cycle of immigrant hostility and native suspicion which denied suffragists essential urban votes.

Fortunately for the cause, the last stages of the suffrage battle were marked by a more enlightened attitude. The most humane figures in the NAWSA had never ceased reminding their sisters, as Julia Lathrop put it, that

> . . . the ignorant vote is not the working vote. Working women in great organized factories have been having, since they began that work, an education for the suffrage. They are not the ignorant voters nor are wives of workingmen; at least, they know in part what they need to safeguard themselves and their homes.[4]

As the social feminist movement grew in strength and understanding during the Progressive era, it helped bring suffragists to an awareness of the complex nature of urban life and work. And, perhaps most importantly, the movement's leaders discovered that the immigrant vote could be won. In 1906 woman suffrage was narrowly defeated in Oregon, but Anna Howard Shaw was impressed that it got the most votes during those hours when workingmen cast their ballots. This lesson was learned elsewhere, and in 1917 New York was carried by the slim majority run up in New York City, where the immigrant working classes gave woman suffrage its margin of victory while the rest of the state split evenly.

Although the movement as a whole did not entirely recover from its nativist infection, by the time America entered the First World War suffragists had learned enough to meet the resultant xenophobia with some dignity and restraint. Their Americanization work was conducted with sanity and

4. *History of Woman Suffrage*, V, 345.

a degree of compassion, and, thanks especially to Carrie Chapman Catt, they never forgot that loyalty had to be deserved. The maturity thus demonstrated by the suffrage movement in its final stages went a long way toward making up for the chauvinism of its bleak years. The fact remains, however, that if the ballot had not meant so much to suffragists, if they had truly cared more about the social ends which the vote was supposed to facilitate, they would not have let themselves become so carried away by momentary passions. Beneath the apparent, and sometimes real, plausibility of their case was an obsessive desire for the suffrage itself, irrespective of what it could do for them. This is not to pass judgment on women who, whatever their faults, labored mightily in a good cause, but rather to point out that if they had been less emotional and more analytic the feminist movement would not have fallen into such disarray once it seized the Holy Grail.

Again, it has to be said that they had much to be emotional about. The position of American women at the end of the nineteenth century was better than it had ever been before—indeed, it was almost as good as it was ever going to be—but native-born, middle-class women were still subject to slurs and restrictions which were not so much harmful as humiliating. Mary Putnam Jacobi spoke for many, if not most of them, when she wrote:

> No matter how well born, how intelligent, how highly educated, how virtuous, how rich, how refined, the women of today constitute a political class below that of every man, no matter how base born, how stupid, how ignorant, how vicious, how poverty-stricken, how brutal. The pauper in the almshouse may vote; the lady who devotes her philanthropic thought to making that almshouse habitable may not. The tramp who begs cold victuals in the kitchen may vote; the heiress who feeds him and endows universities may not. The half-civilized hordes pouring into our country through the open gates of our seaport towns, the Indian if

settled in severalty, the negro on the cotton plantation,—all, now, or in a few years, have a vote. But the white woman of purest blood, and who in her own person, or that of her mother or grandmother has helped to sustain the courage of the Revolutionary war, to fight the heroic battle of abolition, and to dress the wound of the Rebellion—this woman must keep silence. The women who embrace half the education, half the virtue, and but a fraction of the illiteracy or crime of the community—remain excluded from the franchise, buried behind this dense cloud of often besotted ignorance.[5]

5. Jacobi, "*Common Sense*," pp. 73–74.

3

the structure of social feminism

*t*he great majority of women who took an interest in public matters during the years 1890 to 1920 belonged to social feminist organizations like the Women's Christian Temperance Union and the General Federation of Women's Clubs. When the consequences of equal suffrage and the meaning of feminine emancipation were discussed, it was these women to whom people looked for answers. The good reputation of the New Woman was largely a product of their activities. The hard-core feminist groups—notably the NAWSA and the Woman's party—did not attract many women until late in the game. We need not discuss every women's organization to get some sense of the range of feminine interests during these thirty years, but it will help us understand the collective experience of emerging womanhood if we keep in mind the traits of a representative selection.

. . . .

The Association of Collegiate Alumnae was a classic example of an organization designed to meet needs that were overwhelmingly emotional and subjective.[1] At the time of its founding in 1882, the basic problem of how women should be educated had been solved. Most of the important colleges for women had been founded. Most state universities admitted women on an equal basis with men. Even the reluctant graduate and professional schools were coming around. All this had been accomplished without the aid of any national organization. In a sense, then, the ACA was redundant. At its organizing meeting the venerable Lucy Stone (Oberlin '46) was asked to say a few words:

> She said that [sic] was well for those who had received the advantages of a liberal education to do something toward handing that blessing down to others and though she did not herself see what the practical issues of such an organization were to be she congratulated the members on the auspicious beginning which had been made and wished them success.[2]

Miss Stone knew that the battle for higher education had already been won, thanks to herself and a handful of pioneers. What this veteran suffragist, whose own life was so full of meaning and accomplishment, could not understand was the peculiar situation of the average female graduate in the late nineteenth century.

It was still difficult enough for girls to attend college, so that those who did were unusually dedicated. In college their sense of mission was encouraged by teachers who were

1. The only formal history of the ACA and its successor, the AAUW, is Marion Talbot and Lois Kimball Mathews Rosenberry, *The History of the American Association of University Women* (Boston, 1931). Mabel Newcomer, *A Century of Higher Education for Women* (New York, 1959), is generally helpful. The first two chapters of Christopher Lasch, *The New Radicalism in America* (New York, 1965), deal provocatively with the problems of educated women. The most useful sources for investigating the ACA are its irregular *Publications*. Little else survives, although the AAUW's excellent archives contain later material of much interest.

2. "Minute Book" of the ACA, Archives of the AAUW, pp. 42–43.

not yet certain the experiment was a success. The girls were sustained during their years on trial by peer associations of an intimate and rewarding nature. Each June saw the graduation of larger bands of sisters who had been through four years of communal life pitched at the highest moral, mental, and emotional levels. Suddenly they found themselves not merely alone, but alone in a society that had no use for them. Their liberal education did not prepare them to do anything in particular, except teach, and the stylized, carefully edited view of life it gave them bore little relation to the actual world. In consequence, graduation was often a traumatic experience for those young women who had been educated to fill a place that did not as yet exist. Some responded by turning to philanthropic work, and in time this became almost fashionable. At the outset, however, few opportunities for social service existed, and those that did rarely met the young graduates' requirements.[3]

This was where the ACA came in. It was founded in 1882 by Marion Talbot, a recent graduate of Boston University who had drifted aimlessly after leaving school. Its announced goals were to assist the intellectual growth of its members and help raise the standards of female education. Its main function was to restore the lost fellowship and sense of purpose that its members had possessed as schoolmates. This was true not only of the active members who saw each other regularly but even of those others who languished in the provinces. One such wrote, "I felt as if I had been flung out into space, and the notices of those meetings were the only threads that connected me with the things I had known." [4]

3. Good descriptions of the Victorian college girl's experience can be found in Jane Addams, *Twenty Years at Hull House* (New York, 1910); Florence Kelley, "When Co-Education Was Young," *Survey Graphic*, February 1, 1927; Vida Scudder, *On Journey* (New York, 1937); and L. Clark Seelye, *Early History of Smith College* (Boston, 1923), among others.

4. Quoted by Elizabeth Howe, "The Association of Collegiate Alumnae," *Publications of the ACA*, III (February 1908), 20.

Although the recapitulation of schoolgirl ties was central to the ACA, it did not lack for real work to do. M. Carey Thomas later recalled that "we were haunted in those days by the clanging chains of that gloomy little spectre, Dr. Edward H. Clarke's *Sex in Education*." [5] Published in 1873, this slight book argued that the higher education of women could only be accomplished at the expense of their reproductive capabilities. In Clarke's view, the alternatives were an unlettered womanhood or race suicide. Since he was a professor at the Harvard Medical School, his prognosis commanded some attention and for years advocates of feminine education sought to allay the fears he had raised. One of the ACA's first projects was a study of the pupils at the Girls' Latin School in Boston who, it was alleged, were breaking under the awful strain. More difficult to refute, because true, was the charge that women graduates married later, if at all, than most women and produced fewer children. Even a sympathetic figure like G. Stanley Hall, president of Clark University, declared in his influential study *Adolescence* (1904) that educated women had harder deliveries and more poorly nursed children. In fact, only about half the graduates of women's colleges ever married. Those who did were, on the average, five years older than their uneducated sisters. If only because of this they had fewer children and, it stands to reason, more difficulty in bearing them.[6]

ACA members typically did not marry. If they worked it was usually at schoolteaching. This mutuality of interest led M. Carey Thomas to call the association a trade union for women. It did try to represent women graduates as a class, and it sponsored studies on teachers' income and kindred

5. M. Carey Thomas, "Present Tendencies in Women's Colleges and University Education," *Publications of the ACA*, III (February 1908), 49.

6. G. Stanley Hall, *Adolescence: Its Psychology and Its Relations to Physiology, Anthropology, Sociology, Sex, Crime, Religion and Education* (New York, 1904). Vol. II, Ch. 17 is the most thorough contemporary demographic survey of female college graduates.

subjects, but it most resembled the unions of that day in its restrictive admissions policy. To join the ACA a woman had to have graduated from an institution specifically approved by the association. At first there were few such. By 1889 only six schools had been added to the original list of eight. Until 1963, when it finally gave up the struggle and decided to admit the graduates of all accredited colleges and universities, the ACA (which later became the American Association of University Women) devoted an immense amount of time to its admissions policy. It could never decide what it was trying to accomplish by restricting admissions. For a time it believed that the quality of instruction should determine whether an institution's graduates were eligible to join. Then it was argued that the treatment accorded women students should be decisive. This led to further complications: Should the position of women faculty members be examined as well? What was equal treatment anyway?

Behind the rhetoric was the assumption that sub-standard institutions could be brought up to par by women students eager to join the ACA. Or, at the very least, that meeting those standards would confer sufficient prestige on marginal schools to make them willing to accommodate the association. This remained a dubious proposition. Strong institutions had no reason to conform to the ACA's requirements, and weak ones could not. In practice, the only observable consequence of this policy was that a school already qualified on most counts would sometimes make a further slight effort to secure ACA recognition. Thus the University of Cincinnati built a women's building for its coeds when the ACA indicated that the lack of one was the only obstacle to recognition. No doubt this was a convenience for the University's female students, but it hardly affected the quality of their education.

Nonetheless, the association fiddled endlessly with its admissions policies as if the fate of higher education for women depended on finding exactly the right formula. The resulting discrepancy between time spent and results secured suggests the ACA's main function. If the association's purpose was to influence the quality of higher education for women, the admissions policy was pretty much of a failure. It held membership down (on the eve of World War I the ACA had only about six thousand members) without bringing any commensurate benefits. If, on the other hand, its purpose was to give emotional support to the members, the policy worked quite well. At first it eased the members' postgraduation trauma. Later it helped reconcile them to the small return their splendid educations brought them. By the turn of the century thousands of women had graduated from fine institutions only to become poorly paid, unpromoted schoolteachers. Several ACA studies proved that its teaching members were not only earning less than comparable male teachers but that, at a time when few pension plans existed, only about one-fifth were earning enough to provide for their old age. Whatever distinction membership in the ACA conferred, therefore, was especially necessary for women whose careers belied the promise of their college years.

For the sake of these psychological benefits the ACA passed up many chances to make a larger mark in the world. Because women's education in the South was particularly weak, it refused to recognize the graduates of any Southern institution. This forced the few women eager to raise standards to struggle alone in their own small organization, the Southern Association of College Women. Local branches that wanted to be effective in their communities were hamstrung when active women who happened to have gone to unrecognized schools were lost to college clubs that did not discriminate. The ACA never achieved a critical mass sufficient to command widespread attention until after the war when, as the American Association of University Women, it took a broader view of its possibilities.

The association's usefulness was further limited by its isolation from the mainstream of organized women. ACA members liked to think of themselves as the woman movement's General Staff. This flattering conception was once endorsed by Sarah Platt Decker, an exceptionally vigorous president of the General Federation of Women's Clubs, who wanted to get the ACA actively involved in public work. She observed:

> We are the militia, willing, ready, but not versed in the art. You are the West Pointers, the Regular Army, understanding methods, systems, modes of work, understanding through years of community life in college, the "give and take" of the world outside the four walls, which have been our outlook.[7]

Even this artful encouragement failed to bring the ACA out of its narcissistic isolation. Throughout the Progressive era, when women by the millions were organizing for reform, the association stayed aloof. It did not join the innocuous National Council of Women until 1915. Except for an occasional project, like the joint fellowship it offered for several years with the College Settlement Association, its contribution to social feminism was almost nil.

The ACA's policies were not held against it, publicly at least, by the rest of the woman movement. Most feminists seemed pleased that the banner of womanly achievement was unfurled so bravely. Even if they resented the association's pose, criticizing a sister group was regarded as poor form by most organized women, and they rarely did it. This made good sense at the time, but it prevented social feminists from searching out the ACA's meaning for their own future. They might, for example, have wondered if the ACA's resemblance to professional organizations in general

7. "Proceedings" of the 1904 meeting of the ACA, *Publications of the ACA*, III (January 1905), 40.

was not an ominous sign. Did it not suggest that educated and ambitious women, who had, after all, been exposed to the same curriculum as men, would as professionals behave much like men if given the chance? Might they not as a class continue to look after themselves first and society next, even when they were no longer a small minority?

.   .   .   .

The General Federation of Women's Clubs, with its great size and sprawling structure, was at the opposite end of the organizational spectrum from the ACA. It did, however, have its origins in the same needs of leisure-class women for comradeship and extra-domestic activity. Informal clubs began early in the nineteenth century, but the large department club which was the movement's most effective arm did not flourish until after the Civil War. In 1868 Mrs. Jennie Cunningham "Jennie June" Croly, a well-known journalist, irked by the New York Press Club's refusal to admit women to its dinner for Charles Dickens, resolved to found a rival organization for women. Sorosis, as it was called, was initially made up of career women, but it soon attracted more ordinary women in such numbers that it had to be divided into smaller groups organized around specific themes. These "departments" were imitated by the large, urban, women's clubs formed thereafter. In 1889 when Sorosis sent out a general invitation to celebrate its twenty-first anniversary, sixty-one clubs responded. This inevitably prompted thoughts of federation, and the next year many of these clubs organized themselves into the GFWC. At its first biennial meeting in 1892, the federation had already grown to twenty thousand women in nearly two hundred clubs. By 1900 it had 150,000 members, and before the Progressive era waned it could claim a million or more. Although it was probably the largest secular organization of women to flourish during these years, and, in fact, one of the most substantial national bodies of any type supporting the Progressive impulse, it has attracted little attention from historians. Yet the clubs exercised a real, if elusive, political power, and engaged in public affairs women whom no other agency was able to reach.[8]

The spontaneous, grass-roots character of the club movement was its most important feature. The General Federation grew so great because thousands of clubs already existed. Only a little paperwork was needed to make a national organization. Most of the clubs were devoted to something called "self-culture." What this meant in practice was outlined by a reporter who obviously had been overexposed to club life.

> I have been reporting club meetings for four years and I am tired of hearing reviews of the books I was brought up on.
> I am tired of amateur performances at occasions announced to be for purposes either of enjoyment or improvement. I am tired of suffering under the pretense of acquiring culture.
> I am tired of hearing the word "culture" used so wantonly.
> I am tired of essays that let no guilty author escape quotation.

The woman's club, she concluded, was "a body of women banded together for the purpose of meeting together." [9]

Wasteful as such affairs were, at first they were probably necessary. At the federation's first biennial its president, Mrs.

8. The most recent history of the GFWC is Mildred White Wells, *Unity in Diversity* (Washington, D.C., 1953). Still useful is Mary I. Wood, *The History of the General Federation of Women's Clubs* (New York, 1912). J. C. Croly, *The History of the Woman's Club Movement in America* (New York, 1898), is more of a scrapbook than anything else. The best sources for studying the GFWC are the published proceedings of its conventions and its official magazine which has had many different names and publishers since it began. The federation makes no effort to preserve its documents but does have almost a complete set of its past publications.

9. Josephine Woodward, "Woman's Clubs from a Reporter's Point of View," *Club Woman*, III (December 1898), 83.

Charlotte Emerson Brown, pointed out that women were now free to take responsibilities which their habits and training prevented them from discharging. The club, she argued, was a training ground where they could get the experience and education necessary for their new roles.[1] In the clubs they learned to speak in public, make formal reports, meet and work with strangers, and do in a small way what later they would attempt on a community-wide scale. For less serious members of the growing leisure, or semi-leisure, class of women, the clubs were invaluable. Middle-aged, middle-class women whose children were in school, whose homes were cleaned by servants and supplied commercially with all manner of goods and services, found in club life an antidote to boredom. Even if they were not caught up in the club's philanthropic and civic work, they lent it weight and substance all the same. Women inspired by their new freedoms and stimulated by the reform spirit found clubs useful precisely because they included so many women of good family whose membership, however passive, gave the clubs size and prestige.

The movement's attraction for more conservative women was both its greatest asset and its most limiting factor. The clubs did not really compete with other social feminist organizations, most of which required a much higher level of commitment than clubs could expect. But they did want the same kind of women who belonged to religious groups ranging from conventional church auxiliaries on through the exotic sects like Christian Science, Theosophy, Spiritualism, and the mind-cure religions so popular at the time. The General Federation went to great lengths to avoid antagonizing its cautious rank and file. Although most federation leaders were suffragists, it did not endorse woman suffrage until the eve

1. "Report of the First Biennial Meeting of the General Federation of Women's Clubs," *New Cycle*, V (July 1892), 14.

of victory. Even more suggestive was the federation's handling of the race issue. Though the Civil War had been over for more than a generation when the GFWC was founded, it was still very much alive in the hearts of clubwomen. They remembered it because of the surviving abolitionists who still participated in club life, and because (in the Sanitary Commission and related activities) the war had afforded Northern women their chief opportunity for national service. The federation's most distinguished member was Julia Ward Howe, whose "Battle Hymn of the Republic" was sung or recited at almost every biennial. Women who had been born too late to remember the war itself were taught to revere the heroism it had called up.

While this ought to have made clubwomen sympathetic to the Negro's struggle, in practice it did not. This was not simply because most clubwomen shared the general prejudices of this intensely racist era; rather, it was a consequence of the federation's role in the sectional reconciliation then taking place. The very women who thrilled to the memory of their elders' participation in the war were eager to heal the wounds it had caused. The GFWC held its third biennial in Louisville specifically to demonstrate the new unity of American womanhood it was helping to bring about. Accordingly, when a Negro clubwoman attempted to secure delegate status at the fourth biennial in 1900, the federation was compelled to deny her a seat in order to retain its Southern members. During the next two years, while the GFWC did not, as the Southern state federations wished, go so far as to make race a condition of membership, a complicated scheme was worked out to insure that Negroes would not in the future be seated at biennials. When Jane Addams and the Massachusetts' state federation led a group of dissidents in an attempt to block the move at the Los Angeles biennial in 1902, they were overwhelmed. The *Los Angeles Times* summed up the feelings of most clubwomen when it wrote, "The color line has been passed with little friction, and the question is now a buried issue. The unity of the Federation has been preserved, and North and South have forgotten their difference in a new and stronger union, the result of mutual courtesy and concession." [2]

This is not to single out the federation for reproach —most national organizations in the Progressive era followed a similar course—but only to indicate the extent of its liberalism. On the local level, where clubwomen were probably most effective, they did a great deal of civic good housekeeping. Many a town owed its pure drinking water or public library to them. On the state level they joined with other women's groups to lobby for regulatory legislation benefiting women and children. This was true not only of states like Massachusetts, whose advanced factory legislation owed something to the head start organized women had secured there, but even of small states like Rhode Island, where in 1916 the state federation joined a female popular front to put through a fifty-four-hour law for working women and children. Nationally the Pure Food and Drug Act, the Child Labor Bill, and other typical Progressive measures were passed with federation help. Clubwomen, either through marriage or in their own right, were influential members of their communities. They had access to the power structure and, while they did not vote, they had male friends and relatives who did. Thus, because it was impossible to measure their actual potency, wise politicians conceded some power to clubwomen for safety's sake. Clubwomen did not ask for a great deal, but when they wanted something badly it was prudent to assume that their frustration might have unpleasant consequences.

In theory, nothing human was alien to the General Federation. It passed dozens of resolutions at each biennial

2. Quoted in Wood, *History of the GFWC*, p. 163.

on everything from pure food to pure movies. But the range of its serious concerns was fairly narrow. A consensus among clubwomen existed mainly on what might be called protectionist or conservationist issues. As their official organ put it, "Conservation . . . is the raison d'etre of the General Federation . . . conservation of child life, of womanhood, of civic and national integrity."[3] In practice this meant that the GFWC was strongly in favor of protective legislation for working women and children, and against despoiling the natural environment. These interests were consistent with traditional womanly concerns. As mothers clubwomen worried about working children, as women about their less fortunate sisters, and as homemakers about bad housekeeping on the local, state, and national levels. Clubwomen were not interested in the trusts, the currency, organized labor, disorganized farmers, foreign affairs, or indeed, most other questions that agitated Progressives.

The federation wasted much time on tangential or irrelevant matters. It got hung up on issues like civil service reform, to which thousands, perhaps millions, of woman-hours were devoted. Culture was not left to the individual clubs but received sober and lengthy attention during and after biennials. What most discouraged GFWC officers, however, was the sprawling, unfocused character of the club movement itself. Most clubwomen never got much beyond self-culture and entertainment. They enjoyed being part of the General Federation only if it asked little of them in the way of dues or effort, and so long as it did not embarrass them in their communities. This presented the federation's leadership with a dilemma. They could not develop a powerful organization without alienating the mass of ordinary women that gave the GFWC its weight and prestige, and which it was the federation's special pride to have organized in the first place. No federa-

3. Editorial, *Federation Bulletin*, IV (June 1907), 326.

tion officer was willing to do this, even were a tight structure possible, if only because it would destroy the GFWC's unique position in the woman movement. At times this internal contradiction became so acute that federation leaders found themselves sacrificing, for the sake of the organization, those purposes it nominally existed to advance.

. . . .

Unlike the ACA and the club movement, social settlements did not originate in America and were not developed especially to meet the needs of middle-class women.[4] But as most settlement workers were feminists, the movement (it was not formally organized as the National Federation of Settlements until 1911) affected the condition of women nonetheless. It also testified to the English influence on American reformers during the years 1890 to 1920. Most people, raised on the American dream of a yeoman republic and taught to see their homeland as a pastoral refuge from the stews of Europe, had difficulty grasping the fact that an urban, industrialized society was growing up around them. Once they admitted that the same dismal urban problems as obtained in Europe existed here, too, it was natural for them to seek solutions abroad, where the industrial revolution was further advanced. Germany was instructive, but for most American reformers England was the country to study. Birmingham and London were experimenting with municipal solutions to civic problems. Organized labor was beginning to exercise real political

4. The best account of the settlements during their important years is Allen F. Davis, *Spearheads for Reform: The Social Settlements and the Progressive Movement, 1890–1914* (New York, 1967). Also useful are Robert A. Woods, *Handbook of Settlements* (New York, 1911), and Robert A. Woods and Albert J. Kennedy, *The Settlement Horizon: A National Estimate* (New York, 1922). There are many biographies of leading settlement workers and an abundance of primary material on this subject, as Davis points out in his valuable "Note on Sources."

power. William Morris offered one kind of socialist answer to the social question, the Fabian Society another. Americans profited greatly from English initiatives, although they invariably experienced a sea change en route to the New World. The social settlement idea is a good example of how this process worked.

The first settlement was Toynbee Hall in London. Its founder, Canon Barnett, a minister of the Church of England, was inspired by the attempts of young university men like Philip Toynbee to work with the urban poor and establish a community of interest among the social classes. Barnett wanted to foster self-help among working people, and to help raise their moral and cultural tone. Toynbee Hall itself was a kind of university extension in the slums. Stanton Coit, who founded what was to become the University Settlement in New York in 1886, was moved by the same spirit. To him, "the organization of the intellectual and moral life of the people is the crying need of our day." [5] Within a few years, however, Coit emigrated to England and the movement he had begun soon took quite another tack. In 1889 Jane Addams established Hull House, the most influential of all American settlements, for the express purpose of social action, or, as she put it, "the application of knowledge to life." [6] Her conviction that the place to begin saving the city was in its slums became the animating principle of the great American settlements, displacing the original concern with self-help and character development.

After 1900 the movement burgeoned so rapidly that no one could be sure how many houses existed at any given time. Nor was it always easy to tell a settlement from a church mission renamed. Unlike Hull House, most were not

5. Stanton Coit, *Neighbourhood Guilds: An Instrument of Social Reform* (London, 1891), p. 4.
6. Jane Addams, "A Function of the Social Settlement," *Annals*, XIII (May 1899), 325.

engines of reform. But some dozens of settlements, especially in New York, Boston, and Chicago, became centers of regeneration, and over the years thousands of young women lived in them. Miss Addams, as she indicated in her candid essay "The Subjective Necessity of Social Settlements," founded Hull House to resolve her personal crisis. Like others of her class she had been brought up to know that suffering and poverty existed in the world, and taught to be self-sacrificing and altruistic. But, she continued, "when the daughter comes back from college and begins to recognize her social claim to the 'submerged tenth,' and to evince a disposition to fulfill it, the family claim is strenuously asserted; she is told that she is unjustified, ill considered in her efforts." [7] Jane Addams finally rejected the family claim and discovered in settlement work a way of meeting her own and society's most urgent needs at the same time. Thousands of girls followed her.

Miss Addams brought to the slums a cool, unsentimental view of the working classes. Many of the early female settlement residents had a more romantic sense of mission. The first college settlement began only a few months after Hull House when a small group of women graduates moved into a tenement on New York's Lower East Side. Some were moved by the Russian Populists' example, others thought in terms of a Franciscan-like communion with the dispossessed. At least one, Vida Scudder, was a socialist eager to demonstrate her solidarity with the proletariat in a concrete way. Although a Boston paper thought that "the falling of their young unsullied lives in this vicious dismal quarter seems like

7. This essay was reprinted many times. It is conveniently available in Christopher Lasch, ed., *The Social Thought of Jane Addams* (Indianapolis, 1965), p. 38. See also her essay "Filial Relations," in her first book *Democracy and Social Ethics* (New York, 1902), which was dedicated to her companion Mary Rozet Smith, another victim of the generational conflict.

the falling of a lily in the mud," their example was contagious. Within a year eighty girls were trying for places in the New York house, and two more college settlements had been opened in Boston and Philadelphia.[8] With this growth came the usual proliferation of activities, and before long Vida Scudder had to confess that "within the house physical hardship and personal discomfort have largely ceased to exist. Residents continue to come with the intention of giving their strength and life to the neighborhood; the other motive, almost equally strong in early times, of self-identification with the life and conditions of the poor, has shrunk to a vanishing point." [9]

Part of this change was a consequence of the rapid turnover in settlement personnel. Allen F. Davis carefully examined the lives of three hundred settlement workers and discovered that most did not remain long in the neighborhood. About half the female residents eventually married. The median number of years they spent in settlement work was three. Those who did not marry stayed longer, about ten years on the average, before leaving the settlement for some other kind of social service. Only twenty-two of his sample made a career of settlement work, sixteen of them women, and fourteen of these spinsters.[1] On its twenty-fifth anniversary the College Settlement Association polled its alumnae with roughly the same results. Most of the respondents (141) had resided in the settlement for less than five years (sixty-two for less than one year). Most favored woman suffrage and sympathized with organized labor. Forty declared themselves to be socialists, although only five had gone so far as

8. Quoted in Scudder, *On Journey*, p. 139.

9. *Dennison House College Settlement Report for 1900* (n.p., n.d.), p. 5.

1. See his doctoral dissertation "Spearheads of Reform" (University of Wisconsin, 1959), pp. 1–26. This data does not appear in the published version.

to join a socialist organization.[2] Interestingly enough, few were certain that the settlement had a profound effect on its neighborhood, or that the residents shared intimately in the district's social and intellectual life. They did agree that the settlement was most effective in dealing with women and children.

If the ultimate significance of the settlement movement as a contributor to the Progressive ferment and an important chapter in the history of social welfare is hard to assess, its meaning for feminism seems evident. It met the subjective needs of thousands of women for fellowship and constructive enterprise, and it provided heroic models for emancipated women. In taking their place on the front line of social action, female residents dealt the Victorian stereotype of women a fatal blow. Never again was it possible to generalize with perfect confidence on the essentially fragile and decorative character of the gentler sex. In Jane Addams the movement produced the best-known woman in America and, perhaps, after Queen Victoria, in the world. Many of the other great women in that remarkable generation—Lillian Wald, Mary Simkhovitch, Florence Kelley, Mary McDowell—were or had been settlement residents. No other aspect of the woman movement, except for suffragism itself, received so much attention from the national press. Best of all, the settlements reassured conservatives that liberated women would interest themselves in traditional womanly concerns, the novelty of their approach notwithstanding. Settlements did sometimes become involved in political controversies, but over the years their energies were devoted most of all to the interests of women and children, mainly in the slums. On both counts, then, as models for adventurous young female altruists, and as evidence that the social concerns of free women would not

2. Mrs. Thayer and Miss Florence Converse, "After Twenty-Five Years—Questionnaire," *The CSA 1889–1914* (n.p., n.d.), pp. 34–56.

disrupt the existing order, settlement workers played a key role in the woman movement.

. . . . . .

The National Consumers' League was a small, elite organization of well-educated women.[3] In relation to its size and resources, it was one of the most effective social reform agencies in the Progressive era and an especially good example of the way bright, altruistic women found a social use for their talents. Except for the vastly larger NAWSA, no other feminist group seems to have attracted upper-class women in such numbers.

The first Consumers' League grew out of a mass meeting organized in New York City in 1890 by retail shop girls to publicize their low pay, long hours, and deplorable working conditions. Their presentation was so effective that a committee of prominent citizens was formed to investigate conditions, and in January 1891 it named itself the Consumers' League. Its first president was Josephine Shaw Lowell, a Civil War widow whose service in the Sanitary Commission led her into philanthropy. In 1876 she was appointed the first woman commissioner of the New York State Board of Charities, a post she held until 1889 when her interest in the labor question moved her to resign it. She had come to believe that "the interests of the working people are of paramount importance, simply because they are the majority of the whole people, and the indifference and ignorance and harshness felt and expressed them by so many good people is simply

3. The best account is the unpublished doctoral dissertation by Louis Lee Athey, "The Consumers' Leagues and Social Reform, 1890–1923" (University of Delaware, 1965). See also Maud Nathan, *The Story of an Epoch-Making Movement* (Garden City, 1926), and her autobiography *Once Upon a Time and Today* (New York, 1933). The league's papers are mostly in the Library of Congress.

awful to me and I must try to help them, if I can, and leave the broken-down paupers to others." [4]

Mrs. Lowell's prestige and experience brought other upper-class women into the league, notably Mrs. Maud Nathan, who in 1896 replaced Mrs. Lowell as president. Mrs. Nathan and her husband belonged to the small New York community of Sephardic Jews who since the seventeenth century had played an important part in the city's life. Like Mrs. Lowell, Maud Nathan was willing and able to use her place in New York society to advance the interests of working women. In the nineties league members worked out a program that involved contacting individual store owners whose labor practices were sub-standard, promoting a White List of employers whose policies were more enlightened in hopes that buyers would patronize them exclusively, and publicizing the abuses created by "the rage of the purchasing public for cheap goods." [5] By ignoring personalities, absolving businessmen of direct responsibility, emphasizing the humanitarian aspects of its work, and concentrating on the failings of the anonymous middle-class consumer, the league effected improvements in an area where little had been accomplished. Many stores raised the wages of shopgirls and reduced their working hours. A shop-early campaign to ease the Christmas rush was launched that in time enabled the principal New York stores to close earlier during the season.

By 1899 other leagues had been established in large cities, and the National Consumers' League was organized to coordinate their efforts. Florence Kelley, formerly Chief Factory Inspector of Illinois, became its general secretary. This fabulously energetic woman took hold so vigorously that within a year five state leagues had been formed. In a few years there were ninety local leagues, twenty state leagues, thirty-five auxil-

4. William Rhinelander Stewart, *The Philanthropic Work of Josephine Shaw Lowell* (New York, 1911), p. 358.

5. *Ibid.*, p. 338.

iary leagues, and numerous college branches. The NCL sponsored a White Label campaign, similar to its White List of fair houses, by which clothing manufacturers with good labor policies were authorized to use an NCL label attesting to that fact. In 1901 the league began sending out traveling exhibits in support of the label, and by 1914 some seventy manufacturers—mostly of coarse undergarments demanding, as Josephine Goldmark recalled, "a considerable sense of virtue" to wear—were using it. The league also started investigating on its own and produced reports on conditions in a wide variety of industries. It lobbied actively for protective legislation in cooperation with like-minded groups. After 1907 it concentrated with much success on maximum-hour and minimum-wage laws for working women.

If the NCL had done nothing more than offer a platform for Florence Kelley that would have been enough. But the league also developed a cadre of young women like Pauline and Josephine Goldmark, and Frances Perkins (who became FDR's Secretary of Labor) who complemented the older, socially eminent founders. These full-time activists, with the formidable Mrs. Kelley, made the league at least as effective on the national level as much larger organizations like the GFWC and the WCTU. Smallness can be an asset. The NCL moved quickly when action was required, took positions without exhaustive soundings of its membership, and brought all its human resources to bear on a given problem when necessary. And it enjoyed the support of wealthy and influential women whose social weight offset their lack of numbers.

The NCL was not only a model social feminist organization but a prototypical specimen of the Progressive mentality. It had complete faith in the power of reason to change society. It investigated each problem as fully as possible, then it educated the public on the basis of its discoveries. Finally, it relied on the moral indignation thus aroused to influence public policy. The league lobbied when necessary and valued the ability of influential women to apprise legislators of their duty, but it relied mainly on the Progressive formula of investigation, education, and moral suasion. Florence Kelley, although a lifelong socialist, became convinced that in America desirable social changes were most readily secured by an appeal to reason and morality. Of course it was in everyone's interest to have safe, wholesome products made and sold by healthy, well-paid workers. But the appeal to self-interest, Mrs. Kelley decided, no matter how valid, was the least effective way of changing people's minds on social questions. She and her colleagues, therefore, embraced without reservation the cooperative ethic which distinguished Progressive social thought. Perhaps no other social feminist organization was as much a product of its age.

. . . .

Of our sample of organizations, the National Women's Trade Union League was the last organized and the first dissolved.[6] It was founded in 1903 by an assortment of socialists, social workers, reformers, and a few trade unionists gathered for the annual convention of the American Federation of Labor. The idea came from William English Walling, a wealthy socialist intellectual who had been impressed by the WTUL of England and thought a similar body would be useful in this country. At first the league was pretty much a neglected child of the settlement houses. The founders lacked confidence, and with good reason: working women were mostly unskilled workers with little commitment to their trade.

6. The only history is Gladys Boone, *The Women's Trade Union League in Great Britain and the United States* (New York, 1942). Its papers are in the Library of Congress. For several years it published an excellent journal, *Life and Labor*, which was succeeded in the 1920's for a time by *Life and Labor Bulletin*.

The unions, when not actively discriminatory, were not interested in members whose wages did not permit them to pay full dues, and who remained in the work force for comparatively short periods of time. The women workers were themselves frequently prejudiced against trade unions, wished only to get married and out of the factory, and suffered from all the handicaps of youth, inexperience, and, often, foreign birth or parentage. Little wonder, then, that while five million women were employed in 1900, almost none of them were organized. They earned, on the average, about half the wages of working men.

While it was clear that working women needed help, it was not immediately apparent what the NWTUL could do for them that other groups could not. They needed certain kinds of protective legislation, but the Consumers' League and its allies were already engaged on that front. They needed to be organized, but that was the trade union's job. If the unions were derelict in their duty, it was hard to see how a small band of women could infuse labor leaders with the necessary ardor. One thing the NWTUL might have done was to set up unions of its own where organized labor was unwilling to operate. This possibility was never seriously considered. The NWTUL did organize a substantial number of working women over the years, but always for existing unions. The league nagged and pleaded with the AFL—with little success—to organize women more intensively and to open up restricted affiliates, yet the League never doubted that loyalty to the AFL was indispensible to its mission.

Within its self-imposed limits, however, the NWTUL developed several unique functions. It brought a number of wealthy women into direct contact with the labor movement. Margaret Dreier Robins, its president during most of the Progressive era, was well off, so was her sister Mary Dreier who directed the New York League for many years. They brought in others like themselves, sometimes as active members, more frequently as occasional volunteers. The league also developed a body of working women like Rose Schneiderman, Leonora O'Reilly, Helen Marot, and Pauline Newman. Eventually they dominated the league, which thus became the only feminist organization made up largely of working (or ex-working) women. The NWTUL was more liberal than the AFL and often reminded the federation of its moral shortcomings. In 1909, at its second biennial meeting, it refused to endorse oriental exclusion, though this was a policy strongly favored by the AFL.

This liberalism was not only a consequence of the league's ties with the woman movement but a function of its socialist associations. Although the league was not socialist, many of its best members were. Even more important, it found that of all working girls the Jews were easiest to organize. The league's greatest successes were in the garment trades where Jewish working girls predominated. As Alice Henry, an Australian who edited the league's journal, put it, Jewish girls, "add to courage and enthusiasm, such remarkable gifts of intellect and powers of expression as to make them a power wherever they have become awakened to the new problems." [7] Socialism was the major political influence among Jewish workers, and if the NWTUL expected to organize them it had to treat their politics with respect, if not conviction. It managed to do so, and to pick up a few pointers at the same time, even though this exposed it to criticism and harassment from right-wing labor leaders. Its socialist members pushed the NWTUL to the left a trifle; the league, in turn, pulled them to the right. At the 1911 biennial, Pauline Newman announced that "I have been a revolutionist since I came to this country . . . and if I know how to use my revolutionism, how to put my theory as far as possible into practice, it is due to the Women's Trade Union League of New York." [8]

7. Alice Henry, *The Trade Union Woman* (New York, 1915), p. 135.

8. "Proceedings" of the 1909 Convention, Papers of the NWTUL, p. 7.

Of course, in this context putting one's revolutionism to work meant giving it up. The NWTUL, like most reform groups, was counterrevolutionary. It aimed to destroy the conditions that generated revolt, and in doing so it immersed socialists like Miss Newman and Miss Schneiderman in practical work that was not merely unradical but actually destructive of the goals radicals hoped to reach. Yet, while ultimately the middle-class reform ethic prevailed, the NWTUL retained a distinctive flavor as the only branch of the woman movement in which Jews, socialists, and workers (all three attributes normally being found in the same persons) played important parts.

The league was successful in handling the internal tensions generated by its disparate membership, but it was never able to resolve the contradictions posed by its dual membership in the feminist and labor movements. Its one great purpose was to help organize working women. Yet its relationship with the unions was determined by its place in the woman movement. Most trade unions were uninterested in, and sometimes hostile to, working women as a class. The only female organizations the AFL felt comfortable with were its own malleable auxiliaries. President Samuel Gompers and most other AFL leaders paid some attention to the NWTUL only because women like Mrs. Robins had too much influence to be ignored. Sensible labor leaders saw no reason to offend feminists unnecessarily, and generally they did not. On the other hand, the league's feminism and its middle- and upper-class membership enabled the AFL to keep it at arm's length. Since it was allied with, rather than a constituent part of, the labor movement, Gompers was not obliged to give it any votes at the AFL's conventions, or any money to speak of. Both Gompers and the league insisted on its status as a feminist organization, but for opposite reasons. Gompers used the tactic defensively, while for the league it was an offensive weapon.

In the end, as we shall see, the league gave much more

to the AFL than it ever received in return. Its years of loyalty, in fact, cost it whatever slim chance there might have been of organizing a sizable percentage of the female work force. During the Progressive years, however, the NWTUL flourished, and in doing so added spice and variety to the woman movement. Most of all, it provided a large part of the substance for the feminists' claim to represent the interests of women of all classes and conditions.

.   .   .   .   .   .

Taken together, these organizations fairly represent the range of social feminist activity during the woman movement's golden age—which coincided with the Progressive era. Some, like the ACA, predated progressivism and were not deeply affected by it. Others, especially the NWTUL and the NCL, were in large measure products of that age of reform. All of them answered to some degree the need of emerging womanhood for fellowship and constructive enterprise. All of them, except the ACA, figured importantly in the social-justice wing of the Progressive movement. The ACA is worth noticing, however, for what it suggested about the future of educated women. Everyone was certain that the growing body of women graduates would one day be a great force for good in the country. This was mainly because graduates played a large part in feminist and reform activities at a time when they were few in number. The expectation was that as graduates increased numerically, the percentage involved in social action would remain the same. This proved not to be the case. After 1920 the number of graduates shot up, to the great benefit of the ACA which, as the American Association of University Women, burgeoned in consequence, but the percentage working for social justice declined. Hence the relatively narrow and self-centered ACA was a better index to the future of this class of women than its larger and more important sister groups in the Progressive era.

Except for the ACA, again, none of these organizations existed before 1890, the earliest point at which the Progressive era may be said to have begun. But this fact is somewhat misleading. Women had started organizing in the first years of the nineteenth century, and by the 1870's were doing so nationally. The Association for the Advancement of Women was founded in 1873, the Women's Christian Temperance Union in 1874, and the National and American Woman Suffrage Associations even earlier. Women reached for national influence before they could grasp it. By the 1890's, however, the requisite sub-structure for truly large-scale feminine organizations had come into being. Many women had the time and inclination for public works. They had learned in their clubs and other local institutions the practical requirements of such activity, and several bodies, especially the WCTU, had shown how to make this experience work on higher levels. At the same time the suffragist drift from abstract rights to practical consequences had, as we saw earlier, created a platform upon which feminist and nonfeminist humanitarians could stand. It seems certain that the turn of the century would have witnessed a great expansion in feminine enterprise whether the Progressive movement had existed or not.

Feminism did not, of course, develop in a vacuum. Although it had its own wellsprings, it was also part of the drive for national, rationalized social, political, and economic institutions in the Progressive era. The "search for order," as one historian calls it, was made by women as well as men.[9] Some feminist groups, from the NAWSA itself to the NWTUL, expanded as part of a calculated effort to secure predetermined objectives. Others, the GFWC in particular, grew like weeds for no apparent reason. The creation of individual clubs was easy to understand, but the need to bind them together in elaborate state federations feeding up to the General Federa-

9. Robert H. Wiebe, *The Search for Order, 1877–1920* (New York, 1967).

tion was not. Of the GFWC's first five presidents, only two (Ellen Henrotin, 1894–1898, and Sarah Platt Decker, 1904–1908) were really social feminists. Most leading clubwomen seemed to have regarded organizing as an end in itself. They drew up lengthy and intricate constitutions which they lovingly revised and re-revised. Their meetings were marked by an exaggerated adherence to parliamentary procedure, and they were ready at a moment's notice to create committees which could then hold lengthy hearings and make impressively formal reports. In part, such activity resulted from the prevailing impression that this was the efficient way to go about doing things. Certainly male critics were always impressed by elaborate mechanics. It seems also to have stemmed from the sheer pleasure women derived from bureaucratic minutiae, the novelty of which had not yet been tarnished by custom. All of this suggests a kind of unconscious response to, and sometimes a parody of, the great contemporary impulses that sought to transform a sprawling, continental empire into an efficient nation-state.

Groups like the settlement workers and the trade union women, on the other hand, were unambiguously related to the social-justice movement. While they met their members' subjective needs and worked closely with other feminist organizations, their primary objective was social reform. It is hard to see how they could have developed in the same way independently of progressivism. This was especially true of the leading settlements which were keyed into the era from beginning to end. One can hardly think of an important Progressive thought, word, or deed that did not affect them. In the 1880's and 1890's Henry George's writings inspired some residents, while others responded to academic reformers —the sociologists, economists, and philosophers who were breaking down the principles of Social Darwinism and classical economics. The Social Gospel was vitally important, not only to the numerous religious settlements but even in the secular ones, many of whose residents believed that God had called them to this work.

The settlements were also part of a reaction against the charitable principles of the postwar era. Scientific philanthropy, as expressed in the Charity Organization Societies, assumed that poverty was caused by character defects. Relief was thought to aggravate this condition. Thus scientific philanthropists relied on a mixture of exhortation, espionage, and manipulation, with a minimum of direct assistance, to save the poor from their own vices. Settlement residents found this repellent. They believed poverty was a consequence of objective social conditions which could be changed, and which the poor could be taught to understand and fight. This led residents, on the one hand, to become involved in those political struggles for reforming every level of government that characterized the Progressive era, and, on the other hand, to live and work among the poor. Eventually settlement work became professionalized, a matter of providing specific services to the neighborhood.[1] This, too, was typically Progressive. Indeed, its emphasis on expertise and professionalism was one of the most durable aspects of the Progressive impulse. Long after the dissipation of its moral energies and emotional charges, progressivism lived on through the techniques and institutions it had created.

The NCL and the NWTUL were professionalized from the outset, inasmuch as they depended on small, salaried cadres to do most of the work. But their effectiveness was also related to the leisure-class allies who supported both groups. This became clear after World War I when the sustaining ethic disappeared, and with it most of the volunteers upon which the cadres relied. They continued to do valuable work but never regained the influence they had enjoyed in the Progressive years. Even at their peak they suffered from all

1. See Roy Lubove, *The Professional Altruist: The Emergence of Social Work as a Career, 1880–1930* (Cambridge, Mass., 1965).

the difficulties common to reform groups. They never had enough money. Too few of their branches were dependable sources of womanpower. Their size and income fluctuated from year to year, making it difficult for them to plan very far ahead. All the same, they more than carried their weight in the reform movement. Few public bodies in the Progressive era were more effective in relation to their resources, or more successfully blended a crusading spirit with the practical techniques of reform.

4

ten who led the woman movement

*h*aving discussed the origins of feminism, the development of equal suffrage as its principal demand, and the formal structures which were supposed to exploit the vote when it was won, it remains to say something about the women who led the movement in its glory days. The following social feminists, suffragists, and radicals were selected partly because of their prominence at the time, partly to show how various were the character types and socio-political orientations attracted to the women's cause.

· · · · · ·

In many respects Josephine Shaw Lowell typified the patrician philanthropists of the post–Civil War era. George Fredrickson has shown that the old elite, displaced by an emerging plutocracy, learned from the war that charitable work, like that done by the Sanitary Commission, was a way of regaining lost influence. Philanthropy offered a middle road between entrepreneurial excess and democratic moboc-racy that could be traveled by a fastidious upper class eager to affect national affairs without losing its essential character. Social service and reform could, in fact, be used to advance essentially conservative purposes. Mrs. Lowell fits this pattern rather nicely. The daughter of a Boston Brahmin, she married Charles Russell Lowell, Jr., one of the most brilliant products of that hard-working, high-minded elite. She began her public life by doing war relief work, and after being widowed went on to become a charity organizer. She was a Social Darwinist but believed in pl:ilanthropy because it offered "important and redeeming roles to idle members of the upper classes." [1] Something of a mugwump, she actively promoted civil-service reform and economy in government (Grover Cleveland's resistance to "the folly and extravagance of Congress" enabled her to call him "a great man and a true patriot").[2] Her goal was "a hard-working capitalistic society, saved from materialism, corruption and bad taste by an aristocracy subservient to the highest principles." [3] She was disturbed by the effects of direct relief on the poor.

What this description omits is that capacity for growth and change which brought Mrs. Lowell finally into the mainstream of the social-justice movement. She had begun her career as little more than a schoolgirl, captivated by her romance of war waged in a noble cause. But even before the war ended she had become a widow, a mother, and an experienced welfare worker. Her husband and her brother, Colonel Robert Gould Shaw, who led his black regiment to destruction at the battle of Fort Wagner, were both killed in action. As much as a woman could possibly be, she was of that generation about which Oliver Wendell Holmes, Jr., wrote: "In our youth our hearts were touched with fire. It was given us to learn at the outset that life is a profound and passionate thing." Having matured amidst violence and tragedy, she could hardly have brought much sentimentality to the prac-

1. George M. Fredrickson, *The Inner Civil War: Northern Intellectuals and the Crisis of the Union* (New York, 1965), p. 214.

2. William Rhinelander Stewart, *The Philanthropic Work of Josephine Shaw Lowell* (New York, 1911), p. 67.

3. Fredrickson, *Inner Civil War*, p. 214.

tice of charity. Nor, at a time when scientific philanthropy was dominant, could she be expected to question its doctrines on social organization and character development.

What Mrs. Lowell did, however, was to immerse herself in public welfare problems for more than a generation until she had a record that few men and no other prominent woman could match. Moreover, she was able to re-evaluate her own experience and form new opinions on the basis of it. In 1889 she resigned from the New York State Board of Charities having decided that it was better to save people from poverty than try to rehabilitate them after they had succumbed. She became president of the first Consumers' League in order to help unorganized shopgirls, but she did not shrink from working directly with labor unions even though most of her life had been spent among people who feared and despised them. In 1894 she mediated a dispute between striking tailors and their employers. That same year, at the Conference of Charities and Corrections, she defended the unions that had attacked the "unwise and cruel competition" of prison labor.

By the end of her life Mrs. Lowell had moved beyond mugwump reform and scientific philanthropy. Although she had little feeling for organized workers, she nonetheless made labor's cause her own. She never doubted the rightness or necessity of the Civil War, but did not let its heroic aura blind her to the injustices of other wars. She was an ardent anti-imperialist, certain that the destruction of liberty in the Philippines threatened freedom in the United States as well. Mrs. Lowell gave her strength and money to many progressive activities, whether they conflicted with her earlier beliefs or not. In the process she demonstrated the wisdom of evaluating a public figure's words in the context of his entire life. It is easy to exaggerate the theoretical consistency of practical reformers like Mrs. Lowell by extracts from their hastily written, poorly phrased statements. Mrs. Lowell was guided by certain principles, but they hardly added up to an intelligible system of ideas. She had a strong sense of noblesse oblige tempered by common sense and a reasonable openness to experience—not the worst equipment for a philanthropist and leader of women.

. . . . . .

M. Carey Thomas was the kind of feminist that was easily caricatured. Sharp-tongued, ambitious, a confirmed man-hater, she charged through life, leaving behind her a train of bruised feelings and wounded egos. Bertrand Russell, who met her in 1896, recalled that "she had immense energy, a belief in culture which she carried out with a business man's efficiency, and a profound contempt for the male sex. The first time I met her . . . [her brother] said to me before her arrival: 'Prepare to meet thy Carey.' This expressed the family attitude." [4] Russell's unfavorable reaction was confirmed when he overheard a terrific scene between Miss Thomas and her companion who was leaving to be married. Desertion was bad enough, but to be thrown over for a mere man she found unbearable. Her outrage made an indelible impression on Russell, whose feminist sympathies nevertheless survived the occasion.

In most cases too little is known about the emotional history of individual feminists to make possible speculations about their character development. Miss Thomas is something of an exception to this general rule. While she was born into an average upper-middle-class family, she was severely burned as a child in an accident that left her lamed and disfigured during her formative years.[5] She early demonstrated her remarkable strength by refusing to withdraw from life. But her

4. Bertrand Russell, *The Autobiography of Bertrand Russell, 1871–1914* (Boston, 1967), p. 193.

5. Edith Finch, *Carey Thomas of Bryn Mawr* (New York, 1947).

long convalescence deprived her of a normal childhood and made her more familiar with books than with other girls and boys. Her reading fortified a position on the woman question that she doubtless owed to her Quaker mother. "I can remember weeping over the account of Adam and Eve because it seemed to me that the curse pronounced on Eve might imperil girls' going to college." Besides the bible, "I read Milton with rage and indignation. Even as a child I knew him for the woman hater he was." After reading Michelet's *La Femme*, "I was beside myself with terror lest it might prove true that I myself was so vile and pathological a thing." [6] Finally, she decided it was man, not woman, who was pathological.

Despite her handicap, or more likely because of it, Carey Thomas entered college with an unusual capacity for intellectual self-discipline, driving ambition, and, as Russell put it, a profound contempt for the male sex. Sage College of Cornell University did nothing to change her. No graduate school in America would accept a woman, and so in 1883 Miss Thomas received her doctorate Summa Cum Laude from Zurich University. This inspired her to apply for the presidency of Bryn Mawr College, then under construction, although she was not yet twenty-seven years old. The board appointed a retired physician, James E. Rhoads, as president while Miss Thomas became dean, with the understanding that she would actually manage the college. When Dr. Rhoads retired she succeeded him to the presidency, becoming in name what she had always been in fact.

Miss Thomas was second to none among the college autocrats of this period. Until 1916, when a faculty rebellion forced her to relinquish some authority, all the decisions were hers. The habit of command carried over into her public work, leading Mary Peck of the nwtul to consign Miss Thomas to the

6. M. Carey Thomas, "Present Tendencies in Women's Colleges and University Education," *Publications of the ACA*, III (February 1908), 45–46.

ranks of "scholastic suffragists" who failed to understand what democracy was all about.

> She has put in self-government by her student body as the best form of checks and balances, but at the same time she defends the procedure of asking an objectionable professor or other official to resign without a hearing. This last, together with her well-known adroitness in bringing things to pass diplomatically as she wishes them to be, puts her in the category of those who work for democracy in theory, while they act practically along the line of the divine right of rulers, and illustrates my point that the scholastic view of democracy differs from the conception some of the rest of us have.[7]

At Bryn Mawr, Carey Thomas got her way not only by virtue of her personal force but because her judgment on educational matters, if conservative, was generally good. At a time when few college instructors had Ph.D.'s, all her early appointees did, save only Woodrow Wilson. She distrusted male educators, believing that women's colleges were inferior chiefly because they were run by men, yet she was certain that to equal the best men's colleges Bryn Mawr would have to resemble them. Hence "she created in the Bryn Mawr graduate a woman who had mastered a course of study as tough as Harvard's and who could hold her own against any competitor."[8] This principle was also her main contribution to the ACA. She impressed upon it that where women were concerned a different curriculum was always a poorer one. Carey Thomas understood, as many in the woman movement did not, that in a world where men made the rules those educated to other standards would always be at a disadvantage.

One reason, perhaps, for her clarity of vision was its narrow focus. As an educator Miss Thomas was determined to win

7. Mary Gray Peck, "Some American Suffragists," *Life and Labor*, V (December 1911), 368.

8. Barbara M. Cross, ed., *The Educated Woman in America: Selected Writings of Catharine Beecher, Margaret Fuller and M. Carey Thomas* (New York, 1965), p. 47.

the badges of success, but pedagogically she was imitative, and once she had her doctorate she abandoned research entirely. Hence she reinforced the tendency of women to favor grade-getting and degree-winning over creative or scholarly work, to focus on the symbols of achievement rather than its substance, and thus helped fix the "good-student" syndrome which has since kept so many educated women from realizing their early promise. Being a "good student" in this sense requires diligence, obedience, and complete faith in the school and its teachings. At some point the student who wishes to do really original work must break with the system and make his own way intellectually. He may often, perhaps usually, be wrong at first, but he cannot grow beyond studenthood until he begins to teach himself. It is easier for boys to do this because their conditioning is not so complete as girls'. Boys are expected to be rebellious and wrong-headed, and sometimes their deviant experiences give them the confidence —arrogance really—to strike out on their own. Girls are given no such latitude. Convention presses heavily on them from the start, they become such "good" students, their intellectual docility so firmly established, that most can never be anything more than students.[9]

The tragedy of M. Carey Thomas' life, then, was not her accident, not her racial and sexual prejudices, not her elitism, not even her obsession with duplicating the male educational establishment, but her inability to understand that it was precisely their failures that made the best men's colleges great. If the students at Harvard had been as good as the students at Bryn Mawr, that is to say as pliant and as easily indoctrinated, then Harvard itself would have been good only in the way Bryn Mawr was good. In her later years Miss Thomas' vision broad-

9. Charlotte Perkins Gilman touches on this point frequently in *The Home* (New York, 1903). For an excellent discussion of the relationship between social conformity and good grades on the one hand, and among rebelliousness, creativity, and low grades on the other, see James S. Coleman, *The Adolescent Society* (New York, 1961), pp. 323–324.

ened. She became an active suffragist and in 1915 established, against much internal opposition at Bryn Mawr, what became the first school of social work in the United States organically related to a college or university. In the 1920's she founded a summer school for workers which annually brought real working women to the campus for eight weeks of intensive instruction. But she never understood that she and her sister educators, at the same time they made it possible for women to secure a first-class education, had helped establish an academic ceiling above which few women could rise. Carey Thomas' own accomplishments were born of rebellion; at Bryn Mawr there was no room for rebels.

.   .   .   .

Margaret Dreier Robins was almost the exact opposite of Miss Thomas. A large, dark, handsome woman of great tact and presence, she challenged the feminist stereotype on every count. In 1904, as a young woman in comfortable circumstances, she became interested in the newly founded New York Women's Trade Union League. The following year she met Raymond Robins, who had struck it rich in the Klondike and was devoting all his time to the promotion of religion, organized labor, and reform politics. After a three months' courtship they were married and moved to Chicago, where they occupied a tenement flat in the slums. Both were passionate romantics, wholly caught up in the Progressive ferment. For the next twenty years they gave themselves to the business of reform, she mainly as a suffragist and leader of working women, he in a variety of roles from settlement headworker to Progressive party manager and candidate. They were often separated from each other, but when apart the distance between them was bridged by an endless chain of love letters and telegrams.

"There are times," she wrote, "when it makes me quite heartsick to realize that it is my money alone which enables me to carry out the plans, and that whatever intelligence or character I have would be useless were it not for . . . that." [1] Actually, her modest fortune was the least of her assets, though with the confidence and poise that money begets it nicely supplemented her broader virtues. Like all the leading feminists, she was physically strong. This was an essential condition for eminence in the woman movement. The American railway network made it possible, but hardly easy, to travel anywhere in a reasonable length of time. Mrs. Robins, like her fellow activists, spent a huge amount of time arriving and departing from terminals, sitting up in stifling coaches, and waiting around in dark and dirty train stations at all hours of the day and night. To these discomforts were added the intense strains of the work she traveled to advance. Mrs. Robins functioned in an atmosphere of continual crisis. At its peak the Trade Union League was involved in one strike after another, and it was not unusual for it to be supporting two or three at once. Physically and emotionally this was the most taxing work social feminists could do. Even when the strikes went well, which was seldom, they were exhausting. Yet Mrs. Robins also contributed to the great suffrage campaigns, was active in Chicago civic affairs, and labored for a multitude of embattled causes. Since she was a sensitive, compassionate woman who held nothing back when her sympathies were engaged, the emotional pressure on her was enormous. Raymond Robins saw her as a high strung, nervous person, much like himself in point of fact. Still, she never broke under the strain as he did several times. Her strength was the best kind, not the inner hardness that fortified some feminists but a willed discipline that made her finest instincts the servants of a larger purpose.

Her generous nature was one reason why she was indispensable to the WTUL. Working girls were prickly and insecure, quick to detect slights, and resentful of patronage. Mrs.

1. Mary Dreier, *Margaret Dreier Robins: Her Life, Letters and Work* (New York, 1950), p. 57.

Robins knew this and created a warm, friendly ambience which smoothed over feelings ruffled by the tactlessness of league allies. Visitors to NWTUL conventions were struck by their informal character. Mrs. Robins disregarded the elaborate parliamentary protocol typical of large feminist gatherings. She knew and recognized most of the delegates by name. Indeed, she encouraged a kind of schoolgirl frolicsomeness, complete with cheers and songs, among women whose youth had been spent in factories. This was a deliberate policy. Her great ambition was to make the league a self-sustaining organization of trade union women. To this end she deliberately cultivated promising working girls and made the league as attractive to them as she could. Floyd Dell, then a socialist and feminist sympathizer, admired Mrs. Robins because "she has gone to the workers to learn rather than to teach—she has sought to unfold the ideals and capacities latent in working girls rather than impress upon them the alien ideals and capacities of another class." [2] This was not literally true, for she had clear ideas about what the league should become, but it fairly reflects the qualities that made her distinctive among leisure-class reformers.

The great irony of her career, as we have already noted, was that in making the league a true working-class body she undermined its influence in the union movement. Mrs. Robins came close to despising President Gompers and the executive council of the AFL at times, but she was not intimidated by them. Convinced that AFL support was essential to the league's success, she extracted from it more money and recognition than it really wanted to give. In any event, this was not much. Yet without Mrs. Robins the league would have gotten even less. When she retired in the 1920's it became clear that only her social position, personal influence, and determination had given the league influence with the AFL, whose executives had little use for her. They did, how-

2. Floyd Dell, *Women as World Builders: Studies in Modern Feminism* (Chicago, 1913), p. 73.

ever, respect her, as they did not the women of their own class who succeeded her. This was hardly her fault, but all the same it frustrated the labor to which she had devoted half her adult years. In the end, her life's work did not amount to much; the same cannot be said of her life itself. This impulsive, loving, tenderhearted woman gave hundreds, perhaps thousands, of women opportunities for growth and service that had never existed before. Working-class women were largely excluded from the benefits of feminism and progressivism, but through the NWTUL some at least were brought into effective unions, and those who became active league members were caught up in exciting and rewarding work which was very much worth doing.

Mrs. Robins demonstrated that one could be both feminine and a feminist, that a great cause could be fought for without compromising the dignity and self-respect of those it was supposed to help, and that, terribly difficult though it was, lines of empathy could be thrown over the barrier of class. Even if she had done none of these things, it would still be true that, because she was a thoughtful, considerate person, deeply touched by individual as well as social problems, and exemplifying in her own right the most admirable womanly virtues, those who knew her were better for the experience. Mrs. Robins' effort to liberate working women failed; her life itself was a triumph.

. . . .

Jane Addams has been so much written about that until recently it seemed there was little more to say of her. Yet, as Christopher Lasch points out, the conventional image of "Saint Jane," as her friends wryly called her, concealed a remarkably intricate personality whose complexities are only now becoming apparent.[3] In one sense she was typical of that

3. Christopher Lasch, *The New Radicalism in America, 1889–1963* (New York, 1965).

class of young women in the late nineteenth century who struggled to find uses for their education. Like so many others, she found in social service a solution to her personal problems which promised, at the same time, to answer the more general questions troubling middle-class America as a whole. Miss Addams, however, differed from other important women in a number of crucial ways. She was one of the best writers in both the feminist and social-justice movements, even though many of her pieces were rapidly, on occasion sloppily, composed. She was also a supremely gifted manager and organizer. This combination of executive and literary ability was almost unique in the woman movement.

Her personality was equally distinctive. Although in her day cool, distant women were common, Miss Addams was notably detached. Apart from a few confidants, spouse-surrogates actually, like Mary Rozet Smith, who were privy to her inmost feelings, she kept a distance between herself and her co-workers. Frances Hackett, literary editor of the *Chicago Evening Post* and longtime resident of Hull House, remarked that it had "a bracing, not a mawkish atmosphere." [4] Abraham Bisno, a radical trade unionist who spent much time at the settlement, was especially struck by its astringent character. Unlike the socialist movement, where "human affection was paramount in all relationships," settlement workers seemed to Bisno to lack "that touch of human approach and sentiment which is the only real thing in friendship." [5] In this respect Hull House showed the influence of its founder. Miss Addams was famous for her thoughtfulness to the nameless individuals with whom she came in contact. She habitually gave away her possessions, even to the coat off her back, to those in need. Her refusal to accept the deference everywhere accorded her was legend. But her countless small courtesies and benefactions

4. Frances Hackett, "Hull House—A Souvenir," *Survey*, June 1, 1925, p. 276.
5. Abraham Bisno, *Abraham Bisno: Union Pioneer* (Madison, Wisc., 1967), p. 172.

were reserved for outsiders. Those within her circle had their loyalty taken for granted. Her long-suffering friend and ally, Louise H. De Koven Bowen, never forgot that when Jane Addams closed her cottage on Mrs. Bowen's estate in Bar Harbor, she promptly gave away all its furnishings as mementos to people in the district. Nothing was reserved for Mrs. Bowen except one garbage can, in—it must be recorded—fairly good condition.

But the peculiar feature of Jane Addams' life was not the contrast between her reputation as a universal mother figure forever gushing over the wronged poor, and her real life as a precise, dispassionate social worker. Rather it stems from the failure of this gifted intellectual to admit the obligation her fine mind thrust upon her. She had the strongest intellect of anyone in the settlement movement. Among feminists only Charlotte Perkins Gilman, Elizabeth Cady Stanton, and, perhaps, Florence Kelley were her equals. Her varied writings, sketchy and hastily written though they often were, testify to her great ability. But while Miss Addams did operate as an intellectual, she began her career by repudiating her education. While other women gloried in their college years, Jane Addams condemned them as a "snare of preparation." All college had done, she later wrote, was to lead her to view life in terms of art. It interposed a veil of irrelevant abstractions between herself and reality.

In rejecting academic formalism she also denied the tradition of reasoned inquiry which it imperfectly reflected. For her, the settlement's most valuable function was the "application of knowledge to life." The key word here is "application." What was not immediately useful was immediately discarded. This meant in practice that the settlement was keyed to the intellectually lowest common denominator. "It is not," she once remarked, "that simple people like to hear about little things; they want to hear about great things simply told." [6] Unfor-

6. Jane Addams, "A Function of the Social Settlement," *Annals*, XIII (May 1899), 338.

tunately, difficult ideas are not easily rendered. As a result, the settlements enjoyed their greatest success among the women and children who enjoyed and responded best to the parables and instructive anecdotes of which Miss Addams was so fond. Jane Addams freely acknowledged her debt to William James and, especially, John Dewey, but their main contribution was that they supplied a technical rationale for the instinctive philosophy to which she was already committed. These traits of mind and spirit made her a great teacher, but at the same time they prevented her from thinking through the social questions to which she devoted her life. She never grasped the contradictions that prevented social settlements from rehabilitating slums, nor came to terms with the limitations of conventional feminist thought. Her own writings on the woman question were thin and derivative. She was astonishingly candid about the personal benefits of social service, but otherwise she confined herself to the good women could do if only their energies were released from inhibiting laws and customs.

Finally, one suspects, the very qualities that led her to reject the family claim prevented her from fully experiencing the human reality that she celebrated in her writings and defied convention to encounter. She gave her time, money, and talents entirely to the interests of the poor among whom she lived, yet she was unable to give of herself in the direct, spontaneous manner of the women who founded the first College Settlement. In a sense she rejected all personal claims upon her, familial or otherwise, and remained largely untouched by the passionate currents that swirled around her. The crowning irony of Jane Addams' life, therefore, was that she compromised her intellect for the sake of human experiences which her nature prevented her from having. Life, as she meant the term, forever eluded her.

.   .   .   .   .   .

Anna Howard Shaw was short and fat with a broad, seamed face and a disposition to match. No one else in the woman movement fitted so perfectly the stereotype promoted by anti-suffragists of the sharp-tongued, man-hating feminist. She was raised on a farm near Big Rapids, Michigan, when the western part of the state was still almost a wilderness. Even as a child she sensed her oratorical powers, and as a high school student was already preaching before Methodist congregations. Over her family's objections she went to Albion College in Michigan, and then to Boston University from which she graduated as an ordained minister. Pastoral life did not absorb her, and at the age of thirty-five she entered the medical school of Boston University, which awarded her the M.D. in 1885. Medicine, too, failed to hold her interest. Lecturing continued to be her favorite occupation, and for several years she headed the suffrage department of the wctu. Susan B. Anthony brought her into the nawsa, and in 1904, after the resignation of Carrie Chapman Catt, she became its president.[7]

Dr. Shaw's place in the nawsa resulted mainly from her speaking ability. Everyone agreed that she was a poor administrator, but women thrilled to her denunciations of the masculine establishment and her fervent elaborations of feminine virtue. The transcripts of her largely extemporaneous speeches read badly, and we can get little sense today of the power she had to move women in her own time. This was especially true of hard-core suffragists. Social feminists were less impressed because Dr. Shaw paid scant attention to their enterprises. She was advised and sustained by women like Carey Thomas instead of the more broadly sympathetic feminine reformers. Men admired her least of all. Leading feminists usually had at least a few male supporters; Dr. Shaw seems to have had none. Ardent suffragists could not help but feel some antipathy for the male world, but the best ones did not allow their natural feelings to get the better of them as Dr. Shaw's did on more than one occasion. Mrs. Bowen said of her years later that "she was very witty, but always terribly down on men, and sometimes one really almost winced when she attacked

7. Anna Howard Shaw, *The Story of a Pioneer* (New York, 1915).

them so vigorously that they got red in the face and looked ready to do murder." [8]

Even had she been twice the orator she actually was, these defects would have made Anna Howard Shaw a poor head of the NAWSA. Woman suffrage had to have the male votes which Dr. Shaw persistently antagonized. Congress would not listen to the suffragists until their organized strength commanded its attention, but Dr. Shaw was constitutionally incapable of building, let alone maintaining, such a structure. Hence the NAWSA languished, while Dr. Shaw's personality and policies forced the resignation from its national board of distinguished women like Florence Kelley. Each year from 1910 to 1915 saw substantial changes among the NAWSA's officers as a series of women attempted to give the faltering organization direction and stability. A few states were won for suffrage by vigorous local branches, more were lost. By 1915 the rank and file of suffragists were convinced that stronger leadership was required, and Dr. Shaw stepped down quietly, permitting the election of Carrie Chapman Catt.

Anna Howard Shaw's presidency was a classic example of mismatching the woman to the job. She was a rough-edged individualist in a position requiring tact, subtlety, and managerial expertise. Yet her qualities had their uses, as became clear after America entered the World War. On the Woman's Committee of the Council of National Defense, Dr. Shaw found herself in a position that demanded almost the very traits that had made her presidency so fruitless. The Woman's Committee, as we shall see in greater detail later, was set up by the government as a sop to emancipated women demanding a responsible share of the war effort. Dr. Shaw was appointed chairman because she was well known and available. She proved to be, from the government's point of view, the worst possible choice. From the outset she demanded, and sometimes got, a voice in the halfhearted mobilization of womanpower

8. Louise H. De Koven Bowen, *Open Windows* (Chicago, 1946), p. 209.

stimulated by the war. She nagged and chivied the council into giving her some real support, threatened to resign when it did not, and succeeded in the short time before the war was won in having women made an integral part of the CND's field force. She could not prevent women workers from being exploited during the emergency, but all that force of character and unbending determination could do to protect them was done. Since her war was waged almost entirely in secret, Dr. Shaw never got the credit due her for a gallant struggle against bureaucratic inertia and male chauvinism. Because she was not free to go directly to the public, her fight was doomed from the outset. All the same, she kept her head and fought it out to the end. In her way she was an awesome person, tough, harsh, but not unyielding, more graceful in defeat than victory. Historians have generally underrated her because the full story of her work on the Woman's Committee has not been told. When it is, the true stature of this formidable woman will be evident.

. . . . . .

Carrie Chapman Catt was easily the most admired suffragist of the twentieth century.[9] She was also the most successful. Her abilities were first demonstrated in her work as a teacher, school administrator, and journalist in Iowa, after her graduation from the State College, and later in San Francisco. When her first husband died she returned to Iowa, where her lecturing and suffrage work attracted favorable notice. In 1890 she married again and began working for suffrage on the national level. From 1895 to 1900 she was chairman of the NAWSA's organization committee. Her effort to impose order on the sprawling, highly personalized association failed, but she did such good work that Susan B. Anthony chose Mrs. Catt to

9. Carrie Chapman Catt and Nettie R. Shuler, *Woman Suffrage and Politics* (New York, 1923), is her analysis of the suffrage movement. She left no memoirs.

succeed her as president over her personal favorite, Anna Howard Shaw. Mrs. Catt served only four years. Her resignation, a result of overwork and the strain of her husband's fatal illness, did not, however, take her out of the suffrage movement. She continued her labors as president of the International Woman Suffrage Alliance. In 1912 she joined the suffrage campaign in New York State, and there created an organization that won the vote for women in 1917, a victory that was, in many ways, the decisive event in the struggle for woman suffrage. Even before then, Mrs. Catt's accomplishments in New York contrasted so sharply to the lackluster showing of the NAWSA that she became the popular choice to replace Dr. Shaw. She installed as officers of the NAWSA women like herself, duplicated on a national scale her achievements in New York, and led the suffragists to final victory.

Mrs. Catt's eminence in the movement was a result not only of her organizing talents and executive genius but of her ability to learn from experience. As chairman of the organization committee in the 1890's she was sometimes tactless and impatient. In her later years she was notably sympathetic and politic in her dealings with others. She also overcame her impatience and settled down to the kind of long-range planning that few suffragists were able to practice, however much they paid lip service to the need for it. Her New York campaign in 1915 was a huge enterprise, the biggest to that date, employing all sorts of novel techniques and involving grassroots canvassing never before seen on such a scale. Most thought it was certain to prevail. Yet Mrs. Catt viewed the whole thing as essentially a dress rehearsal for the 1917 campaign. Not only was she right about this, she was also able to persuade her followers so that planning and fund-raising for the next effort began immediately upon the realization of failure in 1915.

To her other merits must be added a broad social conscience. It was a suffragist cliché that votes for women would be votes for social welfare and reform. Mrs. Catt was one of the few hard-core leaders to practice in the post-suffrage era what she had preached before it. She set up the League of Women Voters so that ex-suffragists would have a vehicle of their own for public service. After the suffrage campaign was wrapped up she devoted much of her time to the cause of peace. Insofar as circumstances permitted, Carrie Chapman Catt made good her promises.

The only ground on which she could be faulted was that she played the political game too well. Surrounded as she was by altruists, enthusiasts, and amateurs, it was essential that she keep a firm grip on political reality. In so doing, she often lost the difference between sensible compromise and mere expediency. No racist herself, she tolerated bigotry in the NAWSA as the price of Southern, and sometimes far Western, support. Although something of a pacifist, she endorsed American intervention in the First World War and accepted a position on the Woman's Committee of the CND. When the militant suffragists led by Alice Paul embarrassed the cause by picketing President Wilson, she added her voice to the clamor against them and failed to protest the savage mistreatment they received at the hands of patriots and policemen. Of course, she had excellent reasons in each instance. She could not afford to have woman suffrage become entirely a sectional affair, and her racial policy in the NAWSA was no different from that of most other national organizations. Had she opposed American entry after 1916 she would have done great harm to the cause without gaining anything in return. The militants behaved badly on occasion, and required, in any event, no encouragement from her.

But woman suffrage was not just another political movement; it was above all a great moral enterprise. Moral leaders are not in the same position as ordinary politicians. The first duty of a politician, as Winston Churchill observed, is to get himself elected. The first duty of a reformer is to secure the substance, not just the appearance, of change. Millions of women contributed to the suffrage crusade because they expected the vote to improve markedly the quality of American life. Yet the more suffragists behaved as simply another interest group, trading a principle there for an advantage here, the less capable they became of preserving what had brought them into politics to begin with. In a sense, suffragists were depleting their moral capital so rapidly that the interest on it in the post-suffrage era would be inadequate to their needs. There were, as we shall see later, many reasons why woman suffrage failed to satisfy the claims made for it, yet not the least of these was the degree to which it had already been compromised. Mrs. Catt knew what she was doing, but, like Woodrow Wilson and his League of Nations, she believed that the mechanism once gained would be potent enough to offset the casualties incurred in winning it. This turned out not to be the case. Woman suffrage had few effects, good or bad, on American life. In retrospect this makes the earlier suffragist accommodation to political reality seem less defensible. Mrs. Catt's general approach was perfectly reasonable; still she might have been well advised to listen to her heart more often. Among suffragists she was uniquely rational. How strange that her chief asset should, in the end, have proved also to be her principal liability!

.   .   .   .   .   .

Alice Paul was probably the only charismatic figure generated by the feminist movement in its salad days.[1] Other leaders were widely admired, even loved, but Miss Paul was the only one whose example led women of all ages and stations to risk jail and worse. Of Quaker origins, she graduated from Swarthmore College and went on to study at the New York School of Philanthropy, London University, and the

1. On Miss Paul and the Woman's party, see Inez Haynes Irwin, *The Story of the Woman's Party* (New York, 1921), and Doris Stevens, *Jailed for Freedom* (New York, 1920).

University of Pennsylvania, from which she received the Ph.D. Her early years were devoted mainly to social justice and social welfare. She was a resident in the College Settlement in New York, helped organize working women into trade unions, and then moved to England where she held five different positions in settlements and charitable bodies. She came to England at a time when the fantastic Pankhursts were in full cry. Under the leadership of Emmeline Pankhurst and her daughter Christabel, the suffragist movement had been divided into a majority of orthodox women, known as constitutionalists, who practiced traditional methods, and a spectacular minority, called suffragettes, who employed a kind of guerrilla warfare. Beginning in a small way with verbal protests, public demonstrations, and the like, the suffragettes ultimately practiced arson and sabotage, mutilated art works, and physically assaulted cabinet ministers. When jailed they went on hunger strikes which compelled the government either to force-feed or release them. If let go they promptly began committing outrages again.

Alice Paul was not the first American to think there was a place in the United States for this kind of militancy. Earlier, Harriot Stanton Blatch, Elizabeth Cady Stanton's daughter, had returned from a long stay in England to imbue New York feminists with the Pankhurstian spirit. Her efforts prepared the way for Miss Paul, who in 1912 came back determined to light in American hearts the same fire that burned so fiercely in England. The sources of her special power are hard to grasp. She wrote very little, and her speeches were not widely reported. She did not seek personal publicity. Other women—Mrs. Blatch, Mrs. O. H. P. Belmont, Doris Stevens—more often acted as spokesmen for her movement than she did herself. But Alice Paul was an absolute fanatic. Once committed to a project, not ridicule, criticism, or repeated failure could shake her conviction. This became particularly clear after the 19th Amendment was passed and she took up arms for another amendment to the Constitution that would guarantee equal rights to women in every respect. At the time of this writing, almost half a century after she began agitating for it, she is still a tireless advocate of the equal-rights amendment. Even among the humorless, intense partisans of the woman's cause, Alice Paul was something special. Plain-spoken to the point of rudeness, incapable of recognizing any merits in those who resisted her, she yet had the power to inspire love and trust, and to bring her followers through storms of controversy and abuse with their loyalty undiminished.

The English example which Miss Paul followed so closely cut both ways. By skillfully adapting the dramatic English techniques for securing publicity and embarrassing the government, she made militancy relevant to the American scene. When she landed in America the campaign for a constitutional amendment granting woman suffrage was at such a low ebb that the NAWSA's budget for congressional action was only $10, none of which was actually spent. Within a few years she made it the central concern of American suffragists. On the other hand, she embraced not only the tactics of English militancy but its strategy as well. The Pankhursts had determined to make the party in power responsible for women's votelessness. This made sense in England where the majority party did, in fact, have the power to enfranchise women. But in the United States an entirely different system prevailed. The government often did not enjoy a majority in Congress. Even when it did, its power to coerce individual congressmen was limited. In England party discipline was the rule, in America it was the exception. To secure a suffrage amendment would almost certainly require votes from both parties in Congress, hence the NAWSA's insistence on keeping equal suffrage a nonpartisan measure.

Miss Paul disdained practical calculations of this sort. Starting out as head of the NAWSA's moribund congressional committee in January 1913, she rapidly gave it such momentum and such independent direction that the NAWSA was soon forced to unchair her. Thereafter, as the head of the Congressional Union (later renamed the Woman's party), she went her own way. Her first project, a suffrage march in Washington, D.C., timed to coincide with President Wilson's inaugural procession, had been a smashing event. Five thousand women turned out for a walk that became a virtual riot when gangs of rowdies attacked them. The upsurge of support and sympathy around the country proved Miss Paul was right in thinking that vivid techniques would bring new life to the constitutional amendment. Building on this sentiment, the union campaigned against Democratic candidates in the nine states where women voted in 1914, and the next year began organizing in all forty-eight states. The contrast between union vigor and NAWSA ineptitude helped terminate Dr. Shaw's presidency, and when Mrs. Catt took the NAWSA's helm it was with a mandate to press for the constitutional amendment. This was Alice Paul's most substantial contribution to the cause, although neither she nor her followers ever recognized it as such. Like the Pankhursts, who took credit for a suffrage bill that was actually negotiated by constitutionalists, the American militants always believed that the 19th Amendment was solely a result of their efforts.

Miss Paul never modified her ideas on the basis of later experience. In the 1920's she and her Woman's party worked for the equal-rights amendment with the same spirit and techniques that had informed their suffrage campaigns. Times changed, but the WP did not. In the twenties it enjoyed a certain cachet as the only remaining feminist organization still animated by the old fervor. In time, however, the Woman's party became a feminist equivalent of the Socialist Labor party, doctrinally frozen, sealed off from reality, forever anticipating historical changes that would make the old ways relevant again. Self-destructive as these habits were, they cannot but inspire admiration. Alice Paul and her associates gave themselves freely to a great cause, never regretted the effort it cost, and never whined when events moved against them, as was increasingly the case after 1930. Such heroic persistence even when, or especially because, misdirected, acquires a certain cranky grandeur over time.

.   .   .   .

Charlotte Perkins Gilman was, perhaps, the most intellectually gifted of them all. She was raised in near poverty because her father deserted his family shortly after her birth. With her mother and brother she moved nineteen times in her first eighteen years. She had no regular schooling. Her mother deliberately withheld any show of affection to her children, Charlotte recalled, in order to make them emotionally self-sufficient. At the age of eighteen she entered the Rhode Island School of Design, which led to her meeting Charles Walter Stetson, a painter, whom she married in 1884 when she was twenty-four. She soon became pregnant, at which point the desperate years of neglect, denial, and uncertainty exacted their toll. She fell into a deep depression which worsened when the baby was born. "Here was a charming home, a loving and devoted husband; an exquisite baby, healthy, intelligent and good; a highly competent mother to run things; a wholly satisfactory servant—and I lay all day on the lounge and cried." [2] In fact, she was on the edge of a full-scale nervous collapse. A trip to Los Angeles helped, but on her return she broke down completely.

To save her sanity her husband agreed on a divorce. She took her child back to California, where she struggled for some years with indifferent success to earn her own living. Even before Stetson remarried, she sent their daughter to live with him. In 1895, with her mother dead, her child gone, and having failed to make an adequate living as a writer and lecturer, she

2. Charlotte Perkins Gilman, *The Living of Charlotte Perkins Gilman* (New York, 1935), p. 89. See also the introduction by Carl N. Degler to the latest edition of her *Women and Economics* (New York, 1966).

left California for good. Her autobiography does not explain why, but she decided the following year to visit England to attend the International Socialist and Labor Congress. There she met a number of the Fabians, including Grant Allen, whose books popularizing scientific subjects she much admired. When she told him it was wrong of him to write hack novels purely for money, he informed her that a man's first duty was to support his family—a response which, naturally, she found unpersuasive. At the end of the year she sat down to write out her thoughts on the economic position of women, a topic she had lectured on for years, and in seventeen days produced a rough draft. In fifty-eight days the entire manuscript of *Women and Economics* was completed. The most influential book ever written by an American feminist, it became also an international classic. Thereafter Mrs. Gilman had a ready market for her work, even though for seven years after 1909 she devoted most of it to her magazine, the *Forerunner*, whose contents she largely wrote herself. She wrote many books after *Women and Economics*—*The Home*, as we saw earlier, being an especially important one—but most were based on the ideas brought forward in her masterwork.

Charlotte Perkins Gilman compels our respect first of all by the courage with which she overcame her extraordinary handicaps. Her childhood was desolate and crippling, her first marriage, for which she took all the blame, a fiasco. She failed even to make a home for her only child. Yet she struggled back from the edge of insanity, enjoyed a long and useful career in journalism, married again, this time for good, and finally regained the pleasure of her daughter's company. Her experiences marked her for life, of course. She claimed never to have fully regained her power of concentration after her breakdown, yet she still managed to write twenty-odd volumes of poetry, fiction, and social criticism. She functioned at a low level of sexual intensity, seems to have believed that procreation was the only reason for coitus, and reacted strongly to the decline of chastity after World War I, which she blamed on "sexuopathic philosophy," that is to say, Freudianism. But she was a mother, and a heterosexual, unlike some feminists. Thus the degree of her sexual maladjustment was probably less than might have been expected, given her start in life.

Mrs. Gilman had more success in organizing her personal affairs than her ideas. After her breakdown she made her decisions on a strictly logical basis, down to the ordering of her own death which she accomplished by taking chloroform when cancer made it impossible for her to carry on. Her thought was not nearly so rigorous. She considered herself a socialist, but rejected Marxism. Indeed, she rather enjoyed her anomalous position. In her memoirs she proudly remarked that conservatives thought her a socialist, socialists viewed her as a suffragist, while suffragists were uncertain what she was. One suffragist conceded generously that, "after all, I think you will do our cause more good than harm, because what you ask is so much worse than what we ask that they will grant our demands in order to escape yours." [3] And that was, more or less, how things turned out. But it was not just the extreme character of her demands that led to their frustration. Rather, it was her inability to make clear the social context in which they were to be realized. This was the chief intellectual failing of feminism as a whole, as we saw earlier, yet Mrs. Gilman was in a better position than most to deal with it. After the Tilton-Beecher affair, feminists had assumed that formal emancipation would of itself practically insure equal opportunity. Mrs. Gilman knew it would not, but her solution to the problem was largely mechanical, a matter of revised domestic arrangements which would free women for outside work.

The alternative would seem to have been some kind of socialist order that would provide the institutions—public nurseries, paid maternity leaves, and the like—necessary to fulfill the promise of feminine emancipation. Surprisingly enough,

3. Gilman, *Living*, p. 198.

the key writings of this professed socialist neglected the point. She believed that feminism would have to socialize the home, but she apparently believed it possible to have socialized homes in a capitalist society. Perhaps so, but the American experience in this century offers little encouragement to those who think as she did. Mrs. Gilman was a socialist and a feminist, yet in her mind the two remained separate and distinct causes. In the end, her failure to integrate them prevented her from fully utilizing the insights she had gained from each.

. . . .

Florence Kelley was the only great social feminist with a thorough grounding in Marxist socialism. Her father was "Pig Iron Kelley," a famous protectionist congressman and Radical Republican. On her mother's side she was related to many Quakers whose quiet, persistent reform work made a lasting impression on her. "These methods," she later wrote, "which never provoked opposition or resistance, were far more effectual than appeared upon the surface." [4] She graduated from Cornell University in 1882 and then, on the advice of M. Carey Thomas, pursued her studies at Zurich University. Zurich was a center for exiled radicals from Eastern Europe. They converted her to socialism, which she studied so carefully that she was able to make the first English translation of Engels' *The Condition of the Working Class in England in 1844*. As with so many other young radicals, love and revolution went hand in hand. Among the socialist exiles was a Polish-Russian medical student named Wishnewetzky whom she married in 1884. Their marriage was blessed with three children, but was not

4. Florence Kelley, "Notes of Sixty Years: My Philadelphia," *Survey Graphic*, October 1, 1926, p. 11. This is the first of four autobiographical essays published in the *Survey*. The standard biography is Josephine Goldmark, *Impatient Crusader: Florence Kelley's Life Story* (Urbana, Ill., 1953).

otherwise a success. The heady atmosphere of New York City, to which they moved in 1886, had a stimulating effect on Dr. Wishnewetzky, who began to combine revolutionary politics with get-rich-quick medical schemes. In 1891 she left him and moved with her children to Chicago where divorces were more readily obtained. There she began her career as a professional reformer.

Mrs. Kelley remained a socialist all her life. The effort she put into socialist enterprises, however, was miniscule compared with her heavy involvement in social welfare and suffragist activities. Even the Socialist party of Eugene Debs, which attracted thousands of women in the Progressive era, failed to win her away from the reformism of the Consumers' League. Her writings are not very illuminating in this respect. In an early paper read before the ACA and later published in the *Christian Union* (soon to become the *Outlook*), she distinguished between working-class philanthropy and bourgeois philanthropy. The former was undertaken by the workers themselves, through their trade unions and benefit societies. It strengthened them in their daily encounters with the capitalist system and helped mitigate inequities which someday the revolution would sweep away. Bourgeois philanthropy, on the other hand, was only the means by which capitalists returned to the workers a small fraction of the wealth stolen from them in order to control the "dependent and dangerous classes" and avert the revolution.[5] Yet it was exactly this ameliorative process that she made her life work. How do we explain this paradox?

Part of her movement from socialism to social work was circumstantial. Her maiden effort at political action was frustrated when the doctrinaire Socialist Labor party expelled her after a bizarre series of events in the late 1880's. In Chicago she first made contact with Hull House, which involved her in

5. Dorothy Rose Blumberg, *Florence Kelley: The Making of a Social Pioneer* (New York, 1966), p. 77.

the practical work that absorbed all the residents' available time and energy. This led to her being appointed Chief Factory Inspector of Illinois by Governor John Peter Altgeld, and while his defeat at the polls took away her job, she was convinced by then that intelligent legislation vigorously enforced was the fastest way to remedy capitalism's worst evils. The altruism she easily dismissed in her 1887 paper on philanthropy had come, by the time her first book was published in 1905, to seem a vitally important resource. In *Ethical Gains Through Legislation* Mrs. Kelley argued that the middle-class consumer should demand reforms in the names of justice and expediency. But while it was clear to her that the bourgeoisie stood to gain from measures insuring their right to buy well-made goods produced under healthful circumstances, she became increasingly convinced that this argument was not so persuasive as the appeal to pure altruism. In her last book, *Modern Industry*, she made a conventionally socialist analysis support a highly moralistic conclusion. Large-scale production regulated only by the profit motive led to shoddy goods, "the alienation of the anonymous worker and the anonymous employer," widespread exploitation and injustice, and the collapse of responsibility all along the line.[6] Objective conditions had corrupted the moral, as well as the physical, environment. Like any good socialist, she believed these objective conditions were being undermined by the workings of history.

In her mind, however, the distinction between objective socio-economic factors and the subjective moral elements they bred was all important. The decayed public morality was a consequence of industrialization; yet, she argued, this did not mean that the cause-and-effect relationship was consistent. The reconstitution of industrial life was no guarantee that standards would be raised.

6. Florence Kelley, *Modern Industry in Relation to the Family, Health, Education, Morality* (New York, 1914), p. 122.

> Our industrial epoch has corroded our morals and hardened
> our hearts as surely as slavery injured its contemporaries,
> and far more subtly. There is grave reason to fear that it
> may have unfitted us for the oncoming state of civilization, as
> slave-owning unfitted the white race for freedom and
> democracy, and left its blight of race hatred from which the
> Republic still suffers.[7]

Thus the connection between society and morality was a one-way street. A bad society generated inferior morals, but a good society did not do the opposite. This made very little sense. Either morals were social creations or they were not. The distinction flowed, however, from Mrs. Kelley's experience rather than from strict logic. She had built a successful organization by mobilizing the moral energies of leisure-class women, a fact which made it impossible for her to embrace socialist materialism with her old fervor, or to see any longer the class struggle as the central feature of industrial life.

At bottom, what seems to have aborted her career as a revolutionary is that although she had the mind of a socialist, she lacked the requisite temper. She believed in the long-range program of the Socialist party, but she could not devote herself to it while misery and want stalked the land. She needed immediate results, and they were to be gotten only through bourgeois reformist organizations like the NCL. Her abundant energies, and the impatience they contributed to, made it impossible for her to work for a distant revolution when so much needed doing now. Thus her emotional needs militated against her theoretical perceptions. This response, so typical of American radicals, might well be called the pragmatic fallacy, because by concentrating on reform at the expense of revolution one ended up with neither. Nonetheless, Mrs. Kelley's decision did her credit. It requires a certain hardness of character to put abstract propositions, like The Revolution, ahead of human wants, and to work for a distant event when present evils are

7. *Ibid.*, pp. 133–134.

so compelling. With the advantage of hindsight we can see that the problems of poverty and injustice, especially racial injustice, were so deeply rooted that only something like Eugene Debs's Cooperative Commonwealth was adequate to the country's needs. Yet their very virtues prevented generous, impassioned men, and women even more, from heeding the call of reason. Their hearts cried out so insistently that the claims of intellect went unmet. The example of Florence Kelley is especially dramatic, therefore, not by reason of its uniqueness, but rather because she was one of the few reformers whose mind was sufficiently disciplined and whose experience sufficiently broad to lead her beyond reformist maxims. That she succumbed to them all the same indicates how desperately high were the odds against socialism in the United States.

. . . .   ˙

Vida Scudder was born into a leisure-class Boston family. When she was a year old her father, a Christian missionary, was killed. Her mother never remarried and, except for Vida's college years, the two lived together until Mrs. Scudder's death. Vida entered Smith College in 1880, and after graduation studied at Oxford for a time. In 1887 she was hired by Wellesley College to teach literature, which she did until her retirement in 1927. It was unusual for women with private means to pursue a career, but Vida Scudder enjoyed even a greater distinction, for in England she heard Ruskin speak and became a socialist. For the largest part of her long life she was both a socialist and an energetic Episcopalian. Although she was a pioneer settlement resident and a supporter of many good causes, it was as a writer that she made her chief contribution to the movement for social justice.[8]

8. In addition to her autobiography *On Journey* (New York, 1937), see also her *The Church and the Hour: Papers by a Socialist Churchwoman* (New York, 1917).

Where socialism was concerned she was the exception that proved the rule. Very few middle- and upper-class women became socialists. They were repelled by dialectical materialism (which few of them understood in any event), horrified by the class struggle, and certain that socialism was a threat to church and family. Vida Scudder had overcome these doubts and fears herself, hence she was in a good position to combat them. The existence of Christian socialism demonstrated that one need not be an atheist to be a radical. This was a crucial point for, although they were not doctrinaire or sectarian, from Jane Addams on down religion was important to most social feminists. Even Florence Kelley returned to the Quaker religion in her later years. None of the women we have described in this chapter were avowed atheists. Vida Scudder, therefore, reassured her readers that Christianity and socialism were compatible, orthodox Marxists and the capitalist press notwithstanding.

Christian socialism never flourished in this country despite its relevance to the issues at hand. The main reason for this, it would seem, was the doctrine of the class struggle, and the class-consciousness it promoted. Margaret Dreier Robins once wrote that she and her husband "do not believe in the philosophy of the class struggle as an interpretation of past social history, nor as the method of future development in civilization. We believe that the whole progress of social order has been toward individual freedom, rather than toward collective domination." [9] As time was to show, these were dominating sentiments among Progressive social reformers. They had rejected the anarchic individualist of the late nineteenth century, and the Social Darwinist attempt to make "the survival of the fittest" the highest law of human development, but not in order to enshrine their opposites. Most of those who lived to see the New Deal objected to its relatively modest infringe-

9. Unsigned draft of a letter to "Carrie," September 16, 1907, Robins Papers, State Historical Society of Wisconsin, Madison.

ments on individual rights, which suggests how alien to them was the socialist desire for an entirely managed economy.[1]

Progressives in general, and the women among them in particular, were nevertheless as interested in order and stability as in justice—sometimes more so. Campaign rhetoric (TR's "We stand at Armageddon and battle for the Lord," for example) was misleadingly pugnacious. The most important political blocs attempted to frame platforms on which most Americans could stand. The Progressive party in 1912 had the best one, but all the bourgeois parties were struggling, some more successfully than others, toward the same goal. The socialists were alone in declaring that class conflict was the central fact of life in a stratified society. Even if it were true, this proposition was unacceptable to social reformers who were determined to rationalize, not destroy, the class system. What they minded was not the existence of the proletariat and the bourgeoisie but the dangerous gulf between them. They expected to bridge it by eliminating the exploitation of labor and by promoting institutions like settlement houses and public schools which encouraged cooperation between the classes. The more sophisticated accepted trade unions, despite their admitted class-consciousness, as essential to industrial stability. In the long run, they believed, collective bargaining would reduce social tensions by providing an orderly means for resolving conflicts of interest. But this was as far as most Progressives were willing to go.

Those who believed with Vida Scudder that only the classless society would bring an end to class conflict could not, try as they might, reverse these feelings. Miss Scudder attempted to show, most notably in an essay for the *Atlantic Monthly*, that proletarian class-consciousness was a positive force.[2] It promoted brotherhood and internationalism, pointed

1. On this point, see Otis L. Graham, Jr., *An Encore for Reform: The Old Progressives and the New Deal* (New York, 1967).
2. Vida Scudder, "Class-Consciousness," *Atlantic Monthly*, CVII (March 1911), 320–330.

the way to a healthier family life and a more wholesome patriotism, and was not divisive, selfish, or crassly material. Most of this argument, however, missed the point. Even if socialism enjoyed all the virtues Miss Scudder claimed for it, the fact remained that in the foreseeable future it would aggravate the very tensions reformers were trying to ease. Social feminists in particular, while they were not panicked by radicalism, and in all innocence often made radical statements themselves, were more determined than men to secure domestic tranquility. Most envisioned the good society as a happy home writ large. Those few who did not were isolated or ignored. Not even Vida Scudder, for all her gentility (and gentleness), modesty, careful prose, and general inoffensiveness, could change the minds of women eager to diminish conflict in the world, and certain that their maternal virtues were the keys to human progress. When highly intelligent women like Jane Addams rejected socialism on moral grounds, and politically sophisticated ones like Florence Kelley abandoned it, in all but name, for practical reasons, how could the great mass of women be expected to do otherwise?

.   .   .   .

These ten women illustrate important tendencies in the development of American feminism. Seven of the ten were college graduates, indicating what a disproportionate contribution the handful of educated women made to the cause. Five of them were spinsters, two were widowed during the years of their greatest effectiveness, and two divorced—although Mrs. Gilman later remarried. Only two of them had children, and in both cases the mothers had little to do with raising their progeny, who were farmed out to friends and relatives for long periods of time. It was quite true, therefore, that success as a public woman was almost always secured at the expense of the family claim. This has often been the case with successful men, of course, but paternal neglect has not been fatal to domestic life. It was evident that a modest level of social service, in women's clubs and the like, was no threat to the family, but that large feminine ambitions, however selfless, did pose a fundamental challenge to it.

Feminism attracted many different kinds of women. Miss Thomas, Miss Paul, and Dr. Shaw conformed in many respects to the sharp-tongued man-haters depicted by generations of anti-feminists. Eminent women, feminists among them, often drew comfort and inspiration mainly from one another, and their sororital impulses doubtless passed over into lesbianism at times. The Victorian code denied sexual relief to single women, while it sanctioned intimacies among them that in the post-Freudian era would be viewed with alarm. When to this was added the natural hostility of ambitious women to the men who stood in their way, it was inevitable that some kind of homosexuality, whether overt or not, would often result. Even so, most organized women were married, and among their leaders happy marriages were not unknown. Carrie Chapman Catt was twice married (Sara Platt Decker, the best known president of the General Federation, was married three times), and Margaret Dreier Robins had an extraordinarily warm and happy relationship with her husband. On the fringes of the movement there were always free spirits like the Claflin sisters, although few advertised their sex lives so widely. The range of personalities encompassed by the woman movement was broader than its enemies were willing to admit, if not so great as its partisans liked to think.

The socio-economic range was, of course, much narrower. All these women came from the middle and upper classes. Dr. Shaw and Mrs. Gilman were the poorest, but their families were definitely not working class. Of all the branches of the woman movement, only the Trade Union League gave working women an important place. In relation to population, the very rich were better represented than the very poor. In addition to a few immensely wealthy individuals like Mrs. O. H. P. Belmont, the woman movement attracted a surprisingly large number of monied women. In our small group at least four inherited enough to live on, and most had outside resources of some kind.

It is a truism now that people are attracted to even the noblest cause for a variety of reasons—many of them highly subjective and emotional in character. Feminism was no exception to this rule. Of our sample three women—Jane Addams, Mrs. Gilman, and, at the age of sixteen, Vida Scudder —experienced severe emotional disorders. Carey Thomas was scarred in mind as well as in body by her accident. Alice Paul's passionate career as martyr and charismatic folk hero was hardly normal. By and large, feminists were complicated people; had they been otherwise, they would not have become feminists. When woman's role was defined entirely in domestic terms, those women who rejected domesticity almost had to be neurotic. This was the case in the nineteenth century, and the early feminists, admirable as they were, had many peculiarities.[3] As feminism became more respectable and broadly based, it attracted more average women. The impressive thing about the women's clubs, for example, was precisely the ordinary character of their membership, leaders included.

Social feminists as a group were better balanced than hardcore suffragists. While there was no one-to-one relationship, generally the more narrowly preoccupied with women's rights was an individual, the more likely she was to seem odd. Partly this was a matter of social prescriptions, for women were defined as passive, small-minded domestic creatures, and success demanded contrasting traits. Social feminism was attractive to many women because it enabled them to function on a larger stage and at the same time exhibit such womanly attributes as compassion, nurture, and child-centeredness. The professions that appealed most to women were teaching and social work, which were compatible with the prevailing definition of woman's nature. But the most radical suffragists did not merely

3. See, for example, Robert E. Riegel, *American Feminists* (Lawrence, Kans., 1963), especially Ch. 8.

appear to be deviant, they actually were. Their rejection of the social feminist compromise that enlarged women's sphere of action while channeling their energies in, usually, acceptable ways was a product of their profound alienation. Social feminists wanted the vote on the perfectly reasonable ground that it would advance their reforms. Ardent suffragists wanted it for its own sake.

It does not diminish in any way the justice of their cause to say that women were drawn to it for emotional reasons. The character of these emotions, however, greatly affected the course of their struggle. The chief feature of social feminism was that it created roles for women that militated against their full emancipation. Their benevolent enterprises met women's desire for useful and satisfying work without touching the sources of their inequality. It was in this sense an all too rational accommodation to the needs of its participants. Extreme feminism, on the other hand, was generated by emotions so intense as to preclude the serious analysis of their social context essential to genuine equality. Militant feminists were activists, not theorists, but the role they played was too unstable to permit the degree of intellectual sloth that in fact characterized them. Social feminists could afford to be lazy in this regard because their functions were essentially permanent. Generations later, millions of women still find satisfaction in the enterprises launched by their reforming predecessors. The hard core, however, depended on volatile enthusiasms which were really impossible to control. Defeat eliminated the faint of heart, but so did victory—by persuading women that the job was essentially done. Because the militants could not develop institutions like those which sustained social feminists, they were vulnerable to sharp changes in the climate of opinion.

If the extreme feminists had been more reflective and less emotional—which is to say, if they had not been extremists— they might have been able to reason their way to a socialist solution of their dilemma. In retrospect it seems clear that some kind of socialism, whether democratic (Sweden) or not

(U.S.S.R.), is essential to women's full emancipation. Socialist ideology commits left-wing governments to equalitarian practices, even when the governors are not themselves especially keen on the sex question. The socialist battery of welfare aids and protective laws gives mothers the institutional support required to maintain their careers. In Sweden even unwed mothers are supported and protected, thus fulfilling Ellen Key's dream of a society where women could live a rounded life without asking anything of man except his sperm. Theoretically, as we saw earlier, it is possible that the solution toward which radical nineteenth-century feminists were groping was also feasible. Free love, or group marriage, or some other radical redefinition of the domestic unit might have the same effect as the welfare state on women's opportunities. But the continuing popularity of orthodox monogamy makes socialism a better bet in the foreseeable future. Women are not operationally equal to men anywhere in the Western world, but they are more nearly so in the welfare states than in socially underdeveloped nations like the United States. In truth, next to the proletariat itself, middle-class women have gained most from the rise of socialism.

As socialism enjoyed small favor in America, even at its peak in 1912, no one was surprised when it made little impression on the woman movement. Extreme feminists were too emotional to appreciate the logic of their position. Social feminists lacked the motivation to undertake a radical analysis of the woman question. They had, after all, resolved their own problems by becoming reformers. They therefore enjoyed all the freedom they could use and, except for the ballot, were essentially satisfied with their status. Those who required socialism were incapable of understanding it, and those who were best able to appreciate its uses had no need for it. Thousands of women did, in fact, join the Socialist party, but most of them were, like Vida Scudder, more interested in the social question than the woman question. The few committed radicals active in the woman movement—Florence Kelley, for example—were drawn away from socialism by the practical urgencies of reform. Even so gifted a woman as Charlotte Perkins Gilman was unable to fully grasp the socialist imperative. All of which made the odds against a thoroughgoing feminine emancipation, astronomically high to begin with, higher still.

5

feminism in the progressive era

*t*he internal weaknesses and contradictions that militated against feminism's ultimate success were obscured by the gains women made in the late nineteenth and early twentieth centuries. The story of their uneven progress has been told before, but it is necessary to review it briefly in order to understand what happened to the woman movement during and after World War I.[1] For the country as a whole the 1890's were years of crisis and uncertainty. The decade opened with a farmers' revolt which led to the Populist uprising. Half the period was taken up with the greatest industrial depression the country had yet seen. It was a violent time marked by great strikes, notably at Homestead and Pullman, and ending with an attack on Spanish power that quickly degenerated into a prolonged, sanguinary colonial war in the Philippines. The rhetorical wars were hardly less desperate. A Populist leader declared his willingness to ride through rivers of blood to secure the people's demands, while the young Theodore Roosevelt

1. The best general account is Eleanor Flexner, *Century of Struggle: The Woman's Rights Movement in the United States* (Cambridge, Mass., 1959). Andrew Sinclair, *The Better Half* (New York, 1965), is lively and provocative.

proposed that a dozen or so of that motley crew be stood against a wall and shot.

For organized women, however, the nineties was a time of growth and accomplishment. In 1890 the two wings of the suffrage movement were united under the title of the National American Woman Suffrage Association. Elizabeth Cady Stanton of the old National WSA became the new organization's first president. When she retired in 1892 to devote herself to divorce reform and anti-clericalism, she was succeeded by her old friend and associate Susan B. Anthony. By this time the suffrage movement had changed greatly from its free-wheeling early days. The members were more prosperous, and the cause itself had become essentially respectable—unpopular certainly, but still one which women could join without sacrificing their places in society or compromising their good names. In 1893 the NAWSA voted to meet in Washington, D.C., only in alternate years instead of annually, thus shifting away from the old national strategy of pursuing a constitutional amendment. At first events seemed to bear out the wisdom of this change, which Miss Anthony had resisted. In 1893 Colorado adopted woman suffrage, and three years later Idaho followed suit. By this time, thanks to the admission of territories where women voted—Wyoming in 1890, Utah in 1896—there were four states in the union with equal suffrage.[2] These victories did not, however, mean that public opinion had changed much on the suffrage question. Idaho and Wyoming were virtually unpopulated. The Mormons of Utah adopted equal suffrage chiefly to preserve their dominance over a Gentile minority composed largely of men. Colorado was the only state with a major urban center and some industry to enfranchise women. After 1896 no more states were won for the cause until 1910.

The rise of feminine confidence in these years owed more to general accomplishments than to the specific activities of suffragists. Between 1870 and 1890 the number of colleges

2. Alan P. Grimes, *The Puritan Ethic and Woman Suffrage* (New York, 1967) focuses on the Far West.

admitting women almost doubled, and the number of female college students increased fivefold. By the century's end graduate and professional schools had, for the most part, yielded to the pressure as well. The percentage of the female population that worked in 1890 was comparatively small, but here too many basic patterns had already been established. Women made up about one-sixth of the work force by then, as against one-third in 1950. But the percentage of women who were professionals remained fairly constant (10 per cent in 1890, 15 per cent in 1930, 12 per cent in 1950). Or to put it another way, in 1890, 36 per cent of all professional workers were women, and in 1950 they made up 40 per cent of the total. The degree of sexual segregation in employment categories in 1960 was about the same as in 1900.[3] This is not to gloss over the many changes that have also taken place since 1900, but only to say that they do not compare in importance with the earlier ones. Between 1880 and 1900 the employment of women in most parts of the economy became an established fact. This was surely the most significant event in the modern history of women.

Of course, the employment opportunities that opened up for women in those years left much to be desired. The 90 per cent who were not professionals enjoyed the right to work twelve hours a day, often in squalid circumstances, and always at the lowest wages. Even professional women, mostly teachers, were overworked and underpaid by later standards. Still, educational and employment opportunities did multiply at a remarkable pace, and with them came changes in law and custom that were even more beneficial. Middle-class women gained most from these developments. They went to college and

3. Mabel Newcomer, *A Century of Higher Education for American Women* (New York, 1959), has many useful tables. National Manpower Council, *Womanpower* (New York, 1957), is informative on the historical position of working women. The constancy of sexual segregation was demonstrated by Edward Gross in a paper entitled "*Plus Ca Change* . . . The Sexual Structure of Occupations over Time," given at the 1967 meeting of the American Sociological Association.

monopolized the good jobs that became available. In much larger numbers they took advantage of the leisure secured by the increase in national wealth, the decline of male prejudice, and the new confidence inspired by all of these factors to mobilize on a scale which improvements in transportation and communication now made possible.

The growth of women's organizations was impressive. In 1888 the National Council of Women was formed. Two years later the General Federation of Women's Clubs began its fantastic period of expansion. The Women's Christian Temperance Union was already near the peak of its effectiveness. The first durable settlement house was established in 1889, and by the decade's end the experiment was a clear success with some dozens of settlements in being and hundreds more on the way. In 1899 the several Consumers' Leagues were united into a national organization. Nor was patriotism neglected as women rushed to meet the country's varying needs. In 1890 the Daughters of the American Revolution came into being. Seven years later scattered groups coalesced into the National Congress of Parents and Teachers, bringing some order to the burgeoning PTA movement.

It would be easy to expand this list, but suffice it to say that by 1900 about half of the important American women's organizations had been established, most of them in the 1890's. One could argue, in fact, that at the end of the nineteenth century the emancipation of women was about as complete as it would ever be. What happened after that was largely a matter of expanding beachheads which had already been secured. More women went to college or to work, some further legal disabilities were removed, and so on, but these changes were not so important as the breakthroughs that had been made before. Indeed, as the twentieth century opened, politics was the only area of great interest to women that still denied them a place. It took about a dozen years for women to realize their political deprivation, but once they did this last incongruity was quickly abolished. The organizational revolution of women was part of a larger phenomenon which Robert Wiebe calls the emergence of a new middle class. After describing the formation of many trade and professional associations, he points out that "almost every group within the new class experienced its formative growth toward self-consciousness in roughly the ten years from 1895 to 1905." [4] Although middle-class women were not in the same position as men, they nevertheless demonstrated similar desires for order and community. For our purposes, however, the important thing about the organization of women is that the mere fact of their coming together secured a large part of that freedom of action which feminists had been demanding for so long.

Suffragism excepted, then, the activities of organized women in the Progressive era were not so much a matter of winning new rights as utilizing those which had already been secured. The distance ordinary middle-class women had come, and the liberty of thought and conscience they enjoyed, was demonstrated by the General Federation of Women's Clubs in 1904 when it elected as president Mrs. Sarah Platt Decker. A large, commanding woman, she is best known to students of history for her declaration to the clubs that "Dante is dead. He has been dead for several centuries, and I think it is time that we dropped the study of his *Inferno* and turned our attention to our own." It was said of this able woman that her "sex alone kept her from being a United States Senator from Colorado." [5] She was well known to clubwomen for her liberal sentiments, and in electing her they made an active commitment to the reforming spirit she personified. Mrs. Decker did not disappoint them. She reorganized the federation's committee structure and among many good appointments made Rheta Childe Dorr, a progressive journalist, chairman of the Committee on the Industrial Conditions of Women and Children.

4. Robert Wiebe, *The Search for Order, 1877–1920* (New York, 1967), p. 127.
5. Rheta Childe Dorr, *A Woman of Fifty* (New York, 1924), p. 118.

Mrs. Dorr, in turn, recruited an outstanding body of women, including Mary McDowell, the great settlement headworker from Chicago.

The committee's methods showed what clubwomen could do when properly led. It decided to promote a federal report on the condition of working women and children which social workers and reformers had been urging on Congress for years without success. The committee began by securing the approval of President Roosevelt. Then it started pressuring Congress directly. The women wanted an appropriation of $1 million. Speaker Joe Cannon was determined not to give them a cent. In the end they got $350,000 for the project. This was accomplished by persuading clubwomen of the study's importance and inducing them to demand action from Congress. Mrs. Dorr arranged for meetings between clubwomen and eloquent working girls, and in other ways dramatized the issue so that it became a personal interest of clubwomen. Their reaction was summed up by an anonymous Senator who told Mary McDowell, "Oh, I've heard from home. . . . My wife is a member of some clubs out there and she heard what you had to say about this matter at some convention. Then she telegraphed me to get busy, and all her friends did the same. For the sake of domestic harmony I'll have to do it." [6] Much more than husbandly good nature was involved. Clubwomen lacked power, but not influence. Many of them occupied strategic positions in their communities, and when aroused they made themselves felt, both directly and through their husbands. Leaders like Mrs. Decker who could move them possessed an authority that was no less real for being intangible and elusive. The presidents who succeeded her were not so liberal or compelling, but the General Federation continued to support many progressive measures all the same.

The value of mobilizing behind a given effort and pursuing

6. Howard E. Wilson, *Mary McDowell: Neighbor* (Chicago, 1928), p. 129.

it to the finish was also demonstrated by the Consumers' League. The GFWC's weakness lay in its size and diversity of interests; a kind of centrifugal pressure kept it from concentrating on particular efforts for very long. The NCL was in just the opposite position. It was a relatively compact and efficient organization, and Florence Kelley had pretty much of a free hand in managing it. In 1907, when the Oregon Ten-Hour Law was challenged, Mrs. Kelley and Josephine Goldmark asked Louis D. Brandeis, Miss Goldmark's brother-in-law, to defend it before the Supreme Court. Brandeis agreed, and because the Court had earlier ruled that the state's police power extended to matters of public health, he decided to center his brief on the effects of overworking women and children. In two weeks' time Josephine and Pauline Goldmark, Mrs. Kelley, and other volunteers dug up enough evidence—mostly from European sources—to persuade the Court. It took another thirty years to nail down the points made in *Muller v. Oregon*, but the decision opened the door to many protective laws and gave the league a mission it was well equipped to perform.

Thereafter, while the NCL continued to lobby in Congress and the state legislatures for desirable bills, and maintained its campaign for the White Label, logistical support for court tests became its special province. In 1908–1909, with a grant from the Russell Sage Foundation, it supplemented its foreign data with American evidence. When the Illinois maximum-hour law was tested, the NCL was ready with a six-hundred-page brief. In April 1910 Brandeis won the case, enabling Mrs. Kelley to tell her followers that this one event alone justified the league's existence. The NCL next took up minimum-wage laws, sponsoring bills to that effect in a number of states in 1911. When Brandeis was elevated to the Supreme Court, Felix Frankfurter replaced him as the league's chief counsel. The minimum-wage campaign was less successful than the maximum-hour effort. With Brandeis abstaining, the Court divided in the Progressive era, allowing minimum-wage bills to stand; then in *Adkins v. Children's Hospital* (1923) it ruled them unconstitutional. Later, of course, it reversed itself. Nonetheless, the legal research, lobbying, and propagandizing the league did on behalf of both principles paid off handsomely in the end. The NCL sustained this work, in addition to its many other functions, on a budget that never exceeded $10,000 before World War I, and with a membership of perhaps two thousand people. Dollar for dollar and woman for woman, it was the best buy in the history of social feminism.

In a more oblique way, the usefulness of elite units in the women's army was illustrated by the Uprising of the Twenty Thousand in New York City. This great strike began at the Triangle Shirtwaist Company as the culmination of a complex series of events extending over an eighteen-month period. A wildcat strike had been resolved by the formation of a "society" to which only one hundred of the five hundred girls in the shop were admitted. This company union failed to satisfy even those who belonged to it. By September 1909 the girls were demanding a real union. The company responded by firing the leaders, whereupon the entire shop walked out. Leiserson's, another major plant, had already been struck, and the entire trade seethed with discontent. The New York Women's Trade Union League joined the girls and gave them their first important publicity when Mary Dreier was arrested for picketing Triangle. Local 25 of the International Ladies' Garment Workers' Union soon threw all its resources—$4 and a hundred members—into the fray, and demanded a general strike. On November 22, about two months after the girls had first walked out, a mass meeting in Cooper Union heard Samuel Gompers, Mary Dreier, trade union leaders, and socialists debate the issue. Clara Lemlich, a striker who had been assaulted on the picket line, gave a fiery speech in Yiddish that brought the crowd to its feet. A general strike was declared, and everyone took what was said to be an old Jewish oath: "If I turn traitor to the cause I now pledge, may this hand wither from the arm I now raise." [7]

No one had ever seen such a strike before. Never had so many women workers walked out. The strikers, most of them Jewish girls between the ages of sixteen and twenty-five, endured three winter months of hardship, deprivation, and abuse. Their picket lines were attacked by policemen, hired thugs, and prostitutes. They were arrested and fined in great numbers. The police behaved brutally, the employers meanly, and the strikers magnificently. It was a classic strike with everyone playing those roles assigned them by the romantic imagination of the era. Moreover, it took place in full view of press and public, not in a remote mining camp or company town but in America's largest city. The high drama thus revealed, and the unambiguous nature of the cause, brought middle- and upper-class female sympathizers out in unprecedented numbers and gave the NYWTUL its first big chance to show what it could do in an emergency. It turned out to be quite a lot.

The league organized a volunteer force of seventy-five allies and nine lawyers, and furnished nearly $30,000 in bail money. Its headquarters became a strike center so efficient that it could organize a parade of ten thousand workers on short notice. To its efforts were added those of upper-class sympathizers, called "uptown scum" by the employers' association. Mrs. O. H. P. Belmont staged a mass meeting that brought seven thousand people into the Hippodrome. With Miss Anne Morgan and Mrs. J. Borden Harriman she raised $1,300 at a single meeting of the fashionable Colony Club. The strike itself was inconclusive. Many of the larger shops were organized, most of the smaller ones were not. The strike cost about $100,000, a fifth of which was raised by the NYWTUL. It proved, however, to be invaluable for the ILGWU. In 1909 the

7. Gladys Boone, *The Women's Trade Union Leagues in Great Britain and the United States* (New York, 1942), p. 78. The *Survey* reported the strike very carefully. See, for example, Constance D. Luepp, "The Shirtwaist Makers Strike," December 18, 1909, pp. 383–386.

union was insignificant. In 1914 it was the third largest in the AFL. The New York Women's Trade Union League profited also. The uprising put it on the reform map, as it were, and multiplied its membership and resources.

The National WTUL was moved by these events to build a strike fund, hire a full-time secretary, and employ a lecturer, Frances Squire Potter of the University of Minnesota, to spread the good news that the working woman's day had come. When another great strike took place late that same year, the WTUL was ready for it. This was the Chicago garment strike which began September 22, 1910, when a handful of girls walked out to protest a wage cut at Hart, Schaffner and Marx's Number Five Shop. Within three weeks the movement snowballed to the point where some forty thousand workers were out and the men's garment industry prostrate. It was a larger and more representative strike than the New York uprising and included men and women, Jews and Gentiles of many nationalities. The base of outside support was broader also. In addition to the usual labor and socialist allies, the strikers were supported by such varied groups as the Illinois Federation of Women's Clubs, ministerial associations, and even the Chicago City Club (male) which urged a settlement on terms favorable to the workers. Mrs. Robins swung into action with the league's strike committee, demanded and got a seat on the principal strike committee, and went immediately to work raising money and distributing relief. When the strike ended fifty days later, the Chicago WTUL had raised $70,000, most of which went to the commissaries the league established to distribute relief supplies.

As so many of the strikers were married men with families, Chicago witnessed even more heroism and self-sacrifice than New York. Alice Henry visited an Italian family whose mother had just given birth to her fourth child, one of 1,250 born to striking families that winter. She was proud of her husband for staying on the picket line, even though his family was cold and hungry. "It is not only bread we give the children," she told

Miss Henry. "We live by freedom, and I will fight for it though I die to give it to my children." [8] To Alice Henry it was "like living in a besieged city." Want and courage were equally abundant, and confusion was general—even though Carl Sandburg and other friendly newsmen did their best to provide a clear running account of events. So many groups were involved on both sides and conditions changed so rapidly that no one could keep on top of the story. In the end, the United Garment Workers (AFL) ignobly signed a separate peace. The most durable consequence of the strike was the creation of an independent union, the Amalgamated Clothing Workers, made up of those, like young Sidney Hillman, who were dissatisfied with the ambiguous performance of the UGW.

These strikes broadened the sympathies of organized womanhood and enlisted the energies of women who had previously stayed aloof from the social struggle. Their shared experiences helped prepare the way for the Progressive campaign of 1912, which was based on these emotions and this kind of action. The NWTUL, the women's organization most closely connected with these events, gained most from them. In 1911 the National League reported that the New York branch had almost doubled in size, the Boston group had increased by one-third, and Chicago was now the largest of all with 725 members. The league entirely merited this growth. It had efficiently conducted a large share of the housekeeping chores in both strikes, while at the same time performing, from a bourgeois point of view, the indispensable job of blunting the class hatred aroused by such emotional conflicts.

The line was clearly drawn between labor and management in these strikes, but with so many middle- and upper-class allies involved on labor's side it was harder for the workers to see them as class conflicts. This fact was attested to by *The Diary of a Shirtwaist Striker*, a revealing piece of left-wing

8. Alice Henry, *The Trade Union Woman* (New York, 1915), p. 106.

propaganda published after the New York uprising, which attempted to discredit the allies' motives. Why, the writer asked herself, did so many affluent women support the strike? "I shouldn't wonder their conscience pricks them a bit—they must be ashamed of being fortune's children while so many of the girls have never known what a good day means. The rich women seem to be softer than the men; perhaps it's because they ain't making the money—they're only spending it." [9] The immensely rich Mrs. Belmont, a redoubtable fund-raiser during the uprising, posed a special threat. Of her the pamphlet said, "If she is affected by the girls' sufferings, why doesn't she try to do something more for us? If she really feels about it the way I do, why don't she come down among us, feed the hungry and warm the cold? I didn't see her even once and I don't believe any of the girls did." [1] This was, of course, hardly fair. Had Mrs. Belmont dashed around handing out bread and blankets she would surely have been condemned as a patronizing Lady Bountiful. In any event, there were prosperous women like Mary Dreier who walked the picket lines, went to jail, and involved themselves intimately in the strikers' lives.

. . . .

If these strikes showed advanced feminists at their best, the Lawrence strike which followed soon after demonstrated their limitations. The events at Lawrence are well known and easily summarized. A general strike erupted among the unorganized textile workers of Lawrence, Massachusetts, on January 12, 1912, in response to a wage cut. Confusion raged among the leaderless operatives until Local 20 of the Industrial Workers of the World called on its parent body for help. The Wobblies sent in their first team, including the eloquent Joe Ettor; Arturo Giovannitti, poet and journalist; Elizabeth Gurley Flynn,

9. Theresa S. Malkiel, *The Diary of a Shirtwaist Striker* (New York, 1910), p. 10.
    1. *Ibid.*, p. 22.

their famous Rebel Girl; and finally Big Bill Haywood himself. Despite the fierce passions aroused, wholesale brutality by police and militia, fraudulent murder charges against Ettor and Giovannitti, and other provocations, there was comparatively little violence. The Wobbly leadership insisted on a policy of direct action, passive resistance, and solidarity. Skilled and unskilled workers belonging to twenty-seven different ethnic groups rallied behind them, and on March 1 the employers gave in.[2]

Lawrence was in many ways the most significant strike of the Progressive era, because it proved that the status and ethnic differences that divided American workers could be overcome. Not every nationality group in Lawrence responded (the better-established Irishmen and Germans did not), but most did, especially the large Italian and Franco-Belgian contingents. Equally remarkable was the alliance forged between skilled and unskilled workers. The former, in fact, went so far as to agree that the largest share of the wage increase won should go to the unskilled workers who needed it most. The Wobblies' numerous and widely advertised failings in no way detracted from this astonishing triumph. They were, in truth, given to extravagantly bitter and dangerous rhetoric. Their refusal to participate in electoral politics denied them allies among elected officials and weakened the Socialist party. Their refusal to act as a regular bargaining agent and to make formal agreements with employers kept them from developing a solid base among workers. All the same, for a shining moment at Lawrence the Wobblies overturned the conventional wisdom and revealed unimagined possibilities.

It was perhaps inevitable that the door to an alternate future for America which the IWW opened briefly at Lawrence would soon be shut for good. Socialists provided the Lawrence strikers with a good deal of help, but they were dismayed by the Wobblies' language, angered by their refusal

2. The best account by far is Melvyn Dubofsky, *We Shall Be All: A History of the Industrial Workers of the World* (Chicago, 1969).

to play the electoral game, and committed to a policy of boring from within the AFL. Before long the Socialist party would expel its Wobbly members and fatally divide the radical movement. AFL leaders, whose own position had been won by narrowly promoting the interests of skilled workers had, in the short run, nothing to gain and much to lose from the dangerous play being made by the IWW. They would not, as a matter of record, accept the principle of industrial unionism until they were forced to by the Congress of Industrial Organizations more than a generation later. Given these facts, one would not expect that the hearts of ordinary Progressives, social workers, social feminists, and the like, with their devotion to piecemeal reform, would quicken at the spectacle of Lawrence. Even so, there is something to be learned from the way the social feminist vanguard responded to the crisis.

Two weeks after the strike began the Women's Trade Union League voted to join with the Lawrence Central Labor Union in establishing a relief headquarters. Under its direction eight thousand strikers were given food and clothing. Unlike the strikes in New York and Chicago, Lawrence was not sanctioned by the AFL. Its United Textile Workers, led by John Golden, first ignored the strike committee, then tried to break the strike by sending its members back to work after making a separate deal with the owners. When the majority of workers continued to stay out, Golden ordered the WTUL to stop providing relief. Although disgusted by this attempt to starve the strikers into line, the league complied. This episode posed a fundamental challenge to the relationship between the NWTUL and the AFL, a tie already frayed by the federation's cavalier treatment of its female allies. Sue Anislie Clark, president of the Boston branch, was appalled by Golden's tactics. She wrote Mrs. Robins that "many of those in power in the A.F. of L. today seem to be selfish, reactionary and remote from the struggle for bread and liberty of the unskilled workers." Condemning the league's alliance with the "stand-patters" of the labor movement, she insisted that in the future "we must be free to aid in the struggle of the workers wherever and however we find the 'fight on.'" [3]

The NWTUL's executive board typically decided to confer with Golden and Gompers. On May 2 John Golden explained to it that the UTW could not help the rank-and-file textile workers because most of them were women and children who did not earn enough to be charged full dues. It did not, therefore, pay the union to organize them. Samuel Gompers was a trifle more encouraging. After some backing and filling he agreed to give the NWTUL $150 a month for a year to organize textile workers. This made it easier for the league to follow the AFL line at Paterson, New Jersey, the following year, when the UTW more successfully sabotaged another great Wobbly-led textile strike. The league would probably have gone along with the AFL in any event. It was angry with Golden, sympathetic to the Lawrence strikers, impressed by the Wobblies' strategy—but even so, at the first meeting of the executive board after Lawrence, its policy of working only in AFL-sanctioned strikes was reaffirmed. Henceforth, no matter how badly the AFL behaved or how bright the opportunities elsewhere, the league would not be moved. This assured its future as a tail to the AFL's kite.

Settlement workers responded to the challenge of Lawrence in much the same way and for essentially the same reasons. The dominant figure among settlement workers in New England was Robert A. Woods, whose influence was based on support from both philanthropic and political circles. He was, in fact, a part of the Boston establishment and the closest thing to a settlement boss the movement produced. When Lawrence erupted he sided immediately with John Golden and harassed the strikers in every way he could (for example, by

3. Sue Anislie Clark to Margaret Dreier Robins, undated, Papers of the NWTUL.

getting a court order which forced the strike committee to open its accounts). Such was his influence that throughout the strike the only prominent settlement figure to encourage the strikers was Vida Scudder, no longer a settlement resident in any case. She was roundly abused in the press for her pains.[4] When the strike was won, despite numerous official outrages, Woods peevishly complained that Bill Haywood had been met by the citizens of New England "with only a fitful and almost cowering protest." [5]

The settlement leaders were not wholly unconscious of the poor figure they cut at Lawrence and Paterson. Stirred by these events, the president of the New York Association of Neighborhood Workers said in 1914 that the "settlement movement must free itself from all the ties that bind it to the present industrial and social system and be itself at liberty to teach and work for the real liberty of all human beings." John L. Elliott, head worker of Hudson Guild, called for "an entirely different system of social production." The conference in New York at which these statements were made agreed that the settlements had not done enough in the recent industrial uprisings. Florence Kelley called on them to face up to the new challenges. Paul Kennaday blamed their failings on organizational rigor. Too many settlement boards were undemocratic at heart; too many settlement residents were content to be boarders.[6] All this, while true, was beside the point. It was well and good to say that settlements ought to break the ties that bind, but most at the conference probably understood that it was too late for them to change. The "present industrial and social system" was their chief support, and to break with it would destroy the settlement movement. On the other hand, as was

4. The *Survey* reprinted her speech to show how inoffensive it was, "For Justice Sake," April 6, 1912, pp. 77–79.

5. "The Breadth and Depth of the Lawrence Outcome," *Survey*, April 6, 1912, p. 68.

6. Quoted in "The Task of the Settlement Today," *Survey*, June 13, 1914, p. 296.

dimly sensed at the time, to stay with it meant that the settlements would never be much more than first-aid stations in the urban wilderness.

This is not to say, of course, that a more daring response to the IWW would necessarily have changed the course of American social history, or that social feminists were particularly to blame for failing to take it. The IWW in its pure form could never have prevailed, yet its leaders were absolutely unresponsive to the friendly critics who pointed this out. Even if middle-class reformers, social feminists among them, had made a serious effort to work with the IWW, their chances of altering its policies to the required degree would have been slight. Moreover, they would have exposed themselves to the terrible counterattacks that finally crushed the Wobblies. Nor was it entirely clear at the time that only through such drastic and dangerous methods could the condition of the poor be radically improved. Reformers had enjoyed comparatively little success, but their methods were far from discredited, and they were hopeful that their efforts would soon bring important results. Lawrence was a turning point precisely because liberals learned nothing from it, and they learned nothing from it because they were liberals—which is about as far as this line of speculation can take us.

Lawrence was also obscured by another event in 1912 which gave reformers much more congenial opportunities— Theodore Roosevelt's presidential campaign. Many social feminists and reformers admired TR, who as Governor of New York and President of the United States had been moderately responsive to their appeals. In 1912 he gave them more reason to support him by adopting a set of minimum industrial standards which went far beyond anything yet offered reformers. While the New Nationalism seems to have been based on his desire to rationalize the corporate society then coming unevenly into being, it also included just about every major contemporary reform from the abolition of child labor to equal suffrage. When some women at the Progressive party's convention questioned the wisdom of abandoning the suffragist's traditional nonpartisanship, Jane Addams told them, "When a great party pledges itself to the protection of children, to the care of the aged, to the relief of overworked girls, to the safeguarding of burdened men, it is inevitable that it should appeal to women and should seek to draw upon the great reservoir of moral energy so long undesired and unutilized in practical politics." [7]

The coalition of businessmen, politicians (who admired TR, in Medill McCormick's justly celebrated phrase, because he "understood the psychology of the mutt"), social workers, and feminists was a curious one. Roosevelt regarded some of his more impassioned followers as part of what he later called "the lunatic fringe." Even to Donald Richberg, a reforming lawyer who played an important role in the party, it seemed "there was room on the platform for any one who had seen Peter Pan and believed in fairies." [8] Yet for all their emotional extravagance and evangelical fervor, the reformers were quite realistic about the party's position—more so than the professional politicians in fact. They sang "Onward Christian Soldiers" at the convention, but they knew that TR had faint chance of winning the first time around. What they did believe was that his great personal following gave them a chance to build an organization that could win later on, and thus make good the promises of 1912. They campaigned hard, but their eyes were really fixed on 1916 and 1920. This became clear after TR's inevitable defeat when they set up the Progressive Service, an effort to bring the techniques of social service and social research into politics on a continuing basis. Its divisions

7. Jane Addams, *The Second Twenty Years at Hull House* (New York, 1930), p. 33.

8. Donald Richberg, "We Thought It Was Armageddon," *Survey*, March 1, 1929, p. 724. For a full account of the social-justice movement's contribution to the Progressive party, see Allen F. Davis, *Spearheads for Reform* (New York, 1967), Ch. 10.

were led by such prominent reformers as Gifford Pinchot, Jane Addams, Jacob Riis, and Mrs. Robins. The Progressive Service was operating in twenty-one states by 1914, and attracted people like Lillian Wald of the Henry Street Settlement in New York who had stayed aloof from the original effort.

Unfortunately, the professional politicians viewed the Progressive party in quite another way. For them, the campaign had been a gamble that failed. Thereafter they were mainly interested in using the party as a lever to get back into the GOP. Neither the lunatic fringe nor the Progressive Service were of any further use to them, and within a few years they shook out the one and dismantled the other. In 1916 TR liquidated what remained of the effort with a cold message to the Progressive convention urging it to nominate in his stead the conservative Senator Henry Cabot Lodge of Massachusetts.[9] Thus, while the social feminists and social workers were right to join the Progressive party, the odds against them were much greater than they supposed. They sensibly realized it would take time to establish a viable third party, but time was just what they did not have. The professionals were betting on one throw of the dice. If they lost they were prepared to return to the sources from which power and patronage flowed. Under these circumstances the reformers' dedication to the long haul was decidedly romantic, although seemingly just the reverse.

The irony of their situation derives from the fact that while they were practical people and hence drawn to realistic (even though marginal) political mechanisms like the Progressive party, they wanted things which simply could not be secured in the usual way. Again, we have the advantage of hindsight over them. Had they known that three-quarters of a

9. For a vivid description of the convention, see John Reed's "Roosevelt Sold Them Out," *The Masses*, August 1916, reprinted in William L. O'Neill, ed., *Echoes of Revolt: The Masses, 1911–1917* (Chicago, 1966), pp. 138–142.

century after the Progressive movement got under way tens of millions of Americans would still be living in poverty, they might have behaved differently. Another thing we can see clearly that the advanced Progressives could not is that their fear of socialism was largely unwarranted. The democratic socialists of northern Europe have abolished poverty in countries whose resources do not begin to compare with those of the United States. And they have done so without destroying the things that most Progressives believed in. The church and the family are still respected institutions. Most property remains in private hands. Even class tensions have declined, much to the dismay of today's New Left.

The Progressive party was important, therefore, for the ungrasped lessons it taught. Just as the Lawrence strike showed that unskilled workers could be organized and that industrial unionism worked, the election of 1912 and the events following demonstrated that the party system did not work, that reformers who pinned their hopes on it were courting failure. In 1912 only the politics of vision was adequate to the country's needs. The weakness of the Progressive party, for all its apparent novelty, was that its politics were still too conventional. The logic of their position ought to have driven advanced reformers into the socialist camp. But, as we have seen, their fears were stronger than their hopes. This became clearer in the 1930's, when many surviving Progressives opposed the New Deal. Even Roosevelt's modest welfare program seemed to them purchased at too high a price.

These years (especially 1912–1914) were decisive, therefore, precisely because the country did not take a new direction. This meant that the workers would not be organized on a large scale for another generation, that a welfare state would not be built, and, as we saw earlier, that women would not be emancipated from the home. Domestic freedom was a function of those elaborate social services that only socialists were willing to provide. Organized women were nevertheless undiscouraged by these non-events. For one thing, they shared the dominant values of their class and failed to see that, unlike bourgeois men, they stood to benefit directly from the welfare state. For another, while the specific social-justice measures they endorsed often did poorly, the cause of woman suffrage began to make headway. The emotional losses sustained in one area were therefore offset by gains in the other.

. . . .

In 1910 Washington State broke the fourteen-year slump when it voted for woman suffrage. The next year, after a brilliant campaign featuring billboard ads, electric signs, essay contests, and much else, California did the same. In 1912 three more small states were added to the suffrage column, and in 1913, thanks to the Progressive party which held the balance of power in the Illinois legislature, women gained the presidential vote in that state. These events had a stimulating effect on the suffrage movement, and flagging local organizations in many states now began to work in earnest. At the same time it was clear that while decades of patient labor were beginning to pay off for suffragists, the state-by-state route would be a long and exhausting one. In 1912, for example, strong campaigns in Wisconsin, Michigan, and Ohio were all defeated. This set the stage for Alice Paul's arrival in Washington, D.C., with a handful of activists determined to revive the dormant federal woman-suffrage amendment. As we have seen, she got spectacular results from the beginning. She embarrassed the NAWSA, but she nonetheless forced it to take up the federal amendment. In 1914, while her Congressional Union was vigorously campaigning against Democratic candidates in the states where women did vote, orthodox suffragists were losing referenda in five states and winning in only two. In 1915, while the CU was organizing in all forty-eight states, NAWSA affiliates were losing referenda in New York, Massachusetts, Pennsylvania, and New Jersey. The point did not escape regular suffragists.

The period 1910–1915 marked the turning point in the struggle for woman suffrage. No important state except California was won, but the victories in small states released energies never before available to suffragists. It now became possible to wage substantial campaigns in many states at once. The momentum thus generated carried over from one election to the next so that defeat did not, as in the past, lead to a suspension of suffragist activity. By 1914, when the General Federation of Women's Clubs endorsed woman suffrage, it was clear that the cause enjoyed the support of masses of ordinary middle-class women. Thereafter the problem was no longer one of making woman suffrage respectable and of educating women to desire it. Instead, it was a matter of finding ways to translate womanly enthusiasm into political pressure. The Congressional Union had done much to generate that enthusiasm and had shown the NAWSA what direction to take; but it, and its successor, the Woman's party, were too extreme for most women.

The election of Mrs. Catt as president of the NAWSA solved all of these problems. She understood that the federal amendment's hour had come. She harnessed the energies unleashed by the Woman's party as the militants themselves never could. And she made the NAWSA a genuine national organization with a chain of command and channels of communication adequate to its task. In pursuing the federal amendment Mrs. Catt realized that local work could not be neglected, since after passage the bill would still have to be ratified by thirty-six state legislatures. It would never do to lose in the states what had been won in Washington. Finally, the NAWSA at last had sufficient funds thanks to its new drive which increased contributions, and to Mrs. Frank Leslie who bequeathed $2 million to Mrs. Catt in aid of the cause. After her election Mrs. Catt drew up a battle plan that she estimated would take six years to execute. As it happened, only four were required, but otherwise the schedule of events unfolded much as Mrs. Catt had expected. This is not to minimize the effort demanded of suffragists. It was perhaps inevitable that American women would sooner or later be enfranchised. That it turned out to be sooner was because millions of women and millions of dollars were mobilized by a brilliant leadership.

6

. . . .
the woman movement and the war

*a*s the Great War broke out just when American women were reaching organizational maturity, it was inevitable that they would expect to play a part in its resolution. Women had long thought of themselves as uniquely pacific in temper. Many belonged to the pre–Civil War peace movement, in which Elizabeth Cady Stanton and her friends absorbed Garrison's doctrine of nonresistance. By the turn of the century a female pacifism was clearly evident. The WCTU established its peace department in 1887, and other large women's organizations followed suit. As individuals, women were prominent in the flourishing peace societies of the Progressive era.

Jane Addams was the chief spokeswoman for female pacifists, and her book *The Newer Ideals of Peace* (1907) their main contribution to pacifist literature. In it Miss Addams claimed that the older arguments against war had been invalidated by industrialization. The old ideals had been "too soft and literary"; what was needed were vigorous new ones based on the facts of urban life. Like William James, she was searching for a moral equivalent of war. She failed, however, to find it. The new ideals, she hoped vaguely, would be generated by the immigrant masses. "It is possible that we shall be saved from warfare by the 'fighting rabble' itself, by the 'quarrelsome mob' turned into kindly citizens of the world through the pressure of a cosmopolitan neighborhood." [1] This was pretty thin stuff. The main thing to be said in its favor was that no one else in America had anything better to offer. There were, broadly speaking, two schools of thought on war. Imperialists like Theodore Roosevelt believed that war was an essential counterweight to the softening and emasculating tendencies of the affluent society. More popular was the characteristic notion of progressives that the irresistible upward movement of civilization, exemplified by themselves, was rendering warfare between great nations obsolete.

Almost the only work of substance during these years to anticipate future realities was Norman Angell's *The Great Illusion* (1913). Angell tried to show that a major war would not produce the expected results. You could not under modern conditions capture a nation's trade by conquering the nation itself, and the cost of such a conquest could not be recovered by forced reparations. Moreover, the destruction of a country's economy would have adverse effects on all those who did business with her. With remarkable foresight Angell predicted much of what actually happened. The defeat of Germany did not improve England's trading position. The Empire proved more of a liability than an asset. Reparations bore no relation to the war's cost. In the end, the Allies were forced to encourage German recovery because their own economic health demanded it. Angell suffered the prophet's customary fate. Not only did he fail to arrest the course of events, but because his was the best-known anti-war book of the day, in the public mind it was lumped with all those fatuous works that had declared a general war to be impossible.

The outbreak of hostilities caught most Americans off guard, but it was especially unsettling to women who had persuaded themselves, partly by misreading books like Angell's,

1. Jane Addams, *The Newer Ideals of Peace* (New York, 1907), p. 18. On the peace movement as a whole, see Merle Curti, *Peace or War: The American Struggle* (New York, 1936).

that great wars were a thing of the past. The scale and savagery of the war exposed the pitiful inadequacy of their analysis and reduced them to silence. Then, two European women came along to awaken American feminists to their duty as citizens of the most important neutral power.

Of the two, Rosika Schwimmer was certainly the more colorful. A Hungarian journalist and social worker, she was also press secretary of the International Woman Suffrage Alliance, of which Carrie Chapman Catt was president. She was a brilliant and persuasive speaker, but while she could mobilize sentiment she could not organize it thanks to her difficult temperament. Louis Lochner, who saw a great deal of Miss Schwimmer in connection with the ill-fated Ford Peace Ship, said of her: "Eloquence, wit, savoir-faire, forcefulness, a keen sense of the dramatic, a genuine personal charm—all these qualities were at her command, to be used whenever the exigencies of a given situation demanded them." [2] But, he continued, she was "essentially an autocrat." She could not delegate responsibility. She was suspicious and secretive in dealing with Americans who valued openness above everything else. As her correspondence with the Woman's Peace party makes clear, she was given to self-pity and sharp changes in mood. Nevertheless, when Miss Schwimmer came to America in September 1914 she was granted interviews by both President Wilson and Secretary of State Bryan. Her speaking tour around the country, calling on the United States to intervene on behalf of a negotiated settlement, was effective, and a variety of ad hoc peace groups sprang up in her wake.

Hard behind her was Emmeline Pethick-Lawrence, an English feminist of some renown. She had begun her public life in a Christian mission in the London slums and had married a wealthy settlement worker. When the militant suffragists formed the Women's Social and Political Union, she and her husband joined it. They exercised a moderating influence on

2. Louis Lochner, *Henry Ford: America's Don Quixote* (New York, 1925), p. 67.

the militants for some years until Mrs. Pankhurst expelled them for Right Deviationism in 1912. When war broke out Mrs. Pethick-Lawrence was initially carried away by the rush of enthusiasm with which England rallied to the colors. Once the first hectic months were past, she began to wonder if the occasion demanded of feminists this kind of patriotism:

> Had we not spoken and written of the solidarity of women whose main vocation in every nation was one and the same—the guardianship and the nurture of the human race? Could the women of the world remain silent while men in the bloom of their youth were being offered up by many nations for sacrifice? [3]

These thoughts were in her mind even as she did war relief work, but the event which crystallized her resolution was Rosika Schwimmer's request for aid in getting to the United States. She did help Miss Schwimmer, and after being asked to speak at a New York suffrage rally in October she decided to make the crossing and talk about peace as well as votes for women.

At a suffrage rally in Carnegie Hall she first broached her plan for a woman's peace movement and was enthusiastically received. Crystal Eastman formed a woman's peace committee and urged her to contact Jane Addams who, if she became head of the movement in America, would assure its success. The same advice was given Mrs. Pethick-Lawrence in Washington, and so she went from there directly to Chicago where she stayed at Hull House. She found Jane Addams uncertain as to the value of such an organization. Like most American women, Miss Addams was still dazed by events in Europe. But she was elected chairman of the Chicago Emergency Federation of Peace Forces which had been founded in response to the visits of Mrs. Pethick-Lawrence and Miss Schwimmer, and agreed to call a meeting to discuss forming a woman's peace group.

3. Emmeline Pethick-Lawrence, *My Part in a Changing World* (London, 1938), p. 307.

The idea for such a conference seems to have occurred to many women at about the same time. Jane Addams soon received a letter from Carrie Chapman Catt asking her to call for nationwide demonstrations for peace and against preparedness. Mrs. Catt, who was then heading the New York suffrage campaign, had long been interested in disarmament and had associated herself with Miss Schwimmer's visit to President Wilson. Although she was not active in the peace movement, she was close to a number of women who were, notably Anna Garlin Spencer who persuaded her that the national peace societies seemed to have "as little use for women and their points of view, as have the militarists." Mrs. Catt continued: "If I have received the right impression from Mrs. Spencer that the present management of the peace movement in this country is overmasculinized, I think it would be an excellent idea to have the next demonstrations conducted by women alone." [4]

The inception of a women's peace movement, therefore, owed something to the feminist distrust of the male world as well as to the demonstrated incompetence of orthodox peace groups. Mrs. Catt wanted Jane Addams to issue the call to action because if she did so herself it would seem too much like a suffragist ploy. Miss Addams agreed that the men in the peace movement left something to be desired, and, while she usually thought it best to have men and women working together on public issues, "there is no doubt that at this crisis the women are [the] most eager for action." [5] And so, "with a certain sinking of the heart," Jane Addams agreed to take up the work of organizing women for peace, a labor she was never to put down.

The idea of a women's peace meeting had become so irresistible that it overcame both the good judgment and the

4. Carrie Chapman Catt to Jane Addams, December 16, 1914, Papers of the Woman's Peace Party, Swarthmore College Peace Collection.
5. Jane Addams to Carrie Chapman Catt, December 21, 1914, Papers of the WPP.

prejudices of the women involved. Mrs. Spencer was irritated, according to Carrie Chapman Catt, because the meeting was called in response to the initiative of two European women. She detested Mrs. Pethick-Lawrence. Nor was she glad to have an outsider to peace work like Mrs. Catt playing such a prominent role in the affair. For her part, Mrs. Catt was worried that the Washington organizational meeting would be taken over by the militant Congressional Union which was convening at the same time in Washington. She distrusted "the well known habit of all militants to make every one a tail of their kite," and, as leader of the New York suffrage campaign, she could not afford to be identified with a group whose policy it was to campaign against Democratic politicians in the coming elections. Within a week Mrs. Catt's reservations had become more pronounced. She was certain now that the Congressional Union was handling the arrangements for the Washington meeting because of their connection with Mrs. Pethick-Lawrence. This militant penetration was all the more embarrassing because in England the militants had become harshly anti-German and Mrs. Catt, as president of the International Suffrage Alliance, could not offend German women by seeming to associate herself with such sentiments. She agreed to come to the meeting but made it clear to Jane Addams that her suffrage work came first, and that she had no intention of doing anything to compromise her postwar role in the Alliance.

With this mixture of caution, suspicion, enthusiasm, and confusion, the delegates gathered in Washington on January 9, 1915, to form the Woman's Peace party. Mrs. Catt opened the mass meeting on the second day and explained why they had come together:

> The women of this country were lulled into inattention to the great military question of the war by reading the many books put forth by great pacifists who had studied the question and announced that there never could be another world war. But when it was found that their conclusions

were false and the great war came, the women of the country waited for the pacifists to move, and when they heard nothing from them . . . they decided all too late to get together at this eleventh hour.[6]

On the previous day eighty-six delegates from most of the major women's organizations had met to hammer out a platform on which they could all stand. At least six separate platforms were presented, including those of Jane Addams, Anna Garlin Spencer, Emmeline Pethick-Lawrence (who presented the program of Norman Angell's Union for Democratic Control), the New York Federation of Women's Clubs, and Lucia Ames Mead. Mrs. Charles Edward Russell, speaking for the socialists, urged "that attention be paid to the economic factors causing war, namely commercial competition, and that a clause be added indicating the economic basis of war and the cure therefor, the reorganization of industry on a cooperative rather than a competitive basis." [7]

The platform which finally emerged from two days of debate was relatively daring. Of its eleven points the most important called for a conference of neutral nations to work for an early peace, the limitation of armaments and the nationalization of their manufacture (to take the profits out of war), the democratic control of foreign policies, and universal woman suffrage. Of greatest significance were the women's plea for a "Concert of Nations" to replace the "Balance of Power," action toward "the gradual organization of the world to substitute Law for War," and the replacement of rival armies and navies by an "international police." This document demonstrated how cosmopolitan the woman movement had become. Their transatlantic associations had accustomed feminists to thinking and working in global terms, and their immediate response to the war showed how far they had gone beyond most other Americans in shedding the parochial nationalism of an isolated power. While there was little new in their platform

6. Minutes of the Conference, Papers of the WPP, no page numbers.
7. *Ibid.*

—much of it was taken from the program of the English Union for Democratic Control—the comparative ease with which it was adopted suggests that there was something like a consensus on the questions.

The preamble to the platform, written by Anna Garlin Spencer, expressed the simple ideology that bound the women together. Women as the bearers and guardians of life were no longer willing to stand idly by while the fruits of their labor were squandered. "Therefore as human beings and the mother half of humanity, we demand that our right to be consulted in the settlement of questions concerning not alone the life of individuals but of nations be recognized and respected." Harriot Stanton Blatch observed during the meeting that politicians had not tried to end the war because they were neutralized by ethnic rivalries among the voters, and that this made it imperative for nonpartisan women to make themselves heard. But most women seemed to feel that it was their maternal capability which gave them a special interest in peace. Crystal Eastman spoke for many of them when she wrote later:

> From the beginning, it seemed to me that the only reason for having a Woman's Peace Party is that women are mothers, or potential mothers, therefore have a more intimate sense of the value of human life and that, therefore, there can be more meaning and passion in the determination of a woman's organization to end war than in an organization of men and women with the same aim.[8]

No women's organization ever had a more impressive beginning than the WPP. Three thousand people attended its mass meeting on January 10, where Jane Addams was elected chairman. Its officers and sponsors included many distinguished

8. Crystal Eastman to Jane Addams, January 16, 1915, Papers of the WPP. A contrary point of view was that mothers ought to leave it up to their sons to decide if a given cause was worth dying for. Dorothea Brande, "Morale of Women," *New Republic*, September 22, 1917, pp. 218–219.

and influential women.[9] Almost immediately a national headquarters was opened in Chicago and a campaign launched to build sentiment for an American attempt at mediation and arbitration in concert, if possible, with other neutral nations. It is not clear how much faith the women had in neutral intervention to end the war, but so much time and effort was lavished on the scheme that it certainly enjoyed some credibility. Mrs. Catt had little hope for the plan. A conference of neutrals, much less a conference of neutral women, could hardly affect the belligerents, she thought. Her European correspondence had convinced her that passions were running too strongly for the voice of reason to prevail:

> Between these German letters and the French letters my conviction has been emphasized that the world has literally gone mad, and I don't think we could get an international meeting with these warring peoples in attendance. It would be too much like trying to organize a peace society in an insane asylum.[1]

Mrs. Catt played a very small part in the subsequent history of the WPP. She told Jane Addams that her work in New York and the need to preserve herself for an important postwar role in the International Suffrage Alliance would preclude her taking an active interest in the party, much as she sympathized with it. This was characteristic of Mrs. Catt. Her genius as a suffrage leader was for tough, prudent tactics. She focused all her energies on each successive step and disregarded everything else. In the same fashion as she had only

9. Its vice-chairmen were Mrs. Anna Garlin Spencer, Mrs. Henry Villard, Mrs. Louis F. Post, and Mrs. John Jay White. Lucia Ames Mead was secretary, Mrs. William I. Thomas executive secretary, Sophonisba P. Brechinridge treasurer, and Mrs. Elizabeth Glendower Evans national organizer. Among its sponsors were Mrs. Catt, May Wright Sewall, Dr. Anna Howard Shaw, Mrs. Ellen M. Henrotin, Margaret Dreier Robins, Mrs. Booker T. Washington, and Mary McDowell.

1. Carrie Chapman Catt to Jane Addams, January 16, 1915, Papers of the WPP.

nominally involved herself in peace work, so did she only nominally involve herself in war work after American entry. Her convictions did not change, but situations did, and Mrs. Catt was always alert to the demands of the hour.

Her advice was sound enough, but it did not meet the women's need for immediate action. Within a year 25,000 women had joined the WPP, moved by an urgent desire to struggle against the movement of events. The party sponsored a road-company production of Euripides' *Trojan Women* which occupied the local branches wherever it played, and in March helped organize a conference of peace workers which became the National Peace Federation with Jane Addams as chairman. Although the need for a popular front was never more compelling, the differences among the peace groups were too great to be bridged and the federation amounted to little. More promising was the opportunity opened up by the International Congress of Women to be held at The Hague in April 1915. The conference had been conceived by members of the International Suffrage Alliance. They were not able to persuade the Alliance to sponsor such a meeting formally, but gained the support of such leading figures in the woman movement as Dr. Aletta H. Jacobs, president of the Dutch suffrage society, Crystal Macmillan and Emily Hobhouse of England, Lida Gustava Heymann and Dr. Anita Augsburgh of Germany, and others. When the call went out in February it was greeted with enthusiasm by the WPP, which saw in it a unique opportunity to present its plan for continuous mediation.

This scheme had been devised by Julia Grace Wales, an instructor at the University of Wisconsin, approved by the state legislature, and recommended to Congress by Senator Robert M. La Follette.[2] It called for a conference of experts who were to represent the neutral governments without nec-

2. See Walter I. Trattner, "Julia Grace Wales and the Wisconsin Plan for Peace," *Wisconsin Magazine of History*, XLIV (Spring 1961), 203–213.

essarily committing them to a particular program. The conference would meet continuously, recommend solutions and alternatives to the belligerents, and communicate the results of its overtures to all interested parties until an acceptable set of conditions for ending the war was achieved. This was an ingenious and virtually unique proposal that enjoyed wide support. It called for the public action of neutrals without binding any nation, and involved not simply an offer to mediate but the presentation of specific proposals. Moreover, it did not require an armistice, so the belligerents could agree to cooperate with the commission without conceding anything until an accommodation had been reached. Assuming the belligerents wanted a negotiated peace, the plan had much to commend it.

The International Congress of Women was a moving experience for its participants. It passed many resolutions, including one calling for another such congress to be held in connection with the peace conference that would eventually end the war. As might have been expected, however, the public reception to the congress was generally hostile. The belligerent countries on both sides regarded it as an enemy plot. In the United States the tone was set by Theodore Roosevelt who called it "silly and base." [3] The most useful aspect of the congress was its decision to send delegations to the capitals of Europe to confer with responsible officials and advance the plan for continuous mediation. Jane Addams headed one of the two delegations and received courteous hearings from most of the great powers. In Germany Foreign Minister Von Jagow encouraged the women to promote a neutral intervention because "at this moment neither side is strong enough to dictate

3. The *New York Herald* called it "a silly proceeding"; the *Washington Star* an exercise in "utter futility"; the *Pittsburgh Gazette-Times* "a disappointing failure." Midwestern papers were more sympathetic. "Was the Women's Peace Congress a Failure?," *Literary Digest*, May 15, 1915, 1139–1140.

terms and neither side is so weakened that it has to sue for peace." [4] Nothing came of these encounters because European neutrals were too afraid of being drawn into the holocaust to take even the smallest chances, while American policy was too uncertain to permit any initiatives. President Wilson and Colonel House were evasive. Secretary of State Lansing was openly hostile to the idea. His argument that an unsuccessful American attempt at mediation would cost the United States its future influence carried great weight with the President.[5]

Jane Addams believed the war dragged on because the people of Europe did not know the facts. Their leaders "were absorbed in preconceived judgments, and had become confused through the limitations imposed upon their sources of information." [6] Everyone was charged with blinding emotions. This being so, the chances for an early peace would seem to have been negligible. But Miss Addams was reluctant to admit the hopelessness of any situation. If the people could be reached with the truth, it would set them free. If their leaders were properly approached by authoritative neutral sources, they would accept a rational program for ending the war. Most of the people she met in Europe observed this conventional rubric. On one occasion, however, she and her companions were confronted with a more realistic analysis, and their response to it tells us most of what we need to know about their peacemaking capacities. In Berlin they met Professor Hans Delbrueck, a hard-boiled nationalist who wanted to see an end to the war and a restoration of German colonies. Although given to unfortunate teutonisms, he nonetheless provided the women with the best advice they were to receive in Europe. The only way to an early peace, he told them, was for the United States to exercise its power. President Wilson "should tell England that

4. Marie Louise Degen, *History of the Woman's Peace Party* (Baltimore, 1939), p. 106.

5. *Ibid.*, pp. 115–119.

6. Jane Addams, Emily G. Balch, Alice Hamilton, *Women at The Hague* (New York, 1916), p. 92.

he will place an embargo on munitions of war, unless she will accept reasonable terms for ending the war, and let him tell Germany that this embargo will be lifted unless Germany will do the same." [7] The women's response, in the words of Alice Hamilton, was to condemn his idea as "utterly un-American." Jane Addams explained to him that President Wilson would lose all his moral force if he resorted to blackmail and coercion. Delbrueck replied scornfully that "moral influence is nothing," thereby convincing the women of his innate Prussian depravity.

Jane Addams and her friends suffered from a weakness common to all but the radical pacifists—an inability to see that peace could not be won by persuasion alone. This was all the more surprising since she had been on the ground in Europe and knew how strong were the forces that kept the war going. She knew also that in politics moral influence counted for little unless it was backed up by power—votes, money, influential supporters, or whatever. Yet she approached the most desperate political adventure of her life as if sweet reason alone was all that mattered. Allied with this was the failure of pacifists like her to distinguish between levels of force. Obviously, the policy of economic blackmail proposed by Delbrueck involved a kind of violence and was morally unimpressive. But the alternative toward which the country was drifting was the infinitely more violent and immoral one of armed intervention. Their squeamishness gave the women's plans, however intelligently conceived, an inauthentic character and discouraged the kind of political action required to influence policy-makers.

Jane Addams and her associates returned to the United States, where the old public-relations techniques were still pertinent, with some relief. But even at home passions were rising and the politics of reason becoming daily more irrelevant. When the Ford Peace Ship, organized for the perfectly sensible purpose of convening an assembly of neutrals, sailed from New York at the end of 1915, it was so ridiculed by the press as

7. *Ibid.*, p. 30. See also Alice Hamilton, "At the War Capitals," *Survey*, August 7, 1915, p. 419.

to destroy any prospect for its success. By this time the preparedness movement, which laid the groundwork for American intervention, was showing its strength. President Wilson agreed to a moderate expansion of armaments, and the WPP recognized the force of preparedness sentiment shortly thereafter by accepting this increase in hopes it would appease the demand for more arms. A vain hope, it nonetheless testified to the party's desire to remain relevant and was secured over the loud opposition of a minority of absolute pacifists led by Mrs. Henry Villard.

Throughout 1916 America drifted closer to war, and the peace forces were able to take comfort only in their successful efforts to prevent a conflict with Mexico. As described by Arthur S. Link, the distinguished Wilson scholar, the sequence of events was as follows. American troops had been sent into Mexico after the rebel leader Pancho Villa, and had been drawn into contact with the Mexican Army. On June 21 fighting broke out between the two forces, and President Wilson decided to ask Congress for permission to occupy northern Mexico. A war with Mexico was averted thanks mainly to a small anti-war group, the American Union Against Militarism, which publicized the eyewitness report of an American officer showing that American troops had been the aggressors. The AUAM further organized meetings in various cities and stimulated a flood of letters and telegrams to the President. It was assisted by other peace groups, especially the WPP. The change in public sentiment thus engineered, together with more accurate intelligence reports, prompted Wilson to reverse himself. It was one of the very few times in American history when an administration bent on war was thus deterred.[8]

Female pacifists could rightly draw comfort from such a remarkable accomplishment, but otherwise there was little to cheer them. In June the WPP passed out leaflets and put up

8. Arthur S. Link, *Wilson: Confusions and Crises, 1915–16* (Princeton, 1964), pp. 314–318. Lillian Wald, *Windows on Henry Street* (Boston, 1934), pp. 289–298, tells it from the AUAM's point of view.

posters to protest the great preparedness parade in Chicago. But their peace banner "was torn down by patriotic policemen on the ground that it was treasonable, and two of our men friends who tried to defend it were arrested." [9] This incident foreshadowed what was to happen after American entry, when not just Chicago policemen but the entire machinery of justice would treat pacifists as traitors. By the end of the year it was becoming evident that American entry was all but inevitable. On February 28, 1917, President Wilson told representatives of the AUAM and the WPP that America must enter the war in order to have a voice at the peace conference. Knowing that war was certain did not, of course, make its coming easier to bear. When it was declared, the WPP split three ways. Some defected altogether. Deciding that the war was really a great struggle for liberty and justice after all, they supported it with a vengeance. The Massachusetts branch was outstanding in this regard. Mrs. Glendower Evans, a social feminist of long standing and its most prominent member, suddenly discovered that she had been pro-Ally in her heart from the beginning, even though she only realized it when America entered the war.[1]

A radical minority led by Crystal Eastman of the New York City branch took the opposite course. They resolved to continue agitating for an early peace. When the state chairman dragged her feet they called a convention on their own initiative and elected officers from their own ranks. They published a defiant monthly journal, *Four Lights*, until the Post Office took away its mailing privileges. They resisted conscription as long as they could, and lobbied in Albany against the Espionage Bill and universal military training. When Fiorello La Guardia accepted an Army commission without resigning his seat in Congress, they petitioned the Speaker of the House

9. Eleanor Karsten, Report of the Office Secretary, July 1, 1916, Papers of the WPP.
1. Copy of Elizabeth Glendower Evans to Mrs. Raymond Unwin, September 2, 1917, Papers of the WPP.

to make him give it up. They sponsored classes on world politics taught by leading pacifists including Norman Angell and Emily Green Balch, who was later fired by Wellesley College for her peace work. Throughout the war these bright, lively young women demonstrated that it was possible to resist the military spirit without going to jail or compromising one's principles.

Unlike these radical young women, who were comparatively free of responsibilities, Jane Addams had substantial interests to protect. These included not only Hull House itself but the public influence she enjoyed and hoped to use on behalf of a democratic and durable peace settlement. Accordingly, after much anxious soul-searching she decided to work for internationalism during the war and support civilian relief at home. In food conservation she found an especially congenial cause and spoke all over the country on behalf of it. Her position was probably most characteristic of the Women's Peace party as a whole, although the Wilsonian formula of making war in the name of peace was almost equally popular. Very few members followed the radicals' example.

The response of other women's organizations to the war was even less equivocal. Most pledged their support to the government immediately. Those that did not, like the Consumers' League, cooperated with it anyway. The NAWSA, anticipating what war would bring, committed itself in February, well before American entry. When Anna Garlin Spencer of the WPP demanded that Mrs. Catt reverse this decision she was first amused by Mrs. Spencer's hysterical accusations, then angrily snapped back that she was too busy winning votes for women to haggle over trifles.[2] Mrs. Catt took an entirely cold-blooded view of the situation. She had her doubts that the war would make the world a better place to live in, but she never

2. "Suffragists have not quite lost their heads, but I think the Pacifists have." Carrie Chapman Catt to Anna Garlin Spencer, February 19, 1917, Anna Garlin Spencer Papers, Friends Peace Collection, Swarthmore College.

for a moment thought the suffragists had any choice but to endorse the President's policy. They were too near their goal to risk challenging an inflamed public temper. In any case, once women had the vote they would put an end to wars, and the cause of peace would thus best be served by avoiding futile gestures and keeping one's eye on the main chance. The NAWSA would do only enough war work to make its patriotism credible; its main energies would be devoted to winning the vote.

Despite their earlier protestations, the war turned out to be enormously popular with middle-class women. However much their initial response to the war may have been marked by confusion and uncertainty, once the issue was joined most of them left off playing Hamlet and plunged into war work with a zest and enthusiasm that was all the greater for their having been freed from doubt. So wholehearted was their response, in fact, that a grateful if bewildered government found itself snowed under by their demands for a share in the great national adventure. If the government had given the matter any thought at all, it had apparently assumed that American women would loyally but quietly support whatever policies were decided upon. But an organized and aroused womanhood naturally assumed that no great national enterprise could be undertaken without them. Thus the government was caught flatfooted when, as the Woman's Committee's official historian tactfully put it:

> Into turbid, tense, disordered Washington, came the women's tenders of service. It was not known exactly to whom these offers should be referred, or what could be done with them, but it was certain that it would never do to refuse them, for they might be needed, although no one yet knew when and where.[3]

It would have been foolish to ignore this outpouring of patriotic sentiment, and so the administration, with the cer-

3. Emily Newell Blair, *The Woman's Committee . . . An Interpretive Report* (Washington, D.C., 1920), p. 14.

tainty of genius, hit upon the idea of forming a central clearing house to which the women could be sent. Accordingly, on April 21 the Council of National Defense plugged this newly revealed gap in the nation's defenses by creating the Committee on Women's Defense Work under the chairmanship of Anna Howard Shaw. The choice of Dr. Shaw to head this venture was a particularly happy one. As she had just resigned as president of the NAWSA she was free to undertake other lines of work, and consequently she possessed two indispensable attributes from the council's point of view—availability and prestige. Since it was well known that Dr. Shaw was strong on inspiration and weak on organization, her appointment suggests that the council intended the Woman's Committee to be a hortatory and inspiriting force rather than a genuine High Command.

The committee, which went under a variety of official titles but was always known familiarly as the Woman's Committee, was composed mainly of the heads of prestigious women's organizations.[4] Though the weighty character of this group was immediately obvious, its mandate was considerably less so. Its duty, according to Newton D. Baker, Secretary of War and chairman of the Council of National Defense, was simply "to coordinate the women's preparedness movement." The fuzziness of this injunction was all the more apparent because the CND itself was merely an advisory organization and not an executive body, having been set up in 1916 to plan for the mobilization of the home front in case of war. But if no one was quite sure what the women were supposed to do, they set about doing it with alacrity and dispatch all

4. Besides Dr. Shaw it consisted of Mrs. Philip Moore, president of the National Council of Women; Mrs. Josiah Cowles, president of the General Federation of Women's Clubs; Mrs. Maude Wetmore, chairman of the National League for Woman's Service; Carrie Chapman Catt, president of the NAWSA; Mrs. Joseph Lamar, president of the National Society of Colonial Dames; Miss Ida Tarbell; and later Miss Agnes Nestor, president of the International Glove Workers' Union.

the same. A headquarters was secured, and the committee was organized into departments along the lines of the General Federation and the WCTU. Despite the ambiguity of the committee's mandate, American women as a whole expected rather definite things from their mobilization. They assumed that it would be comparable to the mobilization of European women, and those among them who were feminists believed the emancipation of women would be brought nearer as their defense work created a general appreciation of their value. Harriot Stanton Blatch ardently reflected this point of view. She had been to Europe after the war began and believed that Germany was doing so well because it had made full use of its women in the fields and factories. She was especially delighted with the situation in England, which she knew well from years of residence there.

> Throughout my stay in England I searched for, but could not find, the self-effacing spinster of former days. In her place was a capable woman, bright-eyed, happy. She was occupied and bustled at her work. She jumped on and off moving vehicles with the alertness if not the unconsciousness of the expert male. . . . England was a world of women—women in uniforms.[5]

The war was bringing English women all sorts of dividends. They were near to winning the vote, they were gaining admission to new occupations, and, thanks to the allowance laws which supported the families of servicemen, they were close to getting motherhood allowances which they hoped would increase their independence. "The allowance laws may prove the charter of woman's liberties; her pay envelope may become her contract securing the right to self-determination." [6] Mrs. Blatch was convinced that the war would extend the same blessings to American women. Indeed, their only problem

5. Harriot Stanton Blatch, *The Mobilization of Woman-Power* (New York, 1918), pp. 54–55.
6. *Ibid.*, p. 119.

was making sure that American mobilization was complete enough to give them the same chances as European women. It distressed her that while in England 25 per cent of the labor force was in uniform and in France a fifth of the nation bore arms, America had enlisted a puny million and a half men out of a total work force of 35 million. If American women were to enjoy the full benefits of the war, they would have to insist on a much more complete mobilization.

Even as things stood, it was clear to Mrs. Blatch that the war was doing great things for American womanhood. Perhaps a million women had replaced men in industry, where "their drudgery is for the first time paid for." In the past, two-thirds of the positions filled by the New York Intercollegiate Bureau of Occupations were secretarial or teaching jobs; three-fourths of its applicants were now being placed outside these fields as professionals, managers, skilled workers, and so forth. Temporary positions had outnumbered permanent placements, but now the reverse was true, and four times as many women as before the war were being placed at salaries above $1,800 a year. In industry the same wonderful things were happening, for "War requirements may force us to see in the health of the worker the greatest of national assets." [7] The only fly in Mrs. Blatch's ointment was a distressing tendency to enact protective measures solely for working women. Perfect democracy required that male workers be protected in the same way, but there was reason to hope that women workers were coming to understand this.

Not all women shared Mrs. Blatch's enthusiasm for the war as a cause, nor her faith in its contributions to the woman's rights movement. But most felt they could help the war effort, and that in some way they would be rewarded for doing so. They were already reaping dividends from the glow of righteousness which the friends of democracy cultivated at the spectacle of autocracy on the verge of ruin. Then, too, they

7. *Ibid.*, p. 93.

were learning that war was fun. Mrs. Blatch had noted in England "the increased joyfulness of women. They were happy in their work, happy in the thought of rendering service, so happy that the poignancy of individual loss was carried more easily." [8]

Since America suffered few casualties, most women were entirely free to enjoy the novelty of their new situation. Ida Tarbell later thought that her time with the Woman's Committee was the best she ever spent. Alice Hamilton, on the other hand, was sickened by

> the strange spirit of exaltation among the men and women who thronged Washington, engaged in all sorts of "war work" and loving it. I got an impression of joyful release in many of them, as if after all their lives repressing hatred as unchristian, they suddenly discovered it to be a patriotic duty and let themselves go in for an orgy of anti-German abuse.[9]

Miss Hamilton was less than fair to women as a whole, but they did like the war work which gave them opportunities for service and a feeling of intimate participation in great events such as they had never known. Since they were assured by everyone from President Wilson to John Dewey that the war was an exercise in high principle and applied intelligence, they had no reason to doubt the cause they supported or question the lofty ends it was to realize.

The government was happy to encourage their enthusiasms. When Secretary Baker came back from what had to be one of the most skillfully guided tours of the front ever conducted, he informed a conference called by the Woman's Committee that he had not seen an American soldier who

8. *Ibid.*, p. 55. This was later confirmed by an English feminist who noted at the end of the war: "Women have had a good time. Now they are going to struggle to keep it." C. Gasquoine Hartley, *Women's Wild Oats* (New York, 1920), p. 38.

9. Alice Hamilton, *Exploring the Dangerous Trades* (Boston, 1943), p. 193.

was not "living a life which he would not be willing to have mother see him live." Even the trenches were "far less uncomfortable than I had supposed." This led him to think that:

> . . . when those boys come back they will bring a more cosmopolitan view of civilization; that they will bring, also, tolerance and a wider sweep to their imagination; that there will be less selfishness possible when so many of the best men in the world have been engaged man to man, shoulder to shoulder, in a common, unselfish and heroic enterprise.[1]

This made it possible for women who were not feminists to work for the common good. In a survey of the war work of prominent women, evidence of this appeared on every hand. Mrs. Oliver Cromwell Field, president of the American Patriotic Legion, was waging a successful fight to have municipalities forbid the sale of any German-language periodical. Thousands of women were selling liberty bonds, and the full weight of New York Society was being felt in France, where the Bordeaux Cafeteria was operated for the troops' benefit by such luminaries as Mrs. Vincent Astor and the daughter of the late E. H. Harriman. Even Miss Helen Taft, a niece of the former President, caught the spirit.

> She obtained from the Fire Commissioner of one city a fire extension ladder, and a field crew of firemen. Each time a person in the crowd bought a bond Miss Taft climbed another rung of the ladder until she was more than ninety feet in the air. She went up the ladder four times, and offered to dive into a net held by the firemen for a $5,000 subscription. She got the subscription—but it was with the stipulation she did not dive.[2]

The Woman's Committee soon called a conference of women's organizations to systematize the work of such spirited

1. Address to the Woman's Committee Conference, May 14, 1918, Papers of the Woman's Committee, Council of National Defense, National Archives.
2. Anne Emerson, "Who's She in War Work," *Forum*, CIX (June 1918), 747.

volunteers. It met in Washington in June 1917 and immediately came to grips with the thorny question of morality in the training camps. On the one hand, the women feared that a lustful soldiery would debauch pure maidens. On the other hand, it was equally likely that low women would corrupt the innocent young men who had just been rudely snatched from their domestic sanctuaries. One of the first concrete efforts to avert these dangers was made by the Florence Crittenden Mission, whose representative at the conference proudly told of having already "signed up over 1,000 fallen women who have pledged themselves not to go near the camps." [3] Not to be outdone, the Woman's Committee created in July a Department of Safeguarding Moral and Spiritual Forces, whose task it was to guard the chastity of young America. Throughout the war the sexual peril continued to elicit extraordinary attentions. "Reassurance campaigns" were staged to convince mothers that the camps were not hotbeds of vice, and much thought was given to the creation of Woman Patrols and Protective Officers to save young girls from ruin.

After a while it became evident that the government viewed the Woman's Committee as a device for occupying women in harmless activities while men got on with the business of war. Its first assignments—to register women for volunteer work, and to secure food conservation pledges from housewives—were exhausting and meaningless. Few of the millions who registered for service were ever called, and no one was ever able to prove that signing pledge cards inspired women to conserve food. The committee did search out its own opportunities. It cooperated with the Children's Bureau in a nationwide program which resulted in five million babies being weighed and inspected in special health centers established around the country for this purpose. Its voice was added to those insisting that the emergency not be used as an excuse to depress the working conditions of women and children. It

3. Minutes of the Woman's Committee, June 19, 1917, Papers of the WC.

conducted an active propaganda campaign which, though silly and crude at first, was no more so than that staged by the Committee on Public Information. But the Woman's Committee could not disguise the fact that the government preferred to work through other means. Troop welfare was monopolized by the Red Cross, the YMCA, and the Salvation Army. When women did do something well, such as selling war bonds at which they proved to be especially adept, they were taken over by organizations like the National Liberty Loan Committee, an agent of the Treasury Department.

The Woman's Committee resented being shouldered aside and repeatedly attempted to get a specific delegation of authority and independent funds. It pointed out to the CND that while initially the majority of organized women had rallied behind it, their discovery that the WC had no authority and no special assignment led to a falling away. Similarly, since the state branches of the CND were not obliged to support the WC's state divisions, few gave them more than token recognition. Near the end of the war the committee finally forced the CND's hand by recommending that a federal agency with real power be set up to coordinate and direct women's war work. To this end the members submitted their resignations, nominally to give the CND a free hand, really to threaten it with an embarrassing walkout. The CND then agreed to replace its operating arm, the State Council's Section, with a Field Division in which women would have equal representation. It would direct the work of the CND's state organizations and assure women of fair treatment and genuine responsibility. This was, however, not worked out until August 29, 1918, and was consequently never put into effect.

That the committee was not wholly ineffective was largely because of Anna Howard Shaw. The very qualities which had made her NAWSA presidency so debilitating now became assets. As male administrators were determined to give women only token recognition, her stubborn combativeness, rough tongue, and skepticism were invaluable. What her job demanded was not tact or managerial expertise, but rather persistence and courage. She had plenty of both. Her colleague, Ida Tarbell, although not herself a feminist, found Dr. Shaw "delightfully salty in her bristling against men and their ways." We may be sure that the government men were less amused. Dr. Shaw hammered away at them day in and day out. She was not free to complain in public, but she made her views known privately, both to relevant officials and to friends on the outside who could make waves on her behalf. At least one major news story describing the government's shabby treatment of the committee was published during the war, and while there is no evidence that Dr. Shaw was responsible, it was consistent with her views and probably met with her approval.[4] She was certainly responsible for the threatened resignations that forced the CND to give women an equal share in the Field Division.

As important as her prodding of the government was the temperate spirit with which she approached the war itself. She made the customary denunciations of German militarism, but she was alert to its echoes in the United States. When an important women's club asked her to endorse universal military training, she replied bluntly that she was personally opposed to it. The only universal training she approved of would benefit boys and girls alike. "It should be conducted in the schools— not in the military camps but in education camps. It seems to me that training of our young men in military camps prepares them for war rather than the prevention of war."[5] America was at war, she believed, thanks to a defective diplomacy and not because of any military weaknesses UMT would

4. Ralph Block, "American Woman Only Still Denied Her Fair Share of Serious War Work," *New York Tribune*, February 10, 1918, Pt. IV, p. 1. Ida Clyde Clarke, who during the war had celebrated its benefits for women, later concluded that the Woman's Committee was "a grim joke." *Uncle Sam Needs a Wife* (Chicago, 1925), p. 5.

5. Anna Howard Shaw to Mrs. Ira Couch Wood, April 22, 1918, Papers of the WC.

remedy. When the draft age was lowered from twenty-one to eighteen she urged her friends to protest it vigorously. In the same spirit she refused to condemn Jane Addams and other women whose patriotism was suspect, even when pressed to do so.

Dr. Shaw saved the committee from the excesses of other wartime organizations, and she finally squeezed important concessions out of the government. It was a remarkable performance, the more so for being unsung and unheralded. Few knew of it at the time, and after the war women lost interest in the subject. In any event, the committee's real experience conflicted with the official feminist line: that women had contributed mightily to victory and had been richly compensated for doing so. Anna Howard Shaw died in 1919 without disclosing the truth. As a suffragist she had her faults, but as a guerrilla fighter in the corridors of power she was magnificent. If there was irony in her position as an overpraised figure in the history of women's rights, and an unrecognized heroine in the underground struggle for decency in wartime, she seemed unaware of it. All of which gives her a better claim to the admiration of posterity.

.   .   .   .

The experience of the Woman's Committee was not much different from that of most bodies concerned with women's place in the war effort. The shortage of labor did not become acute, and the female work force was enlarged only slightly. This gave women little weight in the government's councils. American feminists had assumed that the European situation would be duplicated here once the United States entered the war. A typically exuberant survey of the state of women had gloated over the employment breakthroughs made possible by labor shortages and concluded: "For the ultimate programme toward which the modern woman today is moving is no less than paradise regained! It may even, I think, have been worth this war to be there." [6] Harriot Stanton Blatch thought work for women was even more important than the vote, for "service to their country in this crisis may lead women to that economic freedom which will change a political possession into a political power." [7] The popular writer Mary Austin was thrilled by women in industry, because when women became absorbed into the work force they were no longer regarded as women but simply as workers. "I should say that three years of this war have set that type of sex emancipation at least a hundred years forward." [8]

But if the emancipation of women had depended on their playing a large role in heavy industry it would never have come about. They were hired in increasing numbers during the war, but not on the scale that feminists expected. Mary Van Kleeck, in an article based on the findings of the Women's Bureau, pointed out that at the peak of the war effort some six thousand women were employed by the aircraft industry, and that while the percentage of women in the iron and steel industry had tripled between 1914 and 1918, only forty thousand women were employed by the industry at the end of the war.[9] Although these increases seemed significant to Miss Van Kleeck because enough women had been hired to demonstrate the feasibility of employing women in heavy industry, the fact was that by 1919 almost half of these women were no longer working in the occupational categories that had been opened up in heavy industry during the war. Feminists were so reluctant to face up to the impermanence of wartime changes that as late as 1921 the *Survey* published an article called "The New

6. Mabel Potter Daggett, *Women Wanted* (New York, 1918), pp. 383–384.

7. Blatch, *Mobilization*, p. 104.

8. Mary Austin, "Sex Emancipation Through War," *Forum*, LIX (May 1918), 617.

9. Mary Van Kleeck, "Women and Machines," *Atlantic*, CXXVII (February 1921), 250–260.

Position of Women" which exhaustively discussed the same Women's Bureau report while ignoring the movement of women out of industrial jobs after the armistice. Feminist dreams died hard.[1]

Since relatively few women were employed by industry during the war, it ought to have been possible to give them a high degree of protection. In fact, the reverse was true. Because there were few women workers in war plants the government never acquired the sense of urgency felt by trade union women and their allies. Here, too, the government was unprepared to make more than ceremonial gestures which affirmed its desire to protect working women without providing the support that would translate this pious hope into reality. The Department of Women in Industry of the Woman's Committee remained little more than a paper organization throughout the war. When Samuel Gompers, chairman of the CND's Committee on Labor, got around to creating a Sub-committee on Women in Industry, he neglected to appoint any trade union women to it. Later, when this omission was brought to his attention, he did appoint trade union women to the sub-committee, but as it had no authority this was only a symbol of official concern. Even if the sub-committee had been given real responsibility, Gompers' appointment of the wealthy Mrs. Borden Harriman as its chairman persuaded radical trade union women that it would not rock the governmental boat.

In June 1918 the Labor Department created a Women in Industry Service as a coordinating agency. At that point there were plans to draft two or three million more men the following year. This would have forced the hiring of large numbers of women and made the WIS an important agency. As it was, the service did become a forerunner of the Labor Department's Women's Bureau, established after the war. Of the other agencies concerned with women workers, the Wom-

---

1. "The New Position of Women," *Survey*, January 8, 1921, p. 539.

en's Branch of the Ordnance Bureau had an Industrial Service Section which was most effective.[2] It was capably led, had a specific assignment to the munitions industry—especially the four manufacturing arsenals that employed women—and was well staffed. Even so, it had only investigative authority. In its exhaustive *Final Report*, the Women's Branch claimed that its principal achievement had been to get more women supervisors in the munitions industry. On the question of equal pay for equal work it noted dryly that the principle was universally endorsed and that "a few employers here and there put it into actual practice." [3] Generally the Women's Branch found that women made less than men to begin with, were promoted more slowly, and were not organized because labor unions seemed uninterested in women members. As a result, after the Armistice most were discharged and the newly opened occupational categories were closed again.

The working conditions of women in less carefully inspected industries were much worse. This was especially true of Negro women, who were the least advantaged sector of the female work force. Mary Church Terrell, a well-educated Negro leader, found that most government agencies would not hire Negro women as clerical workers no matter how great the need. Those that did put them in segregated offices. The Philadelphia Consumers' League discovered that more than half of Negro women workers earned $10 a week or less at a time when a minimum income of $16.60 was required to support a decent standard of living. Summarizing his experiences with

2. The other main bodies were the Woman's Division of the U.S. Employment Service, the War Labor Policies' Board which included women like Grace Abbott of the Children's Bureau, the Women's Department of the War Labor Board, and the Women's Service Section of the Railroad Administration. Representatives of these groups met weekly as a Women's Council organized by Miss Van Kleeck to coordinate the various government programs for women in industry.

3. *Final Report*, Women's Branch, Industrial Service Section, Ordnance Department (Washington, D.C., 1919), p. 55.

the Urban League and other concerned groups, Forrest B. Washington reported that Negro women "have been universally the last to be employed. They were the marginal workers of industry all through the war. They have been given, with exceptions, the most undesirable and lowest paid work, and now that the war is over they are the first to be released." [4]

. . . .

The women who found places for themselves within the government, no matter how frustrated or misused they felt, had it easier than their sisters on the outside, especially those unwilling to abandon their pre-war interests. As a rule, the more intensely an organization concerned itself with purely social questions, the more difficulties it encountered. Thus, while social feminists in organizations like the NCL and the WTUL saw the public lose interest in their activities, organizations like the General Federation which adjusted to the demand that all work be war work had a relatively easy time. The NAWSA was an exception to this rule. As we saw earlier, Mrs. Catt did not intend to have the war interrupt the suffragists' march toward victory. Even before American entry she formulated a strategy to deal with the crisis. There was no question of suffragists abandoning their work for the duration. They had done so during the Civil War only to discover that virtue did not automatically insure reward. On the other hand, Mrs. Catt was fully aware that to ignore the war effort would antagonize the very politicians whose favor was essential to her cause. Accordingly, the NAWSA cooperated with the government, but it continued to campaign for the vote while reminding Americans that a war to make the world safe for democracy ought properly to begin at home. Anti-suffragists immediately charged that the NAWSA was demanding votes for women as a payment for its war work. The *Woman Citizen* replied:

4. Forrest B. Washington, "Reconstruction and the Colored Woman," *Life and Labor*, VIII (January 1919), 4.

. . . Suffragists are asking now for the passage of the Federal amendment as a war measure in order that this country may escape the charge that it has bargained with its women—so much service so much gain. Suffrage for women is a part of that complete democracy so aptly named by Mr. Wilson as the object of this war. It is belittling to the government, not to the women of the country, to withhold grudgingly what it must ultimately give. The government must not make a bargain sale of the democracy it is sending our men to the front to give their lives to maintain. It must start about setting the world right for democracy by giving American women the franchise for democracy's sake, not for the sake of benefits received at the hands of women. It must do this proudly in advance of the price women must pay for this war. Not shamefacedly after that price has been paid.[5]

Yet suffragists were not above suggesting that only the vote would enable them to support the war wholeheartedly. After the Senate rejected President Wilson's personal appeal and defeated the federal amendment, a Liberty Loan speaker said:

Do you know that you have to hurl yourself out at the people below you with super vitality? Do you know that you have to read your own fervor into them? It takes the very heart and soul of you. And my heart and soul are crushed. My spirit is dead. My voice will be lifeless. I shall try my hardest, but my quota will be short.[6]

Fortunately for their sake, suffragists did not often sail such treacherous waters. They had, in any event, safer and more effective ways of arguing that woman suffrage was necessary to the war effort. Perhaps the most persuasive case to be made was the connection between the welfare of working women, industrial productivity, and the vote. Here again the English experience was invoked.

If Englishwomen had had the franchise before the war, England would have been spared the costly and tragic

5. "Suffrage Service in War Time," *Woman Citizen*, June 30, 1917, p. 80.

6. "The Connection," *Woman Citizen*, October 12, 1918, pp. 389–390.

mistake of letting women work in the munitions factories for twelve and fourteen hours a day, seven days in the week —a practice which has now been stopped because experience proved that women who were chronically fagged could not turn out as large a quantity of munitions as they could with reasonable rest.[7]

Less commendable were the suffragists' occasional attempts to prey on loyalist fears. Although the NAWSA's anti-immigrant feelings abated considerably during the war, Mrs. Catt did not hesitate to say that loyal American women, if given the vote, would more than counterbalance the disloyal and pro-German element. This was an urgent necessity because "an enormous number of slackers in war but actors in voting have been revealed in the German counties of South Dakota —the counties which defeated woman suffrage on referendum in 1916." [8] This was a dangerous line to take at any time, but especially so when the NAWSA itself was feeling the effects of a propaganda campaign designed to persuade the country that suffragists were out of sympathy with the war effort. Their best, if not most convincing argument, continued to be the discrepancy between America's democratic war aims and its undemocratic suffrage requirement. This was the position taken by President Wilson in his address to the Senate urging passage of the woman suffrage amendment, and by the women's friends in Congress. In retrospect it seems also to have been their most honorable wartime argument, based as it was on those fundamental principles of justice and fair play which were always the strongest part of the case for woman suffrage. The editors of the *New Republic*, however, did offer an ingenious defense of woman suffrage as a war measure.

> If now you men fail to give women the vote on November 6th, it will not be because we are at war, but because we have not been at war long enough to understand what it

7. "Will You Help Your Country?," *Woman Citizen*, June 23, 1917, p. 64.

8. "The Home Defense," *Woman Citizen*, June 29, 1918, p. 93.

really means. What it means in a nation as thoroughly energized as, for example, Great Britain, is intense cooperative effort on the largest scale. Arbitrarily to draw the line at voting, at a time when every man and woman must share in this effort, becomes an absurd anomaly.[9]

Although the war provided a few new strings to the suffrage bow, it did not automatically guarantee final victory. Few politicians were moved by reason and justice alone, and it was necessary for the NAWSA to lobby its federal amendment first through the House of Representatives, then for fourteen more months until the Senate approved it on June 4, 1919, and finally in thirty-six state legislatures, an agonizing effort which lasted nearly three years and ended only a few months before the national elections in 1920. The NAWSA's task was further complicated by its rival, the Woman's party. In 1916 the WP continued to follow the English example of blaming the party in power, and campaigned against the Democrats in all twelve states where women voted. The WP's strategy failed. Wilson carried ten of the twelve states in which they fought him. Moreover, the idea of holding the party in power responsible was proven false when President Wilson declared for woman suffrage and was unable to carry his party with him. The WP refused to accept this fact of American political life. After its failure in the 1916 elections it decided to picket the White House. This was an even worse error, for the WP picket line went up just before the government declared war on Germany.

In England the militant Women's Social and Political Union suspended its political activities when war broke out, but the WP disregarded both its and the NAWSA's examples and continued to picket the White House after American entry. Their novel tactics and abusive slogans indicting "Kaiser Wilson" made the pickets objects of mob violence. Patriots, often in uniform, physically attacked the women time and

9. "Woman Suffrage in Wartime," *New Republic*, October 17, 1917, p. 344.

again, destroying their banners while the police stood idly by. Then on June 22 the police began arresting, not the assailants but their female victims. When the WP pickets refused to be intimidated, the District courts began sentencing them to jail for progressively longer terms extending up to six months. The jailed women were treated infamously, and when they went on hunger strikes in protest they were brutally force-fed. Eventually their treatment became a matter of public knowledge and the government was forced to pardon the women and put an end to its miniature reign of terror. Compared with the fate of conscientious objectors and the radical critics of American entry, the WP's pickets got off lightly. But the fact remains that they were among the first American victims of the war. No other group of suffragists risked as much or suffered as much as they, nor demonstrated so much courage, resolution, and gallantry.

Their political judgment was less impressive. Although the WP subsequently gave itself credit for the 19th Amendment's passage, its principal contribution was to seriously embarrass an administration that had already been won over to woman suffrage by the patient, skillful efforts of Carrie Chapman Catt and the NAWSA. It is true that the administration, which behaved meanly throughout the affair, deserved to be embarrassed, but the WP's moral victory did not swing any votes in Congress. On the contrary, the WP put the suffrage movement as a whole in the ignoble position of having to repudiate women who were undergoing a kind of martyrdom. The NAWSA did its duty by repeatedly denouncing the picketing as "absurd, ill-timed, and susceptible of grave and demoralizing suspicion," and succeeded in establishing that it was not responsible for, and did not approve of, the WP's behavior. But in doing so the NAWSA gave its implicit consent to the government's policy, thereby strengthening the most repressive aspects of the war effort for the sake of its own unquestionably democratic ends.

Of course, it is hard to see what else the NAWSA could

have done. The press persistently confused it with the WP, and when the pickets committed an especially flagrant act a thousand newspaper editorials blamed the innocent NAWSA, forcing it to send out hundreds of explanatory letters. Mrs. Catt saw the WP's tactics as a childish reversion to the earliest stages of the suffrage movement. It had been appropriate for Miss Anthony to cast an illegal vote in 1872, but the stunt era of suffrage had long since passed. The WP "represent the women who became discouraged by the long-drawn struggle along the old lines, lost heart at exactly the wrong moment and decided that the whole battle had to be fought over again." [1] It was not simply that wartime was the wrong time to revile a President, but that most men were now ready to concede women the vote. The militant campaign was, therefore, especially ill advised. Rather than providing a face-saving mechanism by which men could surrender gracefully, it put their backs up instead.

Still, in its own dramatic way the WP exposed the NAWSA's moral ambiguities. The great strength of Mrs. Catt's organization was its adjustment to the American political system. The NAWSA bargained for votes like any interest group, compromising here, equivocating there, confident that the rightness of its cause justified some cutting of corners. Normally this strategy posed few problems of conscience, but the war created an abnormal environment in which difficult moral decisions had to be made. The NAWSA joined Wilson's Great Crusade with fewer reservations than might have been expected given its initial distaste for the war, only to have the WP raise the vexing question all over again. The WP not only pointed out verbally the distance between America's democratic professions and its undemocratic practices, but was itself an early victim of that gap. It did not really matter, in this context, that the picketing was unwise, and unproductive,

1. "Pickets Are Behind the Times," *Woman Citizen*, November 17, 1917, p. 470.

if not actually self-defeating. The Woman's party had almost certainly given way to the impulse toward destructive, hostile posturing which has afflicted frustrated dissenters throughout American history, but the issue posed was real nonetheless. In allowing their understandable resentment of the WP and their zeal for victory to overcome their sense of justice, the NAWSA suffragists incurred a moral deficit which they would some day have to make good.

In the meantime, however, the NAWSA had a thousand things to do. It had to undertake a respectable amount of war work at the same time it pressed for the suffrage. As we have already noted, this proved to be immensely difficult. Whatever qualms suffragists may have had about their other decisions, events fully justified their refusal to do any more for the war effort than was absolutely essential to demonstrate their loyalty. The NAWSA raised $200,000 for an overseas hospital in France, and participated in many phases of the war effort. It did so without descending to the strident jingoism of so many anti-suffragists. If they felt compelled by circumstance to support the government's designs, suffragists were determined to realize democracy at home in order that these events not be repeated. "For on one thing women are resolved, there will be no more decreeing of war without woman's voice in the decree." [2]

Suffragists also insisted that the war effort not be waged at women's expense. The NAWSA kept track, as best it could, of the activities of working women, and Ethel M. Smith, chairman of its Industrial Department and an active WTUL member, continually reminded suffragists of the need to protect women laborers. The NAWSA also rejected the assumption on which much of the government's war conservation program was based: that women were mainly responsible for the wastage of scarce commodities. Mrs. Henry Wade Rogers, treasurer of NAWSA and chairman of its agricultural committee, incurred Herbert Hoover's wrath by saying publicly that the government

2. "This War to End War," *Woman Citizen*, June 16, 1917, p. 43.

should not expect women to bear the whole weight of the conservation effort, and that speculation in foodstuffs and commercial wastes should be officially discouraged. Hoover feared that such remarks would diminish women's enthusiasm for saving, but Anna Howard Shaw sounded the same note again and again. Soon after her appointment as chairman of the Woman's Committee, she returned from a speaking tour to announce that women were eager to serve, but that "there is a growing sentiment . . . against being scolded by everyone in regard to saving. We women are much more economical than men." [3]

Certainly the most valuable work undertaken by the NAWSA as a result of the war was Americanization. Before 1917 the association's position on immigration, as Aileen Kraditor has shown, was deplorable.[4] But by 1917 suffragists had come to take another view of the question. Part of their reason for disliking foreign-born voters was their belief that immigrants would not vote for woman suffrage. In 1917 New York City voted for their enfranchisement, and suffragists learned that immigrants could be won over. The new light this event shed on their problems, with other moderating factors, inspired the NAWSA to approach the problem of Americanization during wartime in a more genial spirit than would have been possible even a few years earlier. Americanization in this period often meant simply harassing immigrants. Organized women, and especially suffragists, made a genuine effort to approach the immigrant in a fair way. Mrs. F. P. Bagley, chairman of the NAWSA's Committee on Americanization and a member of the Gompers' committee as well, established the tone of her campaign by ruling "Don't Preach. Don't Patronize." The NAWSA's Americanization campaign may not have been strikingly more effective than anyone else's, yet, at the very least, it probably

3. "Barley as Good in Soup as in Beer," *Woman Citizen*, July 14, 1917, p. 122.
4. Aileen S. Kraditor, *The Ideas of the Woman Suffrage Movement* (New York, 1965), Ch. 6.

did not further demoralize the overburdened immigrant population, and it reflected creditably on the good will and good sense of the suffrage movement.

.   .   .   .

Social workers in general had opposed American entry into the war with more vigor than the suffragists. This was especially true of the great settlement workers like Jane Addams and Lillian Wald, who were far more active in the peace movement than their opposite numbers in the NAWSA. But once the war effort was launched, social workers proved to be more ardent than suffragists who were too single-minded about the vote to be swayed for long by other issues, no matter how urgent or compelling. Social workers, on the other hand, were interested in so many causes that their attention swung from point to point according to the direction from which the winds of change blew most strongly.

Before American entry the confused state of American opinion prompted a conservative response from social workers. Their pacific disposition was a defensive reaction to ambiguous circumstances fraught with peril for themselves and their clients. The declaration of war immediately clarified their feelings. Social workers could continue to resist the war spirit, a risky and almost certainly hopeless enterprise, or they could join in the great outpouring of national energy and attempt to guide it into constructive channels. Put this way the question was hardly a matter of choice. Social workers could not refuse a chance to put their skills to full use, and the American war effort, while it affronted their traditional values, offered unprecedented opportunities for the conscious exploitation of national power for beneficent ends. Their position was made all the easier because the explanation for American entry was couched in terms that social workers could swallow without difficulty. The assurances of President Wilson, Secretary of War Baker, John Dewey, and almost the entire Progressive establishment that American entry had transformed the war into a crusade for justice and democracy were not only congenial but in fact inspirational to social workers who were predisposed to favor any cause that could be defended with the humanitarian rhetoric that was the common tongue of American reformers.

Nor were social workers entirely misled on this point, for the war months witnessed a last flowering of the reform spirit. Although the opponents of intervention were savagely suppressed by a mixture of governmental brutality and semi-official vigilantism, many health and welfare measures encountered less resistance than ever before. Social workers and reformers moved into the federal service in large numbers, and a huge army was raised, trained, and sent into combat according to the latest principles of social hygiene.[5] Both the National Conference of Social Work and, to a lesser extent, the National Federation of Settlements reflected the enthusiastic commitment of social workers to the war at home and abroad. The federation at its 1917 meeting acknowledged the feelings of its unregenerate pacifists by unanimously passing a resolution supporting the government's war policies, while noting that a minority of settlement workers opposed all wars on principle. In the same careful way the NFS resolved that it was the "peculiar task" of settlement workers "to oppose in our neighborhoods every attempt to sow the seeds of disloyal and illegal action; and at the same time to uphold the right of honest discussion of questions of public policy, to the end that we may not lose the very soul of democracy in undertaking its defense."[6]

The National Conference of Social Work and the *Survey* were considerably less guarded. Edward T. Devine, chairman of the NCSW's Committee on Social Problems of the War, an-

5. See Allen F. Davis, "Welfare, Reform and World War I," *American Quarterly*, XIX (Fall 1967), 516–533.
6. "National Federation of Settlements," *Survey*, June 16, 1917, p. 265.

nounced that war issues took precedence over everything else. "Freedom, nationality, respect for treaties—for such great causes as these our fathers fought and for them now our sons are called to fight. . . . They are more important, more fundamental, than comfort, physical health, mental development. Until they are assured, the struggle for a normal life, as we have conceived it, is hopeless." [7] Devine found frequent opportunities to express patriotic sentiments in his *Survey* column, now renamed "Social Forces in War Time." But the best guide to his thinking and to that of many other pro-war social workers was his statement on conscientious objection. The first obligation of young male social reformers, he insisted, was to enlist in the Army, which had become the principal instrument of American humanitarianism. For the conscientious objectors Devine had only pity. They had, he believed, failed the nation in its hour of crisis. "They are deserters where they might have been partakers in the national life at one of the supreme moments. They are exerting a divisive, paralyzing influence . . . instead of a strengthening, unifying and invigorating force." Devine knew that the war presented difficulties at home, but he maintained that "the least useful of all people . . . in the defense against such dangers will be those who stand aloof from the emotions and do not share affirmatively in the national undertaking." [8]

Devine's choice of words revealed the primal impulses that thrust like-minded social workers and reformers into the war effort. The opposition to American entry, however well founded, had been negative, divisive, and emotionally unrewarding. The declaration of war enabled all factions to join together honorably in an enterprise that was very much to the taste of social workers. It was unifying, invigorating, and, best

7. Arthur P. Kellogg, "The National Conference of Social Work," *Survey*, June 16, 1917, p. 253.
8. Edward T. Devine, "The First Obligation," *Survey*, August 18, 1917, p. 438.

of all, affirmative. Social workers did not enjoy conflict for its own sake; they much preferred unity and cooperation. The war, simply as a national enterprise without regard to its purposes, involved such a collective outpouring of energies as to bend the will of all but the most determined and resolute pacifist. Even Jane Addams, whose deep anti-war convictions were matched by few others, was not immune to these feelings. She remembered asking herself at the time if individuals had the right to defy society. "Is there not a great value in mass judgment and in instinctive mass enthusiasms, and even if one were right a thousand times over in conviction, was he not absolutely wrong in abstaining from this communion with his fellows?"[9] Jane Addams managed to overcome her romantic attachment to the popular will, but thousands of social workers could not. They were further enticed by the prospects of effective authority. Throughout the Progressive era social workers had been only one of many contending interest groups seeking to impose their vision on a resistant population. Now their most ardent desires—woman suffrage, prohibition, protective laws of many kinds—were being declared war measures and they themselves invited to organize and administer a variety of wholesome programs. It is easy to understand why so many found in the war effort unprecedented opportunities for public service.

Robert Woods, always a spokesman for respectable opinion, caught perfectly the mood of uncritical exhilaration that animated his type of social worker at the war's peak. Having just completed his term as president of the National Conference of Social Work in July 1918, he was in an excellent position to describe the conference's spirit, which he did in an article for the *Survey* fittingly entitled, "The Regimentation of the Free." Social workers, he was pleased to announce, had rediscovered the truth first learned by Florence Nightingale,

9. Jane Addams, *Peace and Bread in Time of War* (New York, 1922), p. 140.

that "the cause of humanity is identified with the strength of armies." [1] The military's needs had inspired a grand coalition of "associated powers," all working together to make not only the armed services but the whole nation better, healthier, and more moral. The cooperative efforts of so many welfare workers had already accomplished much, but "as the essential accompaniment of such progress, and as a result of the cleansing influence of the war, are we not fully ready for a large national program" of social reform? Turning from this attractive prospect he paid tribute to the hearty patriotism of the NCSW, which had "passed beyond the conviction of war justified, and risen into the sentiment of war ennobled. Fear of American partnership on other than democratic motives had disappeared." By this time even the more cautious National Federation of Settlements had overcome its reservations. The *Survey's* cheerful reporter thought "the most striking fact about the eighth annual conference of the National Federation of Settlements . . . was the consciousness of high national purpose. The patriotism that breathed through its meetings was an expression not merely of the fervor of the delegates but of the neighborhoods from which they came." [2]

Not all social workers succumbed to the euphoria gripping so many of their colleagues. One critic protested against her profession's willingness to mobilize for war. The enthusiasm of social workers for centralized, national programs seemed to her misplaced. "The unorganized nation was like a gambler who must stop playing when he had emptied his pockets; the organized is like a gambler enabled by an elaborate financial system to stake all his present possessions and future prospects." Social workers everywhere were only contributing to the general disaster by enabling their countries to expend previously untapped human resources. "A fight to a finish between nations

1. Robert A. Woods, "The Regimentation of the Free," *Survey*, July 6, 1918, p. 395.
2. "The National Federation of Settlements," *Survey*, June 8, 1918, pp. 293–294.

perfectly organized after the modern plan and at all evenly matched, must mean for the vanquished such utter exhaustion as we dare not to imagine, and for the victor a ruin little less complete." [3] Jane Addams spoke for many when she wrote later that "some of us had suspected that social advance depends as much upon the process through which it is secured as upon the result itself; if railroads are nationalized solely in order to secure rapid transit of ammunition and men to points of departure for Europe, when the governmental need no longer exists" why should not the railroads be turned back to their owners? [4]

Miss Addams did experience flashes of hope, as when for a "golden moment" the first Russian revolution seemed to offer an alternative to the endless bloodshed. Many disturbed liberals found in the tsarist collapse a justification for American entry. In this spirit Mary Simkhovitch of Greenwich House wrote that she had doubted whether the Allied cause was overwhelmingly superior to the German, but that "the Russian revolution, following the increased ruthlessness of Germany, resolved that doubt, and made it possible, and, yes, imperative, for many of us to hesitate no longer. America for the world rather than America first is our motto." [5] For people like Lillian Wald and Jane Addams, however, the breakdown of military discipline and the reports of Russian troops fraternizing with German soldiers was the very embodiment of their hopes for a democratic peace. It was a hope further encouraged when the new Russian Ambassador reached New York and on visiting the Henry Street Settlement was surrounded by multitudes of cheering Russian Jews whom he told, "The Jews have got the liberty they earned by valor. They are free." [6] But this promise

3. Rebekah Henshaw, "A Dissenter," *Survey*, July 28, 1917, p. 375.
4. Addams, *Peace and Bread*, p. 135.
5. Mary Simkhovitch, "Social Settlements and the War," *Survey*, April 7, 1917, p. 30.
6. "Tumultuous Welcome for the Russians," *Survey*, July 14, 1917, p. 339.

faded when Russia was forced to stay in the war by Allies who were "so obsessed by the dogmatic morality of war, in which all humanly tangible distinctions between normal and abnormal disappear, that they were literally blind to the moral implications of the Russian attempt." [7]

The reservations of a few settlement leaders did not, of course, prevent the majority from participating actively in the war effort. Although the settlements as a whole were agreed that continuing their regular work was essential, most found it possible to undertake a surprising amount of additional war-related activity. Despite shortages of fuel and other supplies, a falling off of contributions and volunteer workers, and a reduced professional staff, the settlements gave much more than token support to the national enterprise. Woods and Kennedy wrote later that "a large proportion of houses participated in more than eighty of the hundred or more kinds of war work that were developed, and at least two score varieties of service were carried on by all." [8] The work ranged from selling liberty bonds and conserving food to pressing home "patriotic demands." "Settlements were continuously intent on exalting the righteousness of the cause and the honor of its defenders." [9]

The settlements' dual role of interpreting America to the immigrants and vice versa was never more important, and settlement workers, whatever their views on the war, rose heroically to the occasion. Without them the immigrant population would have been even more disaffected. The settlements acted as buffers between their neighborhoods and the larger society, and filtered out as best they could the most hostile, chauvinistic, and repressive aspects of the official ideology. It was hardly the settlement workers' fault that they had no influence over the course of world events, and that the good will,

7. Addams, *Peace and Bread*, p. 101.

8. Robert A. Woods and Albert J. Kennedy, *The Settlement Horizon* (New York, 1922), p. 298.

9. *Ibid.*, p. 303.

energy, and hope which they poured out so generously in their neighborhoods had nothing to do with the broad policies they spoke for but could not guarantee. Perhaps their main failing —one they shared, of course, with most articulate American liberals—was just this readiness to identify so completely with a war over which they had absolutely no control. Max Eastman put his finger on this crucial weakness when he cautioned Upton Sinclair not to assume that by joining their war he had obligated the Allies to accept his conditions. Eastman could see "no disposition on the part of the English . . . to write this laudable plan of Sinclair's into their peace terms." [1] But few American liberals were deterred by such reasoning.

.   .   .   .   .   .

The less liberal and welfare-oriented an organization was, the more easily it adjusted to American entry. For the Association of Collegiate Alumnae, which had virtually ignored the war in Europe, American intervention presented no ideological difficulties whatsoever. Three days after the United States declared war on Germany the ACA met in Washington for its biennial and immediately tendered its services to the government. The association did not plunge thoughtlessly into war work. Rather, with its accustomed caution the ACA resisted the call to arms until it was certain it could make a distinctive contribution. It finally settled on propaganda as its special line of work. Considering the vast machinery which the Committee on Public Information was assembling for this purpose, the need for a private propaganda effort may not have been immediately obvious. But propaganda—or educational activity, as it preferred to call this work—fitted nicely with the association's image of itself. To the extent that it was truly educational it

1. "The Pro-War Socialists," reprinted in William L. O'Neill, ed., *Echoes of Revolt: The Masses, 1911–1917* (Chicago, 1966), pp. 254–255.

was, of course, a suitable enterprise for the ACA, but more importantly it was far removed from the drudgery of bandage-rolling, bond-selling, and food-saving which occupied the mass of patriotic women. An elite requires work appropriate to its status. The glamorous task of inspiring the disloyal to a proper appreciation of their duties was an altogether satisfying resolution of the association's dilemma.

Propaganda work also compensated for a basic deficiency in women's education. College women were fond of saying that their education had equipped them with "trained minds." But the emergency clearly demonstrated that, however splendid their liberal education had been, it had not trained them to do anything in particular. Unless they were willing to attend business or nursing schools, there was little for them to do but teach—an activity in which they were already overparticipating, largely because of this same deficiency. Their enthusiasm for propaganda was therefore entirely understandable. They could not step into demanding positions in business or government, but their education did presumably qualify them to explicate difficult ideas, refute unpatriotic fallacies, and render intelligible the lofty goals of Wilsonian democracy. Thus they got in touch with the Creel Committee, established speakers' bureaus to spread the word, and created a corps of Four-Minute Women as counterparts to the committee's Four-Minute Men who in theaters, schools, and churches delivered canned propaganda. Mercifully, the bulk of the material used by the ACA in this campaign has been lost. But judging from the *Journal* of the ACA during the war period, it was rather superior to the inflammatory prose of the Committee on Public Information, not to mention the poisonous effusions of the national press.

.   .   .   .

From its inception the General Federation of Women's Clubs had demonstrated a steady, if modest pacifism. When the

World War erupted it was understandably upset, and the Woman's Peace party earned the federation's hearty approval. But the federation's peace work in 1915 and 1916 exhibited two characteristics which eased its transition to war work. First of all, clubwomen had little understanding of the war and of what was being said to them about it. When the editor of the *GFWC Magazine* attended the solemn Carnegie Hall meeting welcoming Jane Addams back from Europe in 1915, she heard Miss Addams say, "I do not come back to let loose any more emotion on the world. Those of us who have been in Europe are almost afraid of words. What is needed is careful human understanding to be injected into this over-involved and over-talked situation." The editor's response was to criticize peace meetings for being too dull. What they needed were bands and songs and choruses "shouting for Peace." She wished "some of our club women, bent on arousing an overwhelming sentiment for peace, would try some new method with a strong element of sensationalism in it and let the world watch the effect." [2]

Clubwomen were not about to begin marching and shouting for peace. Mrs. Josiah Evans Cowles, who became president of the GFWC in 1916, clearly defined the federation's position during her tenure as chairman of the federation's peace committee. She herself was much opposed to American entry until quite late in the game. "To go into war," she pointed out in April 1916,

> is to throw away the gains of centuries, and to fill with hate
> the only great nation that has so far risen above its withering
> influence. For our nation stands primarily not for freedom
> nor for democracy, but for international and interracial
> friendships, without which freedom and democracy are alike
> impossible because not permanent." [3]

2. Harriet Bishop Waters, "Editorial Notes," *GFWC Magazine*, XIV (August 1915), 3.
3. Mrs. Josiah Evans Cowles, "Peace; the Right Proportion Between Strength and Duty," *GFWC Magazine*, XV (April 1916), 20.

Mrs. Cowles had nevertheless earlier made it plain that peace could only be won by following the President's lead. Premature schemes and resolutions would embarrass Mr. Wilson and compromise his great design for a warless world. Therefore, the GFWC should concentrate all its energies on educational work to build the sentiment essential to Wilson's plans.

When the President concluded that peace could come only through war, it was easy for the General Federation to continue the support it had already been giving him under more adverse circumstances. It was easier, in fact, to stand by the President in 1917 than in 1916. The federation gladly joined the national effort when war was declared, though it did so with none of the hysterical militarism that marked the contributions of so many other ex-pacifist organizations. The *GFWC Magazine* hailed American entry thus:

> Women realize that we are living in an ungoverned world.
> At heart we are all pacifists. We should love to talk it
> over with the war-makers, but they would not understand.
> Words are so inadequate, and we realize that the hatred
> must kill itself; so we give our men gladly, unselfishly,
> proudly, patriotically, since the world chooses to settle its
> disputes in the old barbarous way. We are even rather proud
> of the minority who stand for principles of preservation,
> and are not ashamed to say so, even though they are called
> cowards. It is this minority that shall provide the leaven
> for a new civilization after this war is worked out. We
> understand when they say they shall not commit murder,
> for war is murder. We are rather glad they look at it in that
> way, for something must come of it if they stand fast.

Later, in this same rambling, effusive, contradictory flow of opinion, the editor anticipated the blessings war would bring.

> We shall exchange our material thinking for something quite
> different, and we shall all be kin. We shall all be
> enfranchised, prohibition will prevail, many wrongs will be
> righted, vampires and grafters and slackers will be relegated
> to a class by themselves, stiff necks will limber up, hearts

of stone will be changed to hearts of flesh, and little by little we shall begin to understand each other.[4]

The confusion, regret, hope, and exaltation expressed in this editorial appear to have been the common responses of clubwomen to American entry. The general disorder did not prevent them from rapidly taking up many kinds of war work. The GFWC raised large sums of money, amounting in the end to more than $5 million, to buy liberty bonds and support the Red Cross and YMCA. In October a Service Office was opened in Washington to coordinate the federation's war work, and later a War Victory Commission was appointed which sent a hundred girls to France to entertain soldiers on leave. The clubs also showed a keen interest in domestic morals. On May 25, 1917, the Reform Department of the Chicago Woman's Club held fifty meetings around the city to rally public sentiment against liquor and prostitutes. Clubwomen were ardent supporters of the Committee on Protective Work for Girls of the Commission on Training Camp Activities, which labored to rehabilitate the younger camp followers. Their zeal for purity encouraged the Army to decline Marshall Foch's generous offer to share the French Army's brothels with American troops, although the Vermont State Federation subsequently did send "four Vermont girls to France to help keep the soldiers contented while waiting for their discharge." Clubwomen were also anxious to preserve the young civilian from cinematic temptations. They everywhere encouraged movie censorship, and in Detroit they succeeded in censoring not only present films but future ones as well. Exhibitors there were persuaded to declare a two-year moratorium on Theda Bara pictures.

It is all too easy to document the instances when clubwomen were silly, impulsive, or misguided. Although their emotions often betrayed them, clubwomen as a whole remained faithful to their best traditions. The General Federation

4. "Editorial," *GFWC Magazine*, XVI (June 1917), 5–6.

avoided jingoism, bitterness, and hysteria. Like the NAWSA, the federation's leadership made it clear that Americanization work was supposed to be positive and not punitive in character. One officer pointed out that while the Army was Americanizing a great many immigrants, nothing was being done to similarly instruct their families. "The women of America can meet this obligation in no better way than by assuming the responsibility of giving the wife and the mother of the soldier the opportunity to acquire new standards and a new language, that they may greet their American heroes on their return as American women." [5] All in all, therefore, the war probably did less harm to the General Federation than to any of the other organizations with which we have been concerned, save only the ACA.

.   .   .   .   .   .

The war challenged the smaller social feminist organizations in ways they could not really meet. Indeed, the Consumers' League suffered even before America entered the war, and from 1915 through 1918 local leagues complained of diminishing support. In 1915 the New York Consumers' League, by far the strongest of the locals, declared it had never seen so many attacks on labor laws in the state legislature. "The Consumers' League has had to fight, not to pass any of the bills in which it was interested, but to hold the ground that was already gained." [6] The league's decline was masked by several facts. It had been fortunate to elect as its new president in 1915 Newton D. Baker, a Cleveland lawyer and civic reformer, who became Secretary of War shortly before American entry. This

5. Mrs. O. Shepard Barnum, "Report of the Department of Education," *GFWC Magazine*, XVII (November 1918), 24.
6. Louis Lee Athey, "The Consumers' League and Social Reform, 1890–1923," (unpublished doctoral dissertation, University of Delaware, 1965), p. 238.

did not mean that the whole force of the War Department was at the league's disposal, for Baker had little time for anything but military affairs. But he did give the league a certain leverage in Washington while protecting it from accusations of disloyalty occasioned by Florence Kelley's opposition to the war. Meanwhile, the New York League was soon fortified for several purely local reasons. When American entry made peace work more dangerous, and apparently less useful, some women shifted their attention to the protection of working women and children. Thus the New York League grew in strength and size, unlike other locals, once war was declared. And the New York chapter, with the aid of like-minded groups, successfully resisted efforts to use the emergency as an excuse to lower protective standards.

The fact remained, however, that the Consumers' Leagues fought a defensive battle to retain existing legislation, and except in New York did so with diminished resources. In addition, the league lost a number of key people to the government. Florence Kelley's position as Secretary of the Board of Control of Labor Standards for Army clothing, a job she acquired by pointing out to Secretary Baker that uniforms were being made in sweatshops, was not overly demanding. But Pauline and Josephine Goldmark had full-time posts in the government, as did other important league members. The league made valuable studies of labor problems related to the war effort—notably a superb examination of Negro women workers—but such studies are only as good as the uses they inspire, and little came of them.

.   .   .   .

The WTUL's experience, although slightly more complex, was much like that of the Consumers' League. The WTUL opposed American entry until it was an accomplished fact, then bowed to the new imperatives which an American war effort decreed.

Margaret Dreier Robins, despite her German ancestry, managed to work up a certain enthusiasm for the war. At its 1917 convention she told the WTUL that "A new economic and social order is emerging in every land, and a new internationalism is being born from the blood and suffering of mankind with all its terrors and conflict . . . let us be glad that we live in this Homeric age." [7] *Life and Labor*, the League's organ, was equally hopeful. It had been strongly against American entry and once war was declared months passed before *Life and Labor* spoke again of the larger issues. When it did, it discussed the riots and suppression of free speech which marked the war effort, but nonetheless concluded that the war created new opportunities for a better society.

Although the WTUL accepted the war less grudgingly than the NCL, this did not give it any special advantages. Income fell off in 1917–1918 despite the increased burdens that war entailed, and the WTUL lost even more women to the government than did the Consumers' League. By 1919 Trade Union League women held thirty-eight government posts of one kind or another, including Agnes Nestor on the Woman's Committee and Mrs. Robins on the Committee on Women in Industry. Mary Anderson was permanently lost to the Women's Bureau. Some of this involved doubling up, which led Rose Schneiderman to complain privately that by always recommending the same women the league created the impression that it had only a few competent leaders. Miss Schneiderman herself, as she well knew, was disqualified from public service by her radical anti-war views. In truth, however, the WTUL was not so plentifully endowed with talent that it could expect to lose people and still carry on its regular work. The National employed one full-time organizer during the war, although Mrs. Robins estimated that twenty-five organizers would be

7. Mary Dreier, *Margaret Dreier Robins: Her Life, Letters and Work* (New York, 1950), p. 132.

needed simply to meet the requests for help it received from working women eager to form unions.

The WTUL could give little help to the great mass of employed women, but it agitated against night work, struggled to maintain existing standards, and took advantage of Washington's new importance by forming a committee to assist the working women of the District of Columbia. In general, the WTUL's policies were much like the AFL's during the emergency, although rather more liberal as always. The league was less provincial than the AFL, in keeping with the cosmopolitanism of the woman movement. A league representative sat at the Hague Congress of Women in 1917, and at its 1917 meeting the league endorsed the plan of Madame Gabrielle Duchene of the Paris White Goods Workers for the insertion of labor clauses into the peace treaty. The WTUL also called for an International Congress of Working Women at the end of the war, and arranged for it to be held in Washington in 1919. In these and other ways it showed itself to be as committed to international cooperation and understanding as were the other arms of American social feminism.

.   .   .   .

In a rough sort of way, then, the hard-core feminists, that is, those women whose reform work was largely concerned with women's rights, found it easy to support American entry because they expected the war to advance their particular interests. Social feminists responded more ambiguously to the challenge of war because they were less certain of its effects. Neither group felt very deeply to begin with about the ideological rationale devised by the government to justify American intervention. Except for the members of the Women's Peace party who were vitally concerned with the specific policies of the belligerents, most feminists gave little thought to the politics of war and peace. At first most of them regarded the war simply as a disaster, or, in Mary Austin's words, "an exhibition of masculinity run amuck." Later, when the United States became involved, most women seem to have believed that Prussian militarism had to be forcibly suppressed, especially because of what it had done to Belgium. But, as we have seen, the hard-core feminists who developed a moderate enthusiasm for the war effort did so because events seemed to be moving in the direction they wanted to go. Assuming the American war effort would be as demanding as that of the European countries, they looked forward to seeing women gain greatly in economic security and political influence. And they expected other fringe benefits to accrue from the spirit of service and cooperation that the war effort promoted.

In fact, the war produced nothing like the great leap forward which feminists had expected. Women did not move into industry in anything like the numbers required for a fundamental change in status, and the new occupations opened up to them by reason of the manpower shortage did not usually outlast the emergency. In a general way the condition of women improved during the 1920's, but this was the result of tendencies that had been long at work. Their enlarged opportunities for graduate and professional study came largely from the momentum generated by the woman movement in the early years of the century, and not as a result of any great need for women specialists.

On the whole, then, the war did not bring feminists discernibly closer to their goals. The Woman's Committee and its sister organizations in the government, while they had a symbolic value which cannot be ignored, had no real effect on the fortunes of the woman's movement, nor was the economic power of womanhood noticeably increased. Yet in a negative way the women had much to be proud of. They did everything the government asked of them, from saving food to buying liberty bonds, and they were prepared to do much more. It was hardly their fault that their services were underutilized by a government which continued to regard them as something less than the great national resource that in fact they were. The feminists who engaged in war work were given no reason for a new birth of confidence in the good faith of the masculine establishment.

Easily the most impressive aspect of their defense work was the generous spirit with which they undertook it. Although women were sometimes as extravagantly patriotic as men, in general feminists were much more appreciative of the moral qualms which made some people pacifists than were the anti-feminists and their masculine counterparts. One did not often find prominent feminists in the ranks of the witch-hunters. On the contrary, as we have seen, the leading suffragists took care to avoid those excesses which disfigured the war work of so many others. Mrs. Catt, as president of the International Suf-frage Alliance, never forgot that after the war she would have to deal with German suffragists again. The strongly interna-tional character of the woman movement was probably more of a sobering influence on American feminists than anything else. They knew there was more to Germany than the Prussian military system, and so they were more truly international than the Wilsonians whose vision of the postwar world community did not extend much beyond a concert of Allies.

Many feminists believed in the President and his promises because it was the only way they could accept the war effort, but having done so they often invested heavily in it. They balanced present losses against future gains and consoled them-selves with the enhanced opportunities the war was bringing to American women. The postwar denouement was, therefore, especially hard on them. They had abandoned their tradi-tional pacifism for the sake of an altruistic, international pro-gram which few American men really believed in, and which could not be advanced by the means Wilson had chosen to use. After the war, organized women were to suffer not only from the conservative backlash which destroyed progressivism but from the knowledge that they had compromised to no purpose. For what it was worth, however, they had the comfort of knowing that they had in most other respects been true to their best principles. This was, of course, worth a great deal, but it was not enough to save feminism as a whole from the consequence of American intervention or from its own unexamined weaknesses.

7

. . . . . .

*the return
to normalcy*

*t*he Armistice did not immediately puncture the euphoria of American reformers who had so successfully, it seemed, used the emergency to advance their own purposes. Even Jane Addams, the least sanguine of social feminists, succumbed in part to their great expectations. At the National Conference of Social Workers in 1918 she cited the wartime control of foodstuffs as evidence that "the social utility motive was being substituted for that of commercial gain." [1] She was also encouraged by the collapse of the tariff system and other indications of a growing internationalism. Feminists and reformers committed to the Wilsonian promise of a worldwide reconstruction in which emancipated women would play a leading part, held a Women's Victory Conference in Washington in February 1919 to build support for the League of Nations and further the interests of democratic women. A permanent committee was formed which included, among others, Mary Anderson, Pauline Goldmark, Mrs. Louis Brandeis, Mrs. Herbert Hoover, Julia Lathrop, and Ida Tarbell.[2] The same spirit was shown by the annual conference of the National Federation of Settlements at which, according to Graham Taylor, the

1. Winthrop D. Lane, "The National Conference of Social Work," *Survey*, June 1, 1918, p. 251.
2. "American Women's Victory Dinner," *General Federation Magazine*, XVIII (April 1919), 9.

settlements showed themselves eager to take on the additional responsibilities their war service had proven them so well fitted to bear.[3] With victory near at hand, suffragists were already turning their thoughts to the challenge facing enfranchised women; early in 1919 they founded the League of Women Voters with a platform largely composed of social goals.[4]

Triumphant womanhood naturally expected a voice at the peace conference. As the NAWSA's journal pointed out, there was "never a war which has been so much in partnership between men and women all the world around." Men, of course, bore the whole responsibility for starting the war, but women had helped to win it and now expected a seat at the peace table as insurance against treaty agreements which would be "fertilizing agents for the seeds of the next war." [5] Accordingly, Jane Addams and other Woman's Peace party members sailed to Europe for another congress of women which, they hoped, would have more effect on world statesmen than had the previous congress in 1915. But Europe at peace was hardly less distressing than Europe at war. Lillian Wald was alarmed by the anti-European attitudes of American soldiers and depressed by the prevailing cynicism and disillusionment. Jane Addams was now convinced that nationalism had become purely malignant.

> The early spontaneity had changed into an authoritarian imposition of power. One received the impression everywhere in that moment when nationalism was so tremendously stressed, that the nation was demanding worship and devotion for its own sake similar to that of the medieval church, as if it existed for its own ends of growth and power irrespective of the tests of reality.[6]

3. Graham R. Taylor, "Neighborhood and Nation," *Survey*, June 21, 1919, p. 464.

4. Carrie Chapman Catt and Jane M. Brooks, "The League of Women Voters," *Woman Citizen*, May 3, 1919, pp. 1044–1055.

5. "Women and Peace," *Woman Citizen*, November 9, 1918, p. 485.

6. Jane Addams, *Peace and Bread in Time of War* (New York, 1922), pp. 174–175.

Harriot Stanton Blatch, who went to Europe specifically to find seeds of hope amidst the ruins of war, returned to say that she had once been "swayed by the propaganda of the war idealists," but now understood that "war breeds in peoples all the qualities which lead to disintegration and demoralization." [7] The peace treaty itself proved equally dismaying. Mrs. Blatch considered it a thoroughly "masculine document." A few prominent American women defended the treaty—Anna Howard Shaw believed the Germans' suffering was ordained by God as a punishment for their sins—but most distrusted it and hoped the League of Nations would compensate for its defects. To Jane Addams the League itself was a great disappointment because of its commitment to business as usual. "The adherents of the League often spoke as if they were defending a too radical document whereas it probably failed to command widespread confidence because it was not radical enough, because it clung in practice at least to the old self-convicted diplomacy." [8]

Returning home, Miss Addams found the country gripped by a fear of radicalism so acute that when she attempted to raise a milk fund for one hundred starving anarchists in the Cook County jail, her old friends and supporters feared to contribute lest they be accused of anarchist sentiments. Organized women were, of course, no strangers to abuse. In the nineteenth century suffragists were regularly accused of promoting free love, former President Cleveland charged clubwomen with ruining the home, and settlement workers were often called anarchists or worse. But until the war such attacks were comparatively infrequent and restrained. The principal anti-suffragist tract linking socialism with women's rights did so in moderate terms by postwar standards. Declaring that woman suffrage was "the corner-stone of socialism," the author, Caroline Corbin, went on to denounce the socialist conception of equal rights in these words:

7. Harriot Stanton Blatch and Alma Lutz, *Challenging Years* (New York, 1940), p. 301.
8. Addams, *Peace and Bread*, p. 211.

> Women are to be lifted up to a physical equality with man
> by placing upon their shoulders equal burdens of labor,
> equal responsibilities of state-craft; they are to be brought
> down from their altruistic heights by being released from all
> obligations of purity, loyalty, self-sacrifice, and made free of
> the world of passion and self-indulgence, after the model set
> them by men of low and materialistic ideals.[9]

Although highly colored and eminently Victorian in its fears, this was not an entirely inaccurate description of what many women expected equality would mean. But anti-suffrage propaganda rapidly deteriorated with the coming of the war and the advances made by suffragists in Europe and the United States. When America entered the war anti-suffragists lost all scruples and inhibitions. The *Remonstrance*, a prominent anti-suffrage organ, which until 1914 had maintained a dignified conservatism on the woman question, abandoned itself to a campaign of slander and vilification. During the war it called the suffragist leaders unpatriotic slackers, afterward it accused them of bolshevism. In the final stages of the ratification struggle it insisted that woman suffrage would lead directly to communism, free love, and the nationalization of women.[1]

Similarly, during the war Mrs. James W. Wadsworth, wife of the United States Senator from New York and an inveterate red-baiter, succeeded Mrs. Arthur M. Dodge as head of the National Association Opposed to Women Suffrage. When the 19th Amendment was ratified the *Remonstrance* was replaced by the *Woman Patriot*, an even more poisonous journal published by a former officer of the NAOWS and partially financed by the Wadsworths. It is best known for having published the "Spider-web Chart," a diagram purporting to show the relationships between Moscow and various liberal women and

9. Caroline Fairfield Corbin, "Socialism and Christianity with Reference to the Woman Question" (Chicago, 1905), p. 10.
1. For example, "Three Steps Toward Chaos," *Remonstrance*, January 1919, p. 1.

women's organizations in America.[2] The *Woman Patriot* was especially interested in Florence Kelley and in Jane Addams and her Women's International League for Peace and Freedom (formerly the Woman's Peace party), but all liberal women's organizations came in for some measure of attention. Other heirs of the anti-suffrage movement who in the 1920's turned to red-baiting feminists included the Daughters of the American Revolution, which had moved from its earlier vaguely benevolent nationalism to the virulent superpatriotism that has characterized it since World War I. Witch-hunting groups often cooperated with one another, but the DAR was especially sympathetic to right-wing veterans' organizations like the American Legion and the Military Order of the World War. In 1927 G. A. Darte, adjutant general of the Military Order, who had already distinguished himself by accusing the YWCA, the WCTU, and the AAUW of harboring elements of the "radical, pink or intelligentsia group," dubbed Rose Schneiderman, now president of the New York WTUL, "the Red Rose of Anarchy" before an admiring audience of DAR members.[3] The list of comparable outrages, impertinences, and the like visited upon organized women in the 1920's is virtually endless. Not even the Woman's party, for all its suspicion of welfare and protective legislation, was immune from right-wing smears. In-

2. The Spider-web Chart was drawn up by an employee of the War Department. Many feminists believed her to have official support because Secretary of War John W. Weeks had been defeated for re-election to the U.S. Senate in Massachusetts in 1918 by the votes of women and thirsted for revenge. Leonard Cline, "Army Fights Women's Societies Because They're in War on War," *New York World*, June 10, 1924.

3. Norman Hapgood, *Professional Patriots* (New York, 1927), p. 173. Miss Schneiderman wrote Darte that she was not and never had been an anarchist. He replied that this was good news indeed, but that he had reliable information, nonetheless, that she was connected with "the American Civil Liberties Union and other organizations." Schneiderman to Darte, May 13, 1927; Darte to Schneiderman, May 16, 1927, Papers of the NWTUL.

dividual members were red-baited, while the party as a whole was described by the *Woman Patriot* as

> like the Communist Workers' party . . . the Woman's Party is organized on a Soviet basis, with 24 occupational councils. . . . This is the vital and distinctive feature of the Soviet system—representation of occupational groups, rather than geographical districts, in politics—to promote internationalism and class loyalty, and to wipe out local self-government and patriotism.[4]

Even today, after half a century of experience with super-patriotism, there is still no really satisfactory response available to its victims. No liberal or leftist can "prove" his loyalty to the satisfaction of professional flag-wavers, and the effort to do so is not only futile but gives greater circulation to the original charges. In the 1920's, however, rightist tactics were still so novel and organized women so unused to attacks upon their loyalty that hate campaigns were more demoralizing to them than was later to be the case. Mrs. Catt attempted several times to put an end to such allegations. In 1917 she circulated a letter refuting the charge that anti-suffragists were unpatriotic, and after the Spider-web Chart appeared she wrote several well-publicized articles exposing the smear campaign against social feminists, especially Florence Kelley.[5] In 1920 the New York League of Women Voters published an excellent pamphlet unmasking the commercial and ideological origins of a rightist lobby in Albany; it anticipated the more elaborate exposés produced later in the decade by Norman

4. Quoted in "Petition Submitted by the Woman Patriot Against Miss Dell," *Equal Rights*, March 13, 1926, p. 38. The Woman Patriot Publishing Company was attempting to block the appointment of Miss Jessie Dell to the Civil Service Commission because of her membership in the WP. It also accused the Woman's party of seeking a dictatorship of women, a charge that, while false, did capture something of the WP's essential flavor.

5. "John Hay, Mrs. Catt, and Patriotism," *Woman Citizen*, November 10, 1917. Carrie Chapman Catt, "Lies at Large," *Woman Citizen*, XII (June 1927), p. 10, and "An Open Letter to the D.A.R.," *Woman Citizen*, XII (July 1927), p. 10.

Hapgood and others.[6] Useful as these exercises were, they failed to silence the malign right or reassure the more timorous women's organizations. Few individuals or organizations were deeply wounded, except in reputation, by these attacks, but they contributed signally to the general loss of nerve which characterized the activities of organized women after the war.

These new political tensions were all the harder to bear because they led to divisions within the women's own ranks as well. As early as February 1919 Lillian Wald sorrowfully announced her open break with Catherine Breskovsky, the beloved "Babushka" of the Friends of Russian Freedom, who had become an ardent enemy of bolshevism. Miss Wald could not yet bring herself to criticize a revolution from which good was still expected. Mary Richmond, a social worker and moderate reformer, summed up the prevailing atmosphere for her professional journal in December 1920.

> There is hardly a profession that does not reflect in its degree this same unrest and demoralization. Teachers in schools and colleges, doctors and nurses back from the war, the clergy of many denominations caught up in a huge, unwieldy substitute for interrelated effort and dropped by it again with a dull thud—all have suffered from the "restless stagnation" of these busy but unfruitful two years.[7]

As these few illustrations suggest, organized women experienced the same emotional devolution which made liberalism in the 1920's so unlike its prewar self. The decline of reform affected women's organizations in a variety of ways. Social feminists were far more dismayed by the postwar reaction than the hard-core advocates of women's rights, who did not immediately lose the momentum generated by their final suffrage campaign. The vulnerability of social feminism in the

6. "Report and Protest to the Governor, the Legislature and the People of the State of New York" (New York League of Women Voters, 1920).

7. Reprinted in Mary Richmond, *The Long View* (New York, 1930), p. 492.

New Era was perhaps best demonstrated by the Consumers' League. Thanks to Florence Kelley it had cherished no illusory hopes as to what could be accomplished under wartime conditions. It had struggled merely to hold the line, and, with the help of its president, Secretary of War Baker, had enjoyed a modest success. After the Armistice Mrs. Kelley could report with satisfaction as "the outstanding fact of the year" that "the National Consumers' League is still in existence and has 82 leagues in fifteen states and the District of Columbia." [8]

There was some reason, then, for the annual meeting in November 1918 to be the gala event that it was. While Mrs. Kelley celebrated the league's survival, Secretary Baker's presidential address gave occasion for a patriotic festival attended by General T. Coleman duPont, the Governor of Delaware, and the press, during which high industrial standards and military victory were equally celebrated. But while the war experience had been less damaging than Mrs. Kelley had feared, neither she nor the league found it easy to set a new course in the uncertain months that followed. The textile industry was given a searching investigation which proved that the output of shoddy had been greatly stimulated by war. This had repulsive consequences, for the rags used in its manufacture were always foul and often contaminated. The meat-packing industry also attracted Mrs. Kelley's attention, and she slammed it with the same vigor that she did the New York state legislature which had failed to grasp the significance of woman suffrage. She informed the state legislators that either women were going to get a minimum wage and a shorter working day or they would strike.[9]

While firing off these broadsides, Mrs. Kelley was also trying to find some way of organizing the widespread but unfocused reaction to economic inflation. As she observed, "Not

8. Minutes of the Council Meeting, November 21, 1918, Papers of the NCL.

9. Florence Kelley, "The Inescapable Dilemma," *Survey*, March 22, 1919, p. 885.

since the Civil War has the public mind been so concentrated upon the cost of living as it is today, and never has such application to one subject produced less visible effect." [1] At this point she seemed to be considering a shift of emphasis away from labor-related problems and toward grievances that affected both middle- and lower-class consumers. But Mrs. Kelley's interest in the consumer was short-lived, and at the end of 1919 the league decided on a ten-year program which subordinated consumer problems to work and welfare measures like the eight-hour day, the elimination of night work for women, passage of the child-labor bill, the establishment of minimum-wage commissions in all states, and compulsory health insurance in industry. The ambitious character of this ten-year plan demonstrated that the league still did not appreciate the gravity of its situation. Having survived the critical war years more or less intact, the CL could not believe that the greatest hazards were yet to come. Soon the league found itself facing challenges from two quite unexpected directions. The campaign of the Woman's party to secure a constitutional amendment making men and women equal in all respects was hotly resisted by social feminists because they believed it would be used to strike down all protective legislation for working women. This was by far the most divisive issue to affect feminists in the postwar era (it receives detailed attention in a later chapter) and was a considerable worry to Mrs. Kelley and other friends of laboring women throughout the twenties.

A more urgent and immediate problem for the league and its allies was the judicial counterrevolution launched by the Supreme Court after the war, particularly its decisions on state minimum-wage laws and the federal child-labor bills. In the Adkins case the Supreme Court wiped out years of effort invested by the league in establishing the legality of minimum-wage laws. Mrs. Kelley was probably even more disheartened by the destruction of the child-labor bill. The prohibition of

1. Florence Kelley, "The Consumer and the Near Future," *Survey*, April 5, 1919, p. 5.

child labor had been, next to equal suffrage itself, the reform most keenly desired by organized women for a generation, and no one had worked harder for it than Florence Kelley. When the first child-labor bill was invalidated by the Supreme Court in 1918, Congress responded by passing another child-labor law in February 1919. This too was struck down in May 1922, and Congress was then persuaded to pass an amendment to the Constitution giving itself the power to regulate and prohibit the labor of children under eighteen years of age. On June 2 it passed the Senate and went to the states for ratification.

Throughout this period the opposition to child-labor reform led by textile manufacturers and their representatives in Congress continued to mount, but the majority of legislators had held firm throughout the eight-year battle. So supporters of the amendment were taken by surprise at the storm of resistance which broke when it was submitted to the states. First to consider it was Massachusetts, a state with superior industrial laws, whose legislature nonetheless ducked the issue by submitting it to a popular referendum. Child-labor reformers were forced to wage a statewide campaign against well-organized and lavishly financed opponents. In urban areas the National Association of Manufacturers and the Associated Industries of Massachusetts led the fight. In rural areas the hostility of the National Farm Bureau and the National Grange was crucial. To these potent organizations were added front groups like the Farmers' States Rights League financed by the Southern Cotton Manufacturers, and a variety of crackpot, superpatriotic groups. While appeals to the self-interest of farmers and manufacturers who used child labor was rational, if unattractive, the irrational attack on the amendment as a Bolshevik plot was apparently most effective. It was charged that the amendment had been drawn up in Moscow and promoted with Russian gold. The ideological case against it was expressed by *The Pilot*, official organ of the Boston Archdiocese, in this manner:

There never was a more radical or revolutionary measure proposed for the consideration of the American people than this so-called Child Labor Amendment, that at one stroke of the pen would set aside the fundamental principles of State rights, and at the same time would destroy parental control over children, and would commit this country forever to the communistic system of the nationalization of her children.[2]

The opposition of the Roman Catholic hierarchy in Massachusetts proved decisive. Cardinal O'Connell asked every priest under his jurisdiction to preach against the amendment and powerfully attacked it himself. Although the amendment was endorsed by the president of the National Catholic Welfare Conference, Father John A. Ryan, and other liberal Catholics, the hierarchy's weight was against them. In the fall elections Massachusetts overwhelmingly rejected the amendment. A few observers thought it was too early in the day to give up hope, but Massachusetts was the turning point, as a disastrous effort in New York the following year demonstrated. By 1930 only six states had ratified the amendment. In a relatively short space of time the old, established child-labor reform movement had been virtually destroyed by what Felix Adler called the "Child Labor Panic."[3]

In a thoughtful review of the Massachusetts referendum the *Survey* blamed its defeat on the climate of opinion. Well-organized opponents financed by the National Association of Manufacturers and similar groups had helped confuse and mislead the public, and there had been a small conscientious group of dissenters led by Joseph Lee, the respected president of the Playground and Recreation Association, who honestly believed that child labor should be locally regulated. The cause also

2. Quoted in Ned Weissberg, "The Federal Child Labor Amendment" (unpublished doctoral dissertation, Cornell University, 1942), p. 122.

3. Felix Adler, "The Child Labor Panic," *Survey*, February 15, 1925, pp. 565–567.

suffered from the general reaction against constitutional amendments inspired by Prohibition, and from those who resented the wartime intervention in business and private affairs. Regardless, the amendment failed mainly because of a nationalist hysteria carried over from the war which made it possible to brand as subversive a whole range of reforms and reformers. Senator Thomas F. Bayard had accused Florence Kelley of being a Soviet agent, and other child-labor law advocates were similarly defamed. A contributor to the *Survey* claimed: "But for the habit of propaganda acquired during the World War it is hardly conceivable that any group of Americans would have had the effrontery so completely to misrepresent the realities of what is actually a very simple question.[4]

In the face of such opposition the child-labor reformers found it difficult to keep their own ranks in order. The National Child Labor Committee itself had been reluctant to undertake a constitutional amendment campaign. In 1922, when the Court struck down the second federal child-labor law, there were many on the committee, including Julia Lathrop, who preferred a "Fabian policy" to another direct assault. Mrs. Kelley was outraged by such faintheartedness, but her own board was reluctant to undertake ambitious counterattacks, and it was only with difficulty that she secured their authorization for a joint effort with other interested groups. Once committed to battle Mrs. Kelley refused to admit defeat. Even after the Massachusetts debacle she continued to think that a public drive like the woman suffrage campaign could be staged, and she spent all the league's money in New York. Finally, the league's executive board ordered her to stop, and with her funds exhausted she had no choice but to accede. Mrs. Kelley continued to support the amendment, but it had been done to death in Massachusetts. Senator Paul Douglas believed that Massachusetts "killed Mrs. Kelley" also.

Florence Kelley lived until 1932, but it was true that these

4. William L. Chenery, "Child Labor—The New Alignment," *Survey*, January 1, 1925, p. 379.

events cut the heart out of both her and the league. It was demoralized by the amendment's failure, yet even before Massachusetts it had begun to shrivel. Mrs. Kelley's feud with the Woman's party, which had admirers in every social feminist organization, the CL included, was divisive, as were her attempts to secure interest in a plan to limit the Supreme Court's power of judicial review. Most destructive of all, perhaps, was the fight over Newton D. Baker's presidency in 1923. When Baker returned home and became head of the Cleveland Chamber of Commerce, he seemed to many Consumers' Leaguers to become increasingly conservative. Mrs. Kelley was deeply grateful to him for having shielded the league in wartime, but when he endorsed the open shop in 1922 and clashed publicly with Samuel Gompers over it, the conflict of interest between his two presidencies became intolerable. Much as Mrs. Kelley despised Gompers, she valued the league's association with organized labor, and in 1923 she supported the Wisconsin economist John R. Commons, who narrowly defeated Baker in the NCL's presidential election.[5]

Baker took his defeat with good grace, but the heated presidential election strained the league's weakened structure to the point where recovery became impossible. Whereas in 1921 the league's income had exceeded $44,000, during the last quarter of 1923 it took in only $2,650. Receipts picked up later, but the NCL faced its severest challenge since the war with sadly diminished human and material resources. In her annual report just after the Massachusetts referendum, Mrs. Kelley observed that "the past year has been the most difficult in the experience of the Secretary, even compared with 1917," and asked her followers to take what comfort they could from the knowledge that "it is doubtful whether any other unpopular organization has survived such deprivation." [6] The league

5. See the excellent account in Louis Lee Athey's unpublished doctoral dissertation, "The Consumers' Leagues and Social Reform, 1890–1923" (University of Delaware, 1965), pp. 244–246.
6. "Report of the Secretary," November 13, 1924, p. 3, Papers of the NCL.

had little to celebrate on its twenty-fifth anniversary, but the event proved to be a brave enough occasion given over largely to eulogies of Florence Kelley. Ex-president Baker generously characterized her as having been a "dangerous woman, not in the sense that loose-witted people might employ the phrase; her work has centered essentially in protecting the home; but dangerous in the sense that she knew what she was talking about." [7]

Baker's use of the past tense was perhaps accidental, but certainly not inappropriate. The years of its greatest accomplishments and effectiveness were behind the league, and Mrs. Kelley was beginning to sense this. In certain respects, she believed, conditions were worse than ever before. While the league had won some permanent victories, notably in securing the constitutionality of maximum-hour laws for working women (although only nine states had established an eight-hour day), "that was before the National Manufacturers Association and the National Industrial Conference Board and many other great national organizations for slowing the national pace had got their stride . . . everything we undertook was far easier and more glowingly hopeful than it is now." [8]

Florence Kelley never thought the struggle for social justice would be a short or easy one. Frances Perkins later recalled that at the outbreak of war, when many were wondering which course to take, Mrs. Kelley told her, "You know at twenty I signed on to serve my country for the duration of the war on poverty and on injustice and oppression, and I take it . . . that it will last out my life and yours and our children's lives." [9] But Mrs. Kelley, like a great engine run too long at full throttle, was beginning to wind down. Age, frustration, the splintering of her organizational base, political defeat, and

7. "Editorial," *Survey*, December 1, 1924, p. 291.

8. Josephine Goldmark, *Impatient Crusader: Florence Kelley's Life Story* (Urbana, Ill., 1953), p. 206.

9. Addresses Given at the Memorial Service for Florence Kelley, p. 29, Papers of the NCL.

the soured public temper placed their stamp upon her. She remained actively in charge of the league until her death, but people no longer called her "Niagara Falls" as they had during her great days in Henry Street. When she died, eloquent and richly deserved tributes were bestowed on her memory. John Haynes Holmes wrote in the *New York Times:* "If our age were the Middle Ages, the late Mrs. Kelley would be canonized and remembered in history as Ste. Florence." [1] At the moving service which honored her passing, Newton D. Baker said she had been the strongest influence in his life, and wrote what should have been her epitaph with the words, "Everybody was brave from the moment she came into the room." [2]

Memorial services are, of course, no place for dispassionate analysis, but Harry Laidler, of whose League for Industrial Democracy Mrs. Kelley was a vice-president, touched on the most incongruous aspect of her public life when he noted that she believed "the profit basis of modern industry was essentially an immoral basis." [3] Mrs. Kelley was indeed a lifelong socialist, but as we saw earlier she had rejected a large part of the socialist formula in favor of more conventional positions. She believed that in America the immediate problems of working women and children were best served by playing upon the moral sensibilities of the middle classes, especially middle-class women. In this context it seems clear that she expected woman suffrage to be decisive. Not only did she express this hope on many occasions, but her whole strategy appears to have been based on the assumption that by organizing women and inspiring them with a higher social consciousness before they gained the vote, it would be possible to lead them to final victory afterward. The tragedy of her particular situation in the 1920's, then, stemmed not from the collapse of the Socialist party, which she had in effect given up on long before, nor even

1. John H. Holmes, "Letter to the Editor," *New York Times,* February 22, 1932.
2. Addresses at the Memorial Service, p. 11.
3. *Ibid.,* p. 25.

from the devastating backlash of the World War, but from the failure of enfranchised women to generate the kind of political power that could be mobilized to advance social reforms.

Her dilemma was not unique to Mrs. Kelley or the league. All social feminists suffered from the long postwar reaction, but there was a special irony in her case. She had abandoned what most American reformers believed to be the chimerical hopes and foolish if not actually vicious theories of revolutionary socialism, only to fail as completely as if she had remained an active radical. Of course, no great life is ever lived in vain, and Florence Kelley did not need to apologize for the uses to which she put her splendid talents. The social payoff from her investment was slight not so much because of her errors in judgment—exaggerating the importance of middle-class sympathy and the potential of enfranchised women—but because of the social and historical context in which she made them. She did everything that a reformer was supposed to do, rang all the right bells, appealed to all the best people and instincts, broke no laws, inflamed no passions, and relied always on the orderly processes of American democracy. In the end, Florence Kelley failed because her estimate of the country's potential for voluntary reform was too generous, her patriotism too deep, and her faith in the United States too great.

. . . .

The later history of the National Women's Trade Union League is much like the NCL's, with some variations owing to its closer ties with the trade union movement, its semi-proletarian membership, and its collective leadership. Having been more committed to American victory, its mood in the immediate postwar period was less grim and detached than the Consumers' League's. The New York WTUL was especially buoyant in these early months. Its moving spirit, Mary Dreier, was chairman of the Women's Joint Legislative Conference which proposed to use women's new political power to lobby through the legislature five new laws for the protection of working women. Nelle Swartz of the league and the New York State Department of Labor spoke for all of them when she said, "The women are presenting a united front as they never did before and we feel confident of success." [4] On March 5 the Conference sent five hundred women to Albany in support of its bills. Their foray was accounted a success, although for the first time their opposition included ultra-feminists who regarded protective legislation for women as discriminatory. The WTUL's June convention was extraordinarily gay. Mrs. Robins gave a fighting speech calling for the full realization of progressive goals. Resolutions were passed against American intervention in Russia and in favor of a league-sponsored International Congress of Women in Washington just before the First International Labor Conference in that city. Feeling ran strongly in support of a free Ireland and against the European food blockade and the Versailles treaty. The convention also called for compulsory health insurance, public ownership of public utilities, trains and communications, mines, packing houses, and grain elevators, and a number of other domestic reforms.

The only jarring note in this otherwise hopeful and high-spirited meeting came when C. P. Fincher told a Philadelphia newspaper that the convention was pro-German. On being questioned, Miss Fincher, a fraternal delegate from Typographical Union No. 2 in Philadelphia, proved to be more concerned with the league's legislative program than its patriotism. She had lost her job when New York banned night work for women or, as she told the delegates, "this Women's Trade Union League became active in amending the laws of New York and confined my working hours between six in the

4. "Women Unite to Protect Women," *Survey*, December 28, 1918, p. 406. Member groups in the Women's Joint Legislative Conference included the New York Consumers' League, the State Federation of Women's Clubs, the YWCA, and the Woman Suffrage party.

morning and six in the evening and legislated me out of a position, while you gave the twenty-four hours to the men working in the industrial field." [5] Miss Finch was admonished and stripped of her credentials, but her peevish outburst with its ultra-feminist pretensions and subversive innuendos was a portent of things to come, more significant in its own way than the serious business of the meeting.

While there was some reason for the league to be optimistic in 1919, much of its confidence was based on ignorance. It sent Rose Schneiderman and Mary Anderson to represent American working women at the peace conference, but they gained little sense of the desperate state of European affairs and returned to the United States convinced that a new era of international cooperation was about to begin. Lacking the European contacts built up over the years by such longtime internationalists as Jane Addams and Carrie Chapman Catt, the NWTUL was not in a good position to judge the hazards awaiting its experiment in cooperation. The first congress of working women in October 1919 was successful in the way that such affairs usually are. Genial statements were made, common principles affirmed, more meetings arranged for, and a permanent organization called the International Federation of Working Women agreed upon. Two years later a second congress was held in Geneva and the formal structure of the IFWW, with Mrs. Robins as president, erected.

The Geneva meeting was a revelation to Mrs. Robins, who finally grasped the immense difficulties of the international program upon which the league had so blithely embarked two years earlier. The NWTUL was distrusted by some European women who considered it mainly a suffragist organization, by others who opposed protective legislation for working women, and by still others who believed that in America women were

5. Proceedings of the 1919 Convention, Papers of the NWTUL, p. 226. See also Henriette R. Walter, "Women as Workers and Citizens," *Survey*, June 21, 1919, pp. 465–466.

organized exclusively in segregated unions. Even though no delegates from the former Central Powers attended the second congress, it was divided in the same way as the rest of Europe. Socialist women were reluctant to cooperate with Catholic women, and all of them feared the communists. Mrs. Robins wrote: "Every group hates every other group, and it is an hour of destruction . . . yet we are bound that constructive action shall somehow take place in Geneva." [6] The delegates, mainly working women, were further demoralized by the economic crisis which threatened their jobs. Their proletarian concerns were impossible for the Americans to understand. Mrs. Robins, for example, was astonished when they refused to send telegrams to the Disarmament Conference in Washington on the ground that as "class-conscious workers they refuse to have any dealings with the bourgeois!" [7]

When the IFWW met again in 1923, the effort to understand and communicate with their European colleagues had become so demanding that the NWTUL was almost glad that new developments provided a graceful opportunity for withdrawal. At this convention a movement led by the British delegation to affiliate the IFWW with the International Federation of Trade Unions succeeded. The NWTUL was placed in an awkward position by this change in direction, because the AFL did not belong to or approve of the IFTU. Mrs. Robins accordingly declined to stand for re-election as president, and after much deliberation the NWTUL voted to resign from the IFWW. Ostensibly this was because its relations with the AFL would be compromised by membership in the IFTU, but more important, it would seem, was the unbridgeable gap between American and European trade-union women, which reflected the distance between the two union movements as a whole. In considering withdrawal, the league's executive board observed:

6. Margaret Dreier Robins to Elizabeth Christman, October 26, 1921, Papers of the NWTUL.
7. *Ibid.*

American women have recognized the necessity for a woman movement within the labor movement. . . . The European labor movements, on the other hand, emphasize class-consciousness and deprecate a woman movement within their class. European working women agree with European working men in this.[8]

Thus, although the WTUL was more thoroughly working class than it had ever been before (at the 1919 convention 90 per cent of the delegates and all the officers save Mrs. Robins were, or had been, workers), it remained too conservative, too bourgeois, too feministic, in short, too American for its European counterparts. Although the league had invested a great deal of time, effort, and money in its European venture now so dismally concluded, the experience had sharpened its self-awareness. The NWTUL did not retire into a complacent nationalism; it maintained some international contacts, especially with oriental women, and continued to press for disarmament and world peace. But the reasons for its, in many ways, incongruous association with the AFL were never clearer.

Although the league was relatively undisturbed by its failures abroad, which gained it nothing except the enmity of isolationist superpatriots, its domestic reverses were quite another matter. In the first brave days after peace was declared, its income shot up to a peak of $52,000 in 1919–1920, but thereafter the postwar recession made itself felt and receipts fell by 50 per cent the following fiscal year. In 1921 it called off its biennial convention for lack of funds and discontinued the publication of its excellent journal, *Life and Labor*. In 1922 Mrs. Robins resigned as president and thereafter played a small role in league affairs. The league managed to hold a convention in that year, but it was a subdued affair, and Mrs. Robins probably spoke for most members when she observed with less than her customary felicity:

8. Minutes of the Executive Board Meeting, October 16-18, 1923, p. 22.

We have been living in these difficult years and life has been hard and ugly, and there are times when it seems that nothing but ugliness stood out and men and women seemed to be moved in numbers by mob action and the mob spirit; we were conscious of the ugliness of life, this ugly thing, and we have all been held by it, it seems so overwhelming in its power.[9]

Despite a financial recovery in 1923–1924, when the league took in almost $50,000, it revival was more apparent than real. It depended for over nine-tenths of its funds on the donations of friends and allies like Mrs. Willard Straight and William B. Thompson, a friend of Raymond Robins, who gave as much as $10,000 at a time. Membership dues and trade-union contributions brought in little more than rent money. Its uncertain sources of support kept the league in debt and made long-term projects impossible under the best of circumstances. When contributions fell off again in 1924, the league undertook what proved to be a permanent retrenchment. Apart from New York and Chicago, where some organizing work continued, the league's only significant activities were its training school and its legislative office in Washington. In 1926 it closed the school, which was extremely costly to operate, and for a time considered closing the Washington office as well.

Had it done so the league would have disappeared as a national organization, because with the decline of its locals the Washington office had become its most visible enterprise. Ethel Smith, who operated with one secretary, few expenses, and at times without salary, was by this time the league's most effective officer. Persuasive, energetic, and politically knowledgeable, she had been more responsible than anyone else for getting the league into the Woman's Joint Congressional Committee in which she played a key role. She also enjoyed the confidence of William Green, Gompers' successor. This counted heavily with the league's executive board, and after heated debate, and in the face of some feeling that special

9. Proceedings of the 1922 Convention, p. 16.

legislation for emancipated working women was no longer appropriate, it was finally decided to move the national headquarters to Washington and consolidate it with the legislative office. On this reduced scale (in 1935 its income was $8,000) the league clearly paid its way as a base for veterans like Ethel Smith, Rose Schneiderman, Mary Dreier, and Elizabeth Christman during the depression. But they were a skeleton crew, for the league no longer attracted ardent youth. In 1950, when it voted to disband, the principal officers had been with the NWTUL for more than thirty years.

In large measure, of course, the league had to fail, because even before the war its resources were pitifully inadequate for what was virtually an impossible task. The war only made things worse. It did not increase the real wages of working women by much "and was in reality more a shifting of groups than an actual tremendous jump in the numbers of those working for payment." [1] In fact, the female share of the work force declined during the period 1910–1920 from 23.4 to 21.4 per cent.[2] Where women retained their new jobs after the war, it was because they were cheaper to employ and more docile than men.

After the war, other elements conspired to frustrate the league. While the percentage of women in the work force did grow during the 1920's, the greatest increase took place in those jobs that were hardest to organize. The number of employed married women grew from 1.9 to 3.1 million, while the percentage of women workers in professional occupations increased from 11.9 to 14.2 per cent and clerical work rose from fifth to third place in the list of female occupations.[3] Thus the

1. Alice Rogers Hager, "Occupation and Earnings of Women in Industry," *Annals*, CXLIII (May 1929), 67.

2. Lorine Pruett, *Women and Leisure* (New York, 1924), pp. 60-61.

3. In addition to the above, see Elizabeth K. Nottingham, "Toward an Analysis of the Effects of Two World Wars on the Role and Status of Middle-Class Women in the English Speaking World," *American Sociological Review*, XII (December 1947), 670.

unmarried industrial worker who was the backbone of the women's labor movement declined in importance, while married professional and clerical workers, historically the most difficult to organize, multiplied. When the high unemployment rate, which never fell below 10 per cent after 1924, is taken into account, it is easy to see why only 2.94 per cent of all working women were unionized in 1924, and why the income gap between male and female workers continued to grow.[4]

The AFL, now very much in decline, continued to demonstrate how little it valued the league. In 1921 the league made a strenuous effort to persuade the federation's executive council that it should issue separate charters to women in industries where the affiliated international unions refused them membership. The AFL had done so on occasion for Negro men in segregated industries, and the WTUL regarded this as ample precedent. The council denied their request, and then added insult to injury. Vice-President Duncan told them he opposed female locals because women were not permanent workers. Locals should be integrated and officered by men who were committed to their trade. Treasurer Tobin of the Teamsters expressed a certain sympathy but declared that he would fight to the end to keep out women coal-team drivers who were dirty, unkempt, and shoeless. The league pointed out that it was unfair of the AFL to discriminate against women when it admitted immigrants. To this Gompers replied that the AFL did indeed discriminate against "Mongolians, or any nonassimilable race" and would continue to do so. Passing over the question of whether women were an assimilable race, Vice-President Mahon of the Streetrailway Men rehashed his union's grievance against women conductors.[5]

4. The discrepancy between male and female skilled and semi-skilled workers increased from 22.8¢ per hour in 1923 to 26.9¢ in 1929. For unskilled workers the differential swelled from 6.3¢ per hour to 10.2¢.

5. From the report of Elizabeth Christman to the Executive Board of the NWTUL, September 22, 1921.

Mrs. Robins and her associates were sufficiently stung by this humiliating rejection to take their proposal to the next AFL convention. While they were certain to be defeated at first, they hoped ultimately to work a change in sentiment. Their resolution did fail, and in time they came to feel that despite their compromises they had offended too many officers of the garment, textile, and streetrailway unions, among others, to ever carry the day. A further complication was the evasive attitude of President Gompers. While continually assuring the league of his support, Gompers never defended the women when they were opposed by the big international unions' baronial chiefs. Mrs. Robins did not trust him, and perhaps he sensed this. Certainly, as Alice Henry pointed out in a letter to her, the AFL executive council has "always had a wholesome respect and fear of you as an individual as well as a President." [6] Even if Gompers had liked them personally and approved of their feminist connections, there remained his opposition to most of the welfare measures the league endorsed—minimum-wage and maximum-hour laws, social insurance, national health schemes, and most kinds of government-labor-management relationships.[7]

The league's commitment to the AFL was increasingly destructive. Louise Altheimer, noting the league's failure to act on its own initiative after the AFL refused to grant separate charters to female locals, observed: "It is only by showing their strength and their capacity for independent action if not recognized on an equal footing with men, that the wage-earning women can hope to gain their rightful place beside the men with whom they must compete in industry." [8] Added to this was the league's abandonment of organizing work. A student

6. Alice Henry to Margaret Dreier Robins, May 20, 1924, Papers of the NWTUL.

7. On this point, see Fred Greenbaum, "The Social Ideas of Samuel Gompers," *Labor History*, VII (Winter 1966), 35–61.

8. Louise Altheimer, "The History of the National Women's Trade Union League Since the End of the World War" (unpublished master's thesis, University of Wisconsin, 1932), p. 77.

delegate to its eighth biennial convention in 1922 later reported that "the purpose of the League as I understand it is to organize the workers into trade union groups, and yet at the convention little time was given to this question, while a great deal of time was devoted to other commissions and reports." [9] Especially since the war, the league had become preoccupied with its internal structure and ever more remote from the organizational work that was its reason for being. Typically, in 1926 when its school for organizers was disbanded and its last contact with the real working women severed, the league's educational committee voted to concentrate on training branch officers. In all these ways, the internal contradictions and built-in weaknesses, apparent even when the league was at its peak, made themselves manifest in the 1920's. The decline of the NWTUL was more significant for the future of women in America than the failures of the Consumers' League, because the NCL was never intended to be anything but a mobile strike force in a war that would have to be won by big battalions. The NWTUL's inability to organize an army of working women guaranteed that female employees would continue to be what they had always been: leaderless, anonymous individuals in a corporate society where organization was the unskilled worker's only salvation.

.   .   .   .   .   .

After 1918 the settlement movement continued to develop along lines established earlier. Income declined for a time because of the postwar recession and the political climate that led nervous donors to withhold funds from conspicuously liberal enterprises. Americanization consumed much energy, but immigration had stopped in 1914 and after the war Congress established a quota system that, in effect, ended this great folk movement for good. The immigrant problem was therefore

9. Report of Letta Perkins, Papers of the NWTUL.

"solved," in a manner of speaking. Prohibition agitated settlements through most of the twenties. Most residents felt it improved conditions in the slums because bootleg whisky was so much more expensive than legal whisky had been that consumption declined. Others felt the damage it did the country as a whole, by inciting defiance of the law and stimulating criminal organizations, outweighed its benefits. The settlement movement generally lost interest in social questions. Jane Addams thought this was because of the war and the subsequent anti-radical hysteria. A more plausible explanation involves the demand for professional status and the growing concern with method and technique at the expense of content that went on throughout the Progressive era.

Social workers wanted to establish a distinct professional identity, and to that end they were eager to isolate a body of knowledge and skill unique to themselves which would command the same respect accorded the expertise of other professionals. Settlement residents shared this concern, and their drift toward professionalism was reinforced by the large institutional commitments that the busiest settlements had made. Perhaps equally consequential was the decay of the residential concept that had been central to the settlement ethic. In the twenties many settlement residents did not actually live in the neighborhood. The men especially, many of them second-generation Americans who coveted a suburban home and the other emblems of social arrival, were more inclined to view settlement work as a job rather than a calling. Under these circumstances the fiction that a settlement was just a big home inhabited by friendly "neighbors" could not be sustained. Indeed, it had not really been true since the first volunteers moved out of their tenement flats and into the comparative isolation of their houses. Having given up the genuine proximity and intimate involvement in the neighborhood's life for which they first went into the slums, they set in motion a process culminating in the impersonal, well-managed institutions of the 1920's, equipped to render a variety of worthy services but largely devoid of the founders' spirit. The early residents' urgent and humane desire to serve their districts more effectively, and themselves provide for needs that could not otherwise immediately be met, had led them in an entirely pragmatic, rational, hardheaded way further and further from their original goals. It was too late in 1920 to lament the decline of a visionary populism which had been living on borrowed time since the day when it was first subordinated to realizable, short-term objectives.

Probably the most damaging blow to the settlement movement was the loss of its social glamour and romantic appeal. The suffragist and the settlement resident had offered stirring models to middle-class girls, but the 19th Amendment and the professionalization of social work left emancipated young women in the 1920's without heroic models to emulate and admire. This was a point often disregarded at the time, and a difficult one to assess in any event. Surely part of the reason why young women seemed so much more interested in their private affairs and the pursuit of pleasure after 1920 was precisely because the adventure had gone out of what had been for a generation or more almost traditional activities. As long as going to college, joining a woman's club, working for the vote, or participating in the social-justice movement called for a certain boldness, and at least a mild taste for adventure, the best and bravest young women were moved to service. When these activities became tame and routine, they ceased to be outlets for spirited youth. Adventure was now to be had, for the most part, in struggling against not social problems but social conventions. Drinking, smoking, dancing, sexual novelties, daring literature, and avante-garde art now filled the vacuum created by the collapse of social feminism. The young do not become reformers simply because work needs to be done, but because they get something out of doing it. Older women who had thrilled to the cadences of social feminism failed to understand why their daughters did not. Yet they had only to see how channel swimmers and film stars had replaced social workers and suffragettes to know the reason why.

.   .   .   .

One of the few social-feminist branches to surpass its prewar level of activity during the 1920's was the peace wing. In one sense this was unexpected, because by the end of the war the women's peace movement had become intensely radical, and radicalism was an appalling liability in the New Era. But this radical phase was short-lived, mainly because it developed from the regular peace workers' failure of nerve in 1917 and 1918 which had left the movement for a time in the hands of its boldest—which is to say its most radical—members. Peace returned the old guard to power. The Zurich congress of women pacifists in 1919 was dominated by the veterans of 1915. Jane Addams was elected president of the Women's International League for Peace and Freedom, established as a permanent body by the congress, and the organization's middle-class, democratic, and reformist character was confirmed. It did become one of the first organizations to criticize the Versailles treaty, it did endorse needed social and economic changes, but the WIL retained insofar as possible the spirit and methods of prewar pacifism. Its position "involving changes in the economic order by nonviolent methods, was a program at once too radical for the right, too restrained for the left, involving too much intellectual discipline for the average woman."[1]

Once their postwar hangover eased, organized American women renewed their interest in peace, but the WIL's peculiar character prevented it from taking the lead in this re-

1. Mercedes M. Randall, *Improper Bostonian: Emily Greene Balch* (New York, 1964), p. 310.

surge of pacifist sentiment. The initiative passed, therefore, to the Committee on the Cause and Cure of War. The cccw, a coalition modeled on the Women's Joint Congressional Committee, was founded by Carrie Chapman Catt in January 1925. Mrs. Catt had never expected much from the war, and the state of postwar Europe inspired her to devote the balance of her public life to preventing another such catastrophe. She was occupied for several years after 1920 in tying up the loose ends of the suffrage campaign. Once this was done she discovered that many women shared her concern about peace, and when she launched the cccw most of the important women's groups joined it.

Another book would be required to summarize the peace work performed in the 1920's by social feminists.[2] Most of it was conducted very much along the old lines, for the Great War had wreaked its awful havoc without providing either male or female pacifists with useful new ideas. Nor were pacifist women able to establish the need for separate women's groups within the peace movement. Under pressure their tendency still was to fall back on what would seem to have been the thoroughly discredited notion of a "mother instinct" sufficiently potent to ward off man-made aggressions. Thus, notwithstanding its intrinsic value, the great amount of peace work done by social feminists during the 1920's avoided, where it did not complicate, the question of who a feminist was and what she ought to be doing. Perhaps some of the appeal of peace work came from that very fact. At a time of great confusion over the postsuffrage role of women, when so many traditional reforms had been tarnished or compromised, the urgency attached to disarmament and similar causes enabled women to work for them without worrying about the ideological and tactical dilemmas in which most social feminist endeavors had become enmeshed. The admirable enthusiasm of

2. A good contemporary account is Florence Brewer Boeckel, "Women in International Affairs," *Annals*, CXLIII (May 1929), 230–248.

the women's peace movement in the 1920's therefore hardly reflected the state of the woman movement as a whole.

.   .   .   .   .   .

The 1920's also marked a turning point in the life of the Association of Collegiate Alumnae, but, unlike most organizations with which we have been concerned in this chapter, the turn was for the better. It adjusted quickly to the postwar deflation so troublesome to more ardent reformers. Unlike its sister groups, the association gained from the war a permanently enlarged sense of its possibilities. Despite its considerable prestige it had always lacked the size, income, and organizational resources to execute substantial projects. After the war it began to expand for the first time in a generation. Its Committee on International Relations, formed during the war, went on to establish the first overseas branch of the ACA in Tokyo, and led in the creation of an International Federation of University Women which solidified the association's interest in a world community of educated women. During the war, state divisions of the ACA were established, and later these became the nucleus of a truly national network of local chapters. Having no political interests that could be damaged by the postwar rejection of reform, the association emerged from the failure of reconstruction with no loss of morale and a better organization. The very social changes that were weakening other women's groups worked to the ACA's advantage. The formation of new special interest groups (such as the National Federation of Business and Professional Women's clubs in 1919) cut into the strength of multi-purpose organizations like the General Federation, while the special constituency of the ACA grew by leaps and bounds. The increased number of women college graduates almost guaranteed an increase in ACA membership, and the association altered its structure to permit further enlargement. In 1921 it merged with the Southern Association of College Women to become the American Association of University Women with several classes of membership allowing previously ineligible women to join the branches.[3]

Thus, while other women's organizations were suffering embarrassing reverses, the association was on the eve of substantial expansion. At its thirty-sixth meeting it passed resolutions in favor of the League of Nations, disarmament, and several laws relating to the health, education, and welfare of all American women. It could congratulate itself not only on the completion of a difficult merger, but on a notably expanded membership (five thousand new members in five years, bringing the total to about twelve thousand) and an expansive new spirit. In 1920 it joined the Women's Joint Congressional Committee, so that in Washington its voice was added to those of virtually all the important women's groups. In 1924 the association voted not to condemn the equal-rights amendment as it had at earlier meetings, but instead to subject the whole question of women's rights in the postsuffrage era to further study. Of itself this was a perfectly sensible decision. But since the equal-rights amendment was expected to benefit skilled and professional women, perhaps at the expense of unskilled workers, it showed again the AAUW's essential class interests. A member of the ACA once pointed out that college worked against the isolationism once so common among middle-class women.

> It is, indeed, a kind of liberation for the student to have shared the purposes, the impersonal interest of a college or university. This "sense of the whole" of which I have been speaking breeds gradually in college women the capacity to work in a team, to submerge themselves the better after they take their places in the world, in group activities. It is a corrective for the over-individualistic attitude which is woman's failing.[4]

3. The complications involved are described in "Proceedings of the 36th Meeting," *Journal of the ACA*, XIV (June–July 1921).

4. Sophie Chantal Hart, "Relation of College Experience to Present Social Demand," *Publications of the ACA*, III (December 1908), 55.

She thought this corporate spirit rendered women better able to work for broad reforms. So it did, but it also encouraged a class-consciousness which was easily adapted to the special in terests of women graduates.

Thus, while the ACA was superficially a part of the drive for associated action that marked the emergence of women as a public force in the Progressive era, it was more fundamentally a reflection of the private concerns and experiences of college women. Whereas large numbers of educated women liberalized the body politic to some extent, when their own interests were concerned, and when they acted corporately as in the Woman's party and the ACA, women graduates were considerably more interest-oriented. It was frequently noted that the lack of class-consciousness among working women made them difficult to organize. The same could not be said of college women. They were easily organized, and in large measure this was because colleges seemed to be more effective socializing agencies than factories. Women workers persisted in regarding their condition as temporary, but college women were transformed by their academic incubators. They emerged from four years of intensive training and social intimacy with a new conception of themselves. Sometimes this identification did not extend beyond a loyalty to their colleges, but often it was widened to include all educated women, as the success of the ACA demonstrated.

. . . . . .

Of all the leading women's organizations, few presented a more confused or confusing aspect with the onset of peace than the General Federation of Women's Clubs. Through most of 1919 the leadership was sustained by patriotic momentum. While the war had "been a supreme struggle for the vindication of civilized ideals and the right of free men everywhere to life, liberty and the pursuit of happiness," the federation recognized that the peace might fail to embody these principles, thereby wasting all the sacrifices made to achieve a military victory. To avert this dire possibility the GFWC strongly supported American membership in the League of Nations.

Lacking foreign ties and associations of any strength, the GFWC could hardly have been expected to take a deep interest in so controversial a topic as the League, so its enthusiasm was relatively short-lived. Of greater importance was the federation's position on domestic issues, where it continued its concern with Americanization which had reached a high pitch during the war. Its magazine carried many articles on the social reconstruction which most women believed to be impending, yet Americanization seemed all the more urgent in the nativist atmosphere of the postwar era. Mrs. Thomas G. Winter, director of Americanization and soon to be president of the federation, sounded both notes in urging clubwomen to attack the immigrant problem. On the one hand, she warned, the country was in danger from revolutionaries "of many grades, from certain intellectuals to 'down and outers'; but they have revolution in their hearts, they have money; they have organization; and they are filled with energy." Clubwomen must respond by Americanizing "ourselves to a higher conception of citizenship and a purification of the body social and politic. We must make democracy more real by fairer laws and enforcements, better housing conditions, better health conditions," and the like. At the same time, "we must make the foreign born in our midst believe in America and love her, and get into the great game with us." [5]

This approach was a congenial one. It enabled clubwomen to express both their fear of the alien and their interest in his welfare. A similar duality characterized the federation's internationalism. While supporting the League of Nations and in small ways attempting to improve the international climate, the GFWC also supported higher tariffs. The desire of clubwomen to have it both ways, to be both nationalist and inter-

5. Mrs. Thomas G. Winter, "An Open Letter to Club Americanization Workers," *General Federation Magazine*, XVIII (December 1919), 15.

nationalist, nativist and assimilationist was, of course, characteristic of a movement devoted to compromise, consensus, and the middle way. But the clubs also suffered from the postwar demoralization which affected their spirit and their organizational structure. Most active clubwomen probably agreed with the Colorado State Federation's resolution attesting to "the crucial need of re-stimulating and re-uniting all women in the service of the Republic" and deprecating "the apparent relaxation of united effort for the public good." [6] But many felt as the directors of the Congress of Women's Clubs of Western Pennsylvania did when, after noting the strain war work had imposed on the clubs, they recommended "that we more strongly feature the social side of the Congress for a time and that the Recreation, Drama and Social Committees be requested to put on a more active program and that the Congress as a group relax a little from their more strenuous activities." [7]

When Mrs. Winter became president in 1920 she found the federation at its lowest point in memory. "There was a great sense of disintegration, and the thing that hit me for the first months of my administration was the constant reiteration of the fact that the General Federation had served its purpose, had been organized, as it were, by some divine providence to work through war time, but there was no more work and it was going to pieces." [8] Mrs. Winter, an exceptionally able and vigorous woman, responded to this malaise by pushing several projects—a headquarters building in Washington, the international relations program—which she believed would rekindle the clubs' enthusiasm, and by visiting every state in the union with her message that the clubs still had a large role to play in the world. Describing her followers as "volunteer

6. Colorado State Federation of Women's Clubs Yearbook, 1919–20 (n.p., n.d.), p. 46.

7. Minutes of the November 23 meeting of the Congress of Women's Clubs of Western Pennsylvania, Archives of Industrial Society, University of Pittsburgh.

8. *Official Report of the Twentieth Biennial Convention* (Washington, D.C., 1930), p. 116.

social workers," she insisted that there remained a great need for disinterested service.

> The Federation has peculiar facilities for this kind of service. It is not a "one idea" organization. It sees life whole and discourages the "one purpose crank." It has all types of women, rich and poor, radical and conservative, city and country, educated and untrained. It is not a class affair. We realize that the things that bind us together are far deeper and greater than the things that separate us—and there is no lesson America needs more at present than just this sense of abiding unity. Class consciousness is one of the greatest dangers both in political life and in industrial life.[9]

Of course the federation was entirely a middle-class organization, reluctant as the leadership was to admit this, but its class character had been masked somewhat in the Progressive period because of its strong support of social-justice measures, its real if limited interest in the problems of working women, and the substantial number of very liberal women active in its affairs. Without jeopardizing its proud status as a part of the woman movement, the federation had been content to make haste slowly, never moving too far ahead of the conservative women who comprised a large share of its membership. Feminists and reformers often wished the GFWC could work faster, but they appreciated the federation's unique ability to engage cautious women in unfamiliar activities. The war and its aftermath did not radically alter the federation's character, yet it helped tip what was apparently a delicate balance between the leadership's progressivism and the membership's conservatism. Mrs. Winter succeeded in restoring the federation's organizational fortunes but not its old enthusiasm for reform and welfare measures. The most liberal elements dropped out of active participation in federation affairs, social feminists like Jane Addams and Florence Kelley spoke rarely at the biennials, and the federation became in-

9. "President Sends First Greetings," *General Federation Bulletin*, I (August 1920), 8.

creasingly preoccupied with domestic and parochial matters at the expense of great national questions. This was especially marked after 1924 when Mrs. John D. Sherman was elected president. Her greatest interest was home economics, and the main project of her administration was an elaborate campaign to increase the use of home appliances—without, however, any serious attention to the level of family income which determined their use.

This is not to say that the GFWC suddenly lost all interest in the causes it had traditionally supported. The changes in the GFWC were more relative than absolute. At a time of general ideological retrenchment the federation backed off less than many organizations. But by comparison with its prewar self it had definitely become more careful and defensive. The tension between progressives and conservative nationalists that characterized middle-class America was reflected in the biennial meetings, which were less homogeneous than before the war. Indeed, a kind of underground and inarticulate struggle came to dominate the GFWC's conventions. In 1922, for example, Shailer Mathews lamented that "this is a bad day for idealists," and a former president, Mrs. Percy V. Pennybacker, made an emotional attack on war that implicitly rejected the federation's support of American intervention. Raymond Robins urged the outlawry of war, and Grace Abbott spoke on the Children's Bureau. But the convention also heard a viciously racist attack on immigration, a more moderate condemnation of the Bolsheviks by Count Ilya Tolstoy, and a confused appeal from a fellow clubwoman to keep the flame of wartime idealism burning by cooperating with the American Legion—which, of course, opposed most of the federation's social program.

The GFWC did not attempt to reconcile these contradictions, a feat it could not have accomplished anyway. In the absence of serious debate or self-examination, the federation adjusted to the strain by moving toward centrist positions where the pressures from each direction neutralized one another. The controversial questions on which it took strong stands were carried over from the Progressive era; on new issues it invariably compromised—disarmament, but not too much disarmament—except on matters of individual morality. Thus it never wavered on Prohibition and consistently endorsed all forms of moral censorship, especially of movies. Film censorship was almost an obsession with many social feminists in this period. The League of Women Voters supported it, and clubwomen ceaselessly investigated and inveighed against the movie industry. They opposed D. W. Griffith's masterpiece, *Birth of a Nation*, because it encouraged race prejudice, and its brilliant sequel, *Intolerance*, for advocating "personal liberty" and placing "individual desire before the common good." [1] Granted that in the early twenties movies were extraordinarily racy and suggestive, even by today's standards, the social feminists' freedom from civil libertarian scruples was noteworthy.

Both traits—compromise and accommodation on all but moral questions, and a lack of regard for personal liberties—distinguished the federation's response to the Red Scare. Just as clubwomen had instinctively recognized that the best policy was to support peace in peacetime and war in wartime, so did they automatically take the establishment line on subversion. On the one hand, they condemned alien radicalism; on the other, they warned that patriotic fears should not be carried to the point where they jeopardized reforms. Mrs. John D. Sherman, during whose presidency (1924–1928) superpatriotic excursions and alarms continued, vigorously advanced both positions. She urged clubwomen to search out communist activities in their schools and churches, "for I have information from the most authoritative sources that it is among our young

1. Florence Butler Blanchard, "The September Symposium and Legalized Censorship," *General Federation Magazine*, XVIII (January 1919), 15–16. Mrs. Blanchard was further irked by a subtitle in *Intolerance* which read, "When a woman ceases to be attractive to men, she goes in for reform."

people, even among our young children that the communists are working steadily and earnestly." [2] At the same time she repeatedly condemned right-wing attacks on social welfare projects and insisted that "the women of the Federation must not be afraid of having their patriotism questioned when their purpose is the betterment of conditions for women and children." [3] But while every postwar federation president was admirably firm on this point, one looks in vain for any suggestion from them that the Constitution protected radicals even if radicals did not protect the Constitution.

. . . .

For social feminists as a whole, the 1920's was a period of defeat and decay. Vanguard organizations like the Consumers' League and the NWTUL received blows from which they were never to recover. More solidly based movements like the GFWC and the National Federation of Settlements beat ideological retreats. This was, of course, the common experience of progressives in a time of reaction. What was distinctive about social feminism was that its decline became permanent. Individual organizations waxed and waned in the years that followed. The Consumers' League rallied during the depression by working closely with various government agencies. The NWTUL was finally dissolved. The ACA flourished. The General Federation had its ups and downs. In the late 1920's it withdrew from the Women's Joint Congressional Committee, depriving that liberal coordinating body of considerable support. In the thirties and forties its social consciousness ex-

2. "Mrs. Sherman Declares Club Work Is Highest Type of Patriotic Service," *Federation News*, October 1927, p. 6. She was also alarmed by the American Association for the Advancement of Atheism, which, among other outrages, proposed to eliminate "In God We Trust" from the coinage.

3. *Official Report of the Nineteenth Biennial Convention* (Washington, D.C., 1928), p. 47.

panded, only to wither in the hostile political climate of the 1950's.

Regardless of the fate of its parts, the woman movement as a whole was dead. After the depression the phrase itself passed out of the language, testifying to the fact that public women no longer felt themselves part of some kind of corporate body, however loosely defined. The sisterly feeling between women's organizations, and the vague unifying ethic accompanying that feeling, did not survive the 1920's. The next chapter will show how this happened.

8

. . . .

the post-suffrage era

*t*he decline of social feminism after World War I was demoralizing to all concerned. Women reformers could, however, console themselves with the knowledge that their frustrations resulted from a nationwide swing to the right rather than any special defects peculiar to themselves. Ardent feminists were denied this comfort. The women's rights movement expired in the twenties from ailments that had gone untreated in its glory days. Chief among them was the feminists' inability to see that equal suffrage was almost the only issue holding the disparate elements of the woman movement together. Once it was resolved, voters who happened to be female were released from the politically meaningless category of "woman." This allowed their basic allegiances to come into play. As a popular journalist pointed out, "the woman 'bloc' does not tend to become more and more solidified, but tends to become more and more disintegrated. Women at the polling places in Vermont turn out to be different from women at the polling places in Iowa; and the differences of locality and of class turn out to overshadow the difference of sex." [1] It quickly became evident that, except on matters like Prohibition and the sex lives

1. William Hard, quoted in "What the American Man Thinks," *Woman Citizen*, September 8, 1923, p. 17.

of political figures, there was no women's vote. It also soon became clear that the anti-suffragists had more accurately foreseen the ballot's limitation than the suffragists. In 1920 it was still possible to argue, as Emily Greene Balch did, that if women voters were often ignorant and inexperienced, "they are also largely free from bad old political habits and traditions, and free to strike out a new political method, not dominated by party, in which social and moral values shall outweigh all others." [2] At the first postwar convention of the International Woman Suffrage Alliance, Carrie Chapman Catt, while admitting that in many countries woman suffrage had come almost by accident as a consequence of the war, still believed "that had the vote been granted to women some twenty-five years ago when justice and logic and public opinion demanded . . . there would have been no World War." [3]

This mood did not last long. By 1922 H. L. Mencken could say:

> Years ago I predicted that these suffragettes, tried out by victory, would turn out to be idiots. They are now hard at work proving it. Half of them devote themselves to advocating reforms, chiefly of a sexual character, so utterly preposterous that even male politicians and newspaper editors laugh at them; the other half succumb absurdly to the blandishments of the old-time male politicians, and so enroll themselves in the great political parties. A woman who joins one of these parties simply becomes an imitation man, which is to say, a donkey. Thereafter she is nothing but an obscure cog in an ancient and creaking machine, the sole intelligible purpose of which is to maintain a horde of scoundrels in public office.[4]

Unjust? Of course. Yet soon many suffragists admitted that fighting for the vote had been more rewarding than getting it.

2. Quoted in Mercedes M. Randall, *Improper Bostonian: Emily Greene Balch* (New York, 1964), p. 282.
3. "Mrs. Catt to the Women of Europe," *Woman Citizen*, June 12, 1920, pp. 45–46.
4. H. L. Mencken, *In Defense of Women* (Garden City, 1922), p. 132.

Mrs. Catt had expected this. Even before women voted in their first national election, she reminded them that they had no obligation to the major parties, for if either had "lived up to the high ideals of our Nation and courageously taken the stand for right and justice as against time-serving, vote-winning policies of delay, women would have been enfranchised long ago." [5] It was partially for this reason that she founded the League of Women Voters, and the experience of 1920 confirmed her judgment. "Suffrage women last autumn numerously confessed that they found real politics 'pale and insipid' when it came time to use their first vote. It seemed sordid and commonplace to be striving merely to elect men whose platforms were so strangely confused they could not find a direct issue. They felt a vacancy where for years there had been purpose consecrated to an immortal principle." [6] A few years later Mrs. Catt noted again that suffragists "are disappointed first of all because they miss the exaltation, the thrill of expectancy, the vision which stimulated them in the suffrage campaign. They find none of these appeals to their aspiration in the party of their choice." [7]

It was one thing for the indomitable Mrs. Catt, whom no political party had anything of value to offer, to take this line; it was quite another for the typical suffragist who had been led to expect something more from the franchise than political tokens (such as the National Committee seats assigned women by both parties). Anne Martin, who several times ran for the Senate from Nevada, was annoyed in 1919 when the National Conference of Republican Women seemed more interested in the clichés of professional politicians than in her own efforts to organize a specifically feminine program. Having given up on the Republicans, she was even more discouraged when in

5. Carrie Chapman Catt, "Which Party Did It?," *Woman Citizen,* September 18, 1920, p. 423.

6. Carrie Chapman Catt, "The League of Women Voters," *Woman Citizen,* April 23, 1921, p. 1188.

7. Carrie Chapman Catt, "Are Women Disappointed in Politics?," *Woman Citizen,* November 3, 1923, p. 14.

1924 the La Follette managers picked a Socialist candidate to run on the third-party ticket, even though she had outpolled him in a previous election. She saw the 1924 election as a debacle for women. Only one was elected to Congress, and she was not among the emancipated candidates supported by the Woman's party. Ignoring the women endorsed by the La Follette party, Miss Martin concluded that all the parties had shown themselves equally bigoted, and that by urging women to work within the established system "Mrs. Carrie Chapman Catt sounded the doom of feminism for many years to come." [8] This was hardly fair to Mrs. Catt, who held no brief for the existing parties but saw no alternative to them, nor was it reasonable of Miss Martin to expect Mrs. Catt to organize another Woman's party when the drawbacks of that policy had, from a social feminist point of view, been so clearly demonstrated by the existing one.

Even so, women with more patience and less personal ambition than Anne Martin found the results of big-party politics disappointing. The first chairman of the Republican Women's Committee of Illinois observed that reform-minded women who joined the regular parties were simply swallowed up. Her experience demonstrated that while the parties were willing to give women symbolic appointments, they were carefully shut out of the decision-making process. This was not so much because they were women as because they were amateurs who did not share the regulars' passion for office. The professionals reasoned correctly that "once in the organization we could be controlled. Our nuisance value was gone. Not only that, our power for good was gone." [9] It was a mistake, she concluded, to think women could reform the party from within.

Emily Newell Blair, who served as vice-chairman of the Democratic National Committee from 1921 to 1928, was less

8. Anne Martin, "Feminists and Future Political Action," *Nation*, February 18, 1925, p. 185.

9. Winifred Starr Dobyns, "The Lady and the Tiger," *Woman Citizen*, XI (January 1927), 20.

disillusioned but hardly more sanguine. She agreed that women had little influence on the parties, that they had been awarded few high offices, and that in general their services had not been adequately compensated. She thought there was a good reason for this. "Members of the party take responsibility and women have been backward about taking it. Their habit is to sit back and then complain because it is not offered them." [1] Mrs. Blair understood the deeper problems enfranchisement had revealed. When women first gained the vote, she noted, male politicians had feared the consequences and treated women with respect and caution. But soon it became clear not only that women would not hang together, but that they would not even support for public office the best female candidates. Since there was no bloc vote, there was no reason for men to cater to it. All of which, she felt, resulted from the fundamental failure of suffragists to think deeply enough about what would happen when the vote was won. Anna Howard Shaw knew the suffragists had let their followers down in this respect. Once victory was assured, she told Mrs. Blair, "I am sorry for you young women who have to carry on the work in the next ten years, for suffrage was a symbol, and now you have lost your symbol. There is nothing for the women to rally round." [2]

Before long it became evident that the League of Women Voters, though it did good work, was no substitute for the NAWSA. It labored on too many fronts; the nature of its activities precluded either the exhilarating victories or heart-wrenching defeats that made life among the suffragists so exciting; and its determined neutrality denied it the passionate loyalties reserved for partisan organizations. Most of all, perhaps, the LWV lost a great many fights, and this did not commend it to younger women who came of age during the years when suffrage was a winning cause. Of course, politics as such di-

1. Emily Newell Blair, "Women in the Political Parties," *Annals*, CXLIII (May 1929), 224.
2. Mary Carroll, "Wanted—A New Feminism: An Interview with Emily Newell Blair," *Independent Woman*, IX (December 1930), 499.

minished in interest during the 1920's, and many women who might otherwise have concerned themselves with public affairs were drawn off into the cultural, social, and recreational pursuits that made the New Era exciting. Marguerite Wells, while attempting to show that women profited from the vote, was forced to admit that "the net effect of suffrage on many clubs has been that they are less, rather than more, prone to 'take action' on political questions." [3] And Rose Schneiderman, although she was careful to point out that she was no more disappointed in women's suffrage than she had been in men's suffrage, admitted that "the women's vote hasn't been of any sensible value in the measures which the Women's Trade Union League want. We started twelve years ago to fight for a forty-eight-hour week. We are still fighting for it, and I can't see that it is a bit easier now, that we make any more impression on the Legislature than we did before we could vote." [4] So much for Florence Kelley's contention that politicians were unresponsive to the needs of working women because they could not vote. The rejoinder that woman suffrage was no worse in practice than man suffrage, although often used, was of course beside the point: a large part of the original justification for it had been that women would vote more sanely than men. If women were going to be no different as voters, there was little purpose to the long struggle except as a matter of simple justice, and mere justice was not why social feminists had invested so much in the cause.

Although the expected gains failed to materialize, there were some fringe benefits. As the genial Edward S. Martin observed in an essay on the disappointment of suffragists, "Nevertheless, woman suffrage is a good thing if only to have it over." The emancipated spirit that won the vote brought other things of greater worth in its train. "Take the matter of

3. Marguerite Wells, "Some Effects of Woman Suffrage," *Annals*, CXLIII (May 1929), 208–209.
4. Quoted in "Is Suffrage Failing?," *Woman Citizen*, March 22, 1924, p. 9.

clothes," Martin continued. "The release of women from clothing in the last thirty years is marvelous and almost all to the good."[5] Indeed, it was one of the great ironies in women's history that dress reform, which the early feminists first practiced and then abandoned because the bloomer costume had so sensational an effect on men, boys, and dogs, in the long run proved more valuable than other reforms which seemed essential at the time. Certainly it did women far more good to shed their crippling foundation garments and multi-layered, confining, and unsanitary costumes than to vote. Today the ballot means little to most of them, but with every breath they draw women have reason to be grateful that capricious fashion did what feminism could not—physically emancipate them from the bonds that taste and custom had forged.

Because the vote brought few of the consequences expected of it, both suffragists and anti-suffragists could draw some comfort from its effects. Ida Tarbell, an old anti-suffragist, believed in 1930 that ten years of votes for women had, just as she predicted, seen women lose their independent power and their capacity for innovation. They had been swallowed up by the parties and lost the special position that had made them effective in the Progressive era. Mrs. Catt admitted that women had had little effect on the political structure, but she felt they had more of a sense of responsibility and exercised more influence over the general condition of the country.[6] Of course, Mrs. Catt could hardly say anything else. She could not admit that woman suffrage was a comparative failure, nor could she offer much in the way of evidence to show it had been a great success. But no one really needed to debate the issue because, unlike Negro suffrage, for example, the granting of votes for women was irreversible. There was some evidence to suggest, however, that while the 19th Amendment effectively

5. Edward S. Martin, "New Freedom for the Girls," *Harper's*, CLIII (August 1926), 391.
6. "Ten Years of Woman Suffrage," *Literary Digest*, April 26, 1930, p. 11.

destroyed anti-suffragism, it did not greatly affect the sentiments on which antis had relied. In 1937 a Gallup poll had shown that only 31 per cent of the electorate would vote for a woman as President. In 1967, when asked the same question, 57 per cent of the respondents declared their willingness to put a woman in the White House. The first poll showed that seventeen years of woman suffrage had not persuaded either men or women of the latter's fitness for high office. While by 1967 this prejudice had declined, it had not done so to the degree that prejudices against Catholics and Jews had. Moreover there was little difference between the public's attitude toward women and Negroes as presidential candidates.[7]

By 1936 it was possible for John Gordon Ross to sum up the results of woman suffrage in terms that require little modification today. In their sixteen years as voters women had overthrown no bosses, and few women in politics had established independent power bases. Women bureaucrats were no better than men—though less corruptible. The vote had not made women mannish, as had been feared, "rather their new responsibilities have brought out only the undesirable traits that women have always had," that is, fussiness, primness, bossiness, and the tendency to make unnecessary enemies. They did not trust each other as candidates. They had not come up with any useful new political ideas. As voters they tended to be excessively moralistic and intolerant. Only about half as many women as men registered to vote, and when they went to the polls they voted as their husbands did. "After a fair trial of sixteen years, it seems just to appraise women's suffrage as one of those reforms which, like the secret ballot, the corrupt-practices acts, the popular election of senators, and the direct

7. George Gallup, "Marked Decline Recorded in Voting Prejudice," *Chicago Sun-Times*, June 4, 1967, Sec. 2, p. 12. The number of respondents willing to vote for a Catholic for President rose from 64 per cent to 89 per cent, for a Jew from 46 per cent to 82 per cent. Gallup did not ask in 1937 how many would vote for a Negro, but in 1967, 54 per cent said they were willing to do so, while 57 per cent would vote for a woman.

primary, promised almost everything and accomplished almost nothing." [8]

Except for a slightly mean-spirited satisfaction in the deflation of suffragist pretensions, this still seems a fair appraisal. The percentage of women who register to vote is much higher now than in 1936, but otherwise the situation is little changed.[9] Ross did, however, admit to one area in which women excelled politically—lobbying. But, he pointed out, they had been successful lobbyists long before they got the vote, and their prowess in this area did not in any way weaken his argument. Quite so, yet it did raise again the possibility that anti-suffragists had been right in thinking that the vote would diminish women's actual influence over politics. Emily Newell Blair later remarked that so long as the woman vote was an unknown quantity, professional politicians were obliged to respect it. Moreover, women in the pre-suffrage years spoke with virtually a single voice as they were never able to do again. Although some women of note opposed equal suffrage, almost none of them was publicly against the purposes of social feminism. In the Progressive era, before women were divided by partisan political

8. John Gordon Ross, "Ladies in Politics," *Forum*, XCV (November 1936), 215.

9. For an up-to-date survey, see Martin Gruberg, *Women in American Politics* (Oshkosh, Wisc., 1968). Among other things, Gruberg concludes that the average difference between the proportion of eligible men and women voters who actually vote is about 10 per cent in favor of men. Women voters are more responsive to personalities than to issues, but where issues do matter to them they are inclined to be more conservative than men toward labor, changes in government, and religious, domestic, and moral issues. They are more liberal than men toward government intervention and ownership, relief, welfare, and social justice measures generally. 1964 seems to have been the only election year in which a majority of women voted for the Democratic rather than the Republican candidate. This was because it was widely (but wrongly) believed that President Johnson would be less likely than Senator Goldwater to lead the country into war. The suffragists did not entirely err, therefore, in thinking that women voters would be pacific, although in practice this has not had much influence.

affiliations, before the German scare and the Russian scare unleashed an hysterical patriotism, before ex-suffragists fell out over their differing conceptions of equal rights, an apparent unanimity prevailed that lent great weight to the woman movement's expressions of opinion. Organized women did not understand the sources of their unity very well. They explained it by references to the bonds of motherhood and other more occult characteristics which supposedly bound them together, but it was no less real for being so misconstrued. As they did not understand the peculiar circumstances responsible for their unity, they could hardly preserve it in the postwar, postsuffrage, and post-Progressive world.

This is not to say, of course, that the woman movement could have been saved if only suffragists had adopted a sounder strategy in their voteless years, or if they had given up entirely on votes for women. The latter was not a real option. Too many years, too many tears had gone into the movement for anyone to arrest it on the eve of victory. Even if suffragists had appreciated that the vote would do organized women more harm than good, they would still have wanted it. Nor could they control the historical processes that were going to make class differences and ideological disagreements more important to women after 1917. But while recognizing that chance and circumstance sharply limited their field of maneuver, it is still clear that suffragists' neglect of certain alternatives was fatal to their larger purposes. They oversold the vote, which meant that both they and the generation that followed them were inevitably disillusioned with public affairs in general. They made too many compromises, from ignobly deserting their embattled sisters in the Woman's party to accepting American participation in a war they disliked. Practical politics made these choices essential, but expediency tarnished the moral quality that was the movement's most precious asset in the postsuffrage era. They failed to think seriously about what was to come after the federal amendment was passed. And, perhaps worst of all, in overconcentrating on politics they neglected other areas—economic, social, domestic—that more profoundly governed women's lives.

It might have been expected that the decline of feminism after 1920 would have been especially hard on the militant suffragists. They had wanted the vote more desperately than most women, and had risked more and suffered more to gain it. Militants lived a richly colored emotional life. Like children, zealots, and romantics, they were either way up or way down, but whether high or low they were always intense, doctrinaire, and assertive. Once their initial euphoria had passed, the members of the Woman's party, more so than other suffragists, found victory hardly less demoralizing than defeat. Previous setbacks had, after all, only been provisional; victory was final. Suffragists had sustained innumerable reverses with their morale intact. But the struggle had gone on for too long, had become, in fact, a way of life. Victory too long delayed loses its savor, and campaigns if endlessly prolonged become self-sustaining and self-justifying. Three generations of women had fought for the vote, and in doing so had become dependent on the cause to give their lives meaning. The vote was no compensation for the effort that had gone into winning it, no substitute for the emotions it displaced. The suffrage army was quickly demobilized. The thought patterns and modes of behavior it had required were not so easily converted to a peaceful, postsuffrage economy.

The NAWSA had anticipated some such denouement by founding in advance the League of Women Voters, a new bottle into which it hoped to pour the old feminist wine. But the prosaic LWV offered nothing to militants who, like discharged commandos, could see no way of using their special skills in the postwar world. Even before most women had a chance to cast their first vote, ultra-feminists were expressing their discontent and searching for ways to maintain the old faith. Mrs. Oliver Hazard Perry Belmont, an immensely rich and determined widow who had become the Woman's party's principal means of support, returned from Europe in July 1920 urging women to boycott the coming elections. "Husband your new power," she instructed them, adding that "suffragists did not fight for your emancipation for seventy years to have you now become servants to men's parties." [1] Her vague admonitions became less opaque a few days later when she announced that the times demanded a new party to save women from the corruptions of big-party politics. Mrs. Belmont's lack of enthusiasm for the party system was widely shared. The League of Women Voters was, of course, scrupulously nonpartisan, in keeping with organized women's traditional aversion to regular politics, but many women were not. Charlotte Perkins Gilman endorsed Mrs. Belmont's position with some fervor:

> The power women will be able to exercise lies with their not joining in the party system of men. The party system of politics is a trick of men to conceal the real issues. Women should work for the measures they want outside of party politics. It is because the old political parties realize that women's influence will be negligible on the inside that they are so eager to get women to join with them.[2]

On February 18, 1921, the old Woman's party was disbanded and a new one created in its stead. Florence Kelley was there and took its number in a slashing report for the *Survey*. She found the new Woman's party's position on the race issue singularly ignoble. The leadership declared that since Southern Negro women were discriminated against equally with Negro men, the principle of equal rights was not imperiled and the party not obliged to intervene. "An inglorious ideal of equality this! Acquiescence in the disfranchisement of millions of women, provided only that the men of their race also are deprived of their constitutional rights." The party's interpretation of equal rights in the industrial field was just as bad. It

1. *Washington* (D.C.) *Times*, July 6, 1920. This and the following quotations from newspaper accounts lack page numbers because they were taken from the copious Belmont scrapbooks now in the possession of the National Woman's party.
2. *New York Call*, July 9, 1920.

was inclined to regard protective legislation for working women as discriminatory, an attitude Mrs. Kelley believed to be both unjust and ill-informed. "How cruel, therefore, is the pretension of certain organizations of professional and business women to decide for the wage-earners, without consulting them, what statutory safeguards they are henceforth to do without." [3] From the day of its birth, then, the battle lines between the new Woman's party and the social feminists for whom Mrs. Kelley spoke were clearly drawn. Although other social reformers were not so quick to react as Mrs. Kelley, she correctly gauged the dedication of the WP to equal rights thus construed, and prophetically warned Newton Baker that the struggle would go on "until an amendment of this general nature is adopted, or the leaders of the Woman's Party all die of old age." [4]

For a time Mrs. Belmont clung to her original conception of the WP as an alternative to the major parties, but soon the WP devoted itself entirely to lobbying for the equal-rights amendment. It was obvious that to tackle every discriminatory statute in the country would require pushing hundreds, if not thousands, of individual bills through state and federal legislatures. In Wisconsin, however, an equal-rights amendment to the state constitution had been easily passed, an event which suggested that resistance to the idea would be light. A federal amendment would, it was hoped, recapture some of the enthusiasm and recall some of the glory that had attended the last great suffrage campaigns. In making these calculations the WP committed two important errors. First, it gravely underestimated the opposition a blanket amendment would meet. In this regard the Wisconsin precedent was misleading, for the Wisconsin equal-rights amendment contained a vital qualification that women were guaranteed complete equality "unless

3. Florence Kelley, "The New Woman's Party," *Survey*, March 5, 1921, p. 827.
4. Florence Kelley to Newton D. Baker, June 3, 1921, Papers of the National Consumers' League, Library of Congress.

such construction will deny to females the special protection and privileges which they now enjoy for the general welfare." [5] Thus social feminists were assured that the amendment would not jeopardize Wisconsin's exemplary welfare and protective legislation. The WP's proposed federal amendment did not contain such an exemption, and hence aroused all the fears which in Wisconsin had been so carefully allayed. Secondly, the WP exaggerated its own potential strength. In one of her manifestos Mrs. Belmont predicted that "our organization will be a colossal thing in a very short time" and that "the day is not far off when the Woman's Party of which I am president will be strong enough to impose any measure it may choose." [6] As late as 1924 Maud Younger, an experienced lobbyist, cautioned the Republican party that if it did not endorse the amendment it would lose its last chance to get on the right side, for the amendment was certain to be passed before the GOP's next convention.

The WP's principal difficulty, however, was its continued failure to understand the social feminist impulse. Having little stake in the mass of protective legislation so painfully erected by a generation of reforming women, the militants could not appreciate their motivations. When ultra-feminists announced their intention to secure an amendment guaranteeing women complete equality with men, they seemed to threaten the chief accomplishments of a number of groups ranging from the Consumers' League to the General Federation. The best legal advisers they could get—Felix Frankfurter, Dean Roscoe Pound —warned social feminists that, as Dean Acheson put it, the courts would take the amendment "to mean that the protection which women have received through legislation, since it is a restriction of their liberty of contract, is no longer possible, and that this new-won equality guarantees to women all the

5. Mabel R. Putnam, *Winning of the First Bill of Rights for American Women* (Milwaukee, 1924), p. 66.
6. Mrs. O. H. P. Belmont, "Women as Dictators," *Ladies Home Journal*, XXXIX (September 1922), 7.

intolerable and antisocial conditions which their brothers in industry now enjoy." [7] Nor was it simply a matter of organizing women so they could command the same benefits as union men—a point sometimes made by the Woman's party. Many social feminists believed that motherhood gave women a competitive disadvantage in the industrial world and made protective legislation a permanent necessity: "investigations have shown a lower resistance on the part of women to the strain and the hazards incident to industry." [8]

By 1924 the Women's Joint Congressional Committee and every important social feminist organization had attacked the equal-rights amendment as a threat to protective legislation for working women. The Woman's party's response was evasive. When Florence Kelley asked Alice Paul if she was opposed in principle to protective legislation, Miss Paul refused to answer, saying only that her board was evenly divided on the question. Some WP leaders were more direct. Gail Laughlin, first president of the National Federation of Business and Professional Women's Clubs and an officer of the WP, opposed all legislation based on sex. "The so-called eight-hour laws for women, glibly called 'protective,' mean the shutting of the door of opportunity to women. If we are to have legislation concerning hours of labor—and I believe we should have that legislation—it should be based along lines of industry, not along lines of sex." [9] The argument that protective legislation was desirable when equally applied to men and women was made so often by the militants that their sincerity on the point seems hardly open to question. *Equal Rights*, their well-edited journal, insisted that sweeping protective laws dated from the period when women as a group were inferior to male workers,

7. Dean Acheson to Ethel M. Smith, September 8, 1921, Papers of the NCL.

8. Alice Hamilton, "For the Sake of the Race," *Woman Citizen*, October 7, 1922, p. 17. She later changed her position and became a supporter of the amendment.

9. "President Laughlin's Trip East," *Independent Woman*, I (February 1920), 12.

but as this was no longer the case such laws had ceased to protect and now limited the opportunities of many women employees.

> We agree fully that the mother and unborn child demand special consideration. But so does the soldier and the man maimed in industry. Industrial conditions that are suitable for a stalwart, young, unmarried woman are certainly not equally suitable to the pregnant woman or the mother of young children. Yet "welfare" laws apply to all women alike. Such blanket legislation is as absurd as fixing industrial conditions for men on a basis of their all being wounded soldiers would be.[1]

In another editorial *Equal Rights* pointed out there would be no reason to fear the effect of an equal-rights amendment on mothers' pensions if fathers were included in the system of family allowances, as was done in France, Belgium, Germany, and other countries. The party resented being called anti-labor. Alice Paul had once helped organize a milliners' union; Josephine Casey, chairman of its Industrial Council, was a wage-earner and a former organizer of the ILGWU; and the party took the same position on protective legislation for working women that Samuel Gompers did for working men.

The Woman's party's case was further strengthened by the adherence of distinguished European women to similar positions. Aletta Jacobs, a Dutch feminist and pacifist, was against special legislation for working women, and in England an influential group of women led by Mrs. Sidney Webb took the same view. In her minority report of the War Cabinet Committee on Women in Industry in 1919, Mrs. Webb advised Parliament to reject the assumption, which she believed was built into the existing legal structure, "that industry is normally a function of the male, and that women, like non-adults, are only to be permitted to work for wages at special hours, for special rates of wages, under special supervision and

1. "Why the Argument," *Equal Rights*, October 6, 1923, p. 268.

subject to special restriction by the legislature." [2] All three of the leading English feminist organizations—Women's Freedom League, National Union, Six Point Group—were of the same mind, although trade-union women continued to support protective laws.

The growth of anti-protectionist sentiments made the Tenth Congress of the International Woman Suffrage Alliance an exceptionally lively one. While the WP's application for membership was turned down, out of respect for the Alliance's longtime president, Carrie Chapman Catt, in other respects the party did very well. Viscountess Rhondda withdrew the application for membership of her Six Point Group in protest against the WP's rejection. Extremist sentiment was so strong that the Alliance's labor committee overwhelmingly endorsed a resolution condemning protective legislation, a resolution only narrowly defeated on the floor. The final resolution was still quite strong, declaring as it did "that any international system of differential legislation based on sex, in spite of any temporary advantage, may develop into a very real tyranny because of the segregation of women workers and by the imposition of fresh handicaps upon their capacity as wage earners." [3] The social feminists in the Alliance barely managed to retain command in the face of this remarkably strong surge of ultra sentiment.

The WP position was not without liberal support in America as well. Judge Ben Lindsey, whose enthusiasm for social welfare was never in question, supported the equal-rights amendment, believing that "what is known as special legislation for women is in fact not for women at all, but for children." [4]

2. "Mrs. Sidney Webb on Industrial Equality," *Equal Rights*, April 7, 1923, p. 61.

3. "Equal Rights Before the IWSA," *Equal Rights*, June 12, 1926, p. 141. For a hostile account of the same events, see Cornelia Stratton Parker, "feminists and Feminists," *Survey*, August 1, 1926, pp. 502–505.

4. "A Telegram from Judge Ben B. Lindsey," *Equal Rights*, March 8, 1924, p. 27.

The Minnesota Farmer-Labor party endorsed the amendment at its convention in March 1924 thanks to the efforts of Myrtle Cain, a Farmer-Labor member of the state legislature as well as past president of the Minnesota WTUL. Among the La Follette candidates for Congress in 1924 were a number of social feminists pledged to support the equal-rights amendment.

If the WP's program attracted the support of progressive men and women, how was the intense opposition it aroused to be explained? Why did Florence Kelley call it "insane" and Mary Anderson describe it as "a kind of hysterical feminism with a slogan for a program"?[5] The larger climate of opinion was partially responsible. Social feminists suffered so many reverses in the immediate postwar period that they were in no mood to countenance, or even try to understand, what seemed to them an open-and-shut case of treachery in the ranks. Demoralized by judicial decisions which appeared to undermine their whole position, they could not respond fairly to proposals that even marginally complicated their position. In fact, the two wings were not so far apart as reformers thought. The Woman's party believed in social welfare, but it reversed the priorities of social feminism by putting equality first and welfare second. Nevertheless, the postwar reaction had shaken both the confidence and judgment of orthodox feminists. During the war, when the Woman's party had posed a much graver threat to the woman movement, the regulars—whatever their private opinions—had maintained their public composure. But now, at a time when the extremists were in no position to threaten seriously the movement's basic interests, its leadership overreacted.

The Woman's party did earn much of the invective directed against it. Haughty and uncooperative under the best of circumstances, the party became truculent in the face of adversity. Mrs. Belmont and some other leaders were extraordinarily

5. Mary Anderson, *Woman at Work* (Minneapolis, 1951), p. 168.

tactless. The party's manifesto began, "Women today, although enfranchised, are still in every way subordinate to men" [6]—a statement which was not so much false as belittling of all that had been done for and by women in the recent past. The WP insisted that all grievances listed in the Seneca Falls declaration of 1848, save only votelessness, still obtained. This sweeping untruth irritated veteran suffragists who by the turn of the century had come to feel, as Susan B. Anthony put it, that "while women still suffer countless minor disadvantages, the fundamental rights have largely been secured except the suffrage." [7] Equally offensive was the WP's claim to be the original suffragists' only heir. "Other women's organizations work for many things and for women incidentally; the Woman's Party works to acquire for women equal rights and opportunities, and this, in sum and substance, is the feminist movement." [8]

The Woman's party sometimes appeared to have virtually a monopoly on the kind of woman condemned by the *American Mercury* as "a rabid feminist, one of the type that sees all history as a struggle between Woman, the beautiful builder, and Man, the eternal brute and wastrel." [9] It continually obscured the merits of its program by flippancies which could only offend the serious. *Equal Rights* concluded one editorial on the probable judicial reaction to its amendment by observing that however "the courts may interpret the amendment, we can rest serene in our reliance on the righteousness of the principle of Equal Right for men and women and not worry

6. Julia W. Johnsen, ed., *Special Legislation for Women* (New York, 1926), p. 99.

7. In her introduction to the *History of Woman Suffrage*, IV, xxvi. Among the 1848 charges that no longer obtained were the following: that women had no property rights, that the divorce laws were weighted against her, that she could not obtain a college education, that nearly all profitable employments were closed to her.

8. Lavinia Egan, "Keeping the Issue Straight," *Equal Rights*, July 28, 1923, p. 188.

9. Chester T. Crowell, "What Price Freedom?," *American Mercury*, VII (January 1926), 98.

as to the details of how it will work out. The establishing of a righteous principle will certainly bring only good results." [1] But, of course, the "details of how it will work out" were precisely what the controversy over the amendment was all about.

Extreme feminists, while superb agitators, were hopelessly bad politicians with no feel for the bargaining and compromises that make the democratic machine go. Agitation had played its part in the suffrage struggle, but it was accompanied by a careful attention to the political arts. The Woman's party was, in this sense, completely unbalanced. Even when it did attempt to play politics, its approach was absurdly unrealistic. By 1924 it had given up its old strategy of attempting to hold the party in power responsible, but it was drifting toward a new and equally implausible theory—that a sufficient number of congresswomen would guarantee passage of the equal-rights amendment. For a time the party planned to support all women candidates, regardless of their position on the amendment, and urged women to vote exclusively for members of their own sex. Eventually the WP decided to support only those women candidates who endorsed the amendment. Five did so, all of them La Follette or minority candidates. All of them, despite the WP's help, were beaten. As usual, the party had gotten much, largely hostile, publicity, but the effort was so great and failure so complete that it never tried this tactic again.

Perhaps the best example of the WP's unreflective militance under conditions demanding some politesse was its performance at the Women's Industrial Conference in 1926. This meeting was sponsored by the Women's Bureau, which invited the WP, with most social feminist organizations, to participate in a discussion on the needs of working women. Not only were the militants heavily outnumbered, as might be expected given their isolated position in the woman movement, but their amendment was not even given a place on the agenda. The

1. "Interpretation of the Equal Rights Amendment by the Courts," *Equal Rights*, March 1, 1924, p. 20.

party's response was to launch a premeditated assault on the conference. The extremists led off by staging a conference of their own two days before the regular conference, touting their amendment and condemning protective legislation for working women. Later they called on President Coolidge bearing the same message. But their principal achievement was forcing the conference to recognize them. The most picturesque account of how this was accomplished appeared in the NWTUL's bulletin:

> At the opening of the afternoon session the Woman's Party delegates launched an obviously planned campaign typical of their most militant suffrage days, and directed it at the Women's Bureau. . . . Gail Laughlin having got the floor, other Woman's Party delegates, responding almost like puppets on a string, one after another and four at a time obeyed the directions of Mabel Vernon, their appointed floor leader, to "get up and yell—you've got good lungs." The rest of the delegates, in self-defense, resorted to hisses and hand-clapping to drown out the din of the Woman's Party voices. The gavel of the chairman made no impression whatever, and the tumult, senseless, almost insane it seemed, raged for nearly an hour. Toward the end of it Anita Pollitzer, of the Woman's Party, made a swift excursion to the press table, where, according to one of the reporters, she asked, "Have we done enough to get into the papers? If we have, we'll stop." [2]

We need not accept this highly colored version to appreciate that the WP had won a victory of sorts. Gail Laughlin's motion to put the question on the agenda failed to pass, but an evening debate was arranged between representatives of the two sides, and the WP gained the delegates' attention for fifty

2. "The Second Women's Industrial Conference and the Assaults Upon It," *Life and Labor Bulletin,* IV (February 1926), 2. Essentially the same description appeared in Ethel M. Smith, "The Woman's Industrial Conference," *Woman Citizen,* February 1926, pp. 13–. More neutral were "The Woman's Industrial Conference," *Independent Woman,* March 1926, pp. 12–, and Ruby A. Black, "Equal Rights at the Conference," *Equal Rights,* January 30, 1926, pp. 402–403.

minutes of close argument. At the end of the conference Miss Laughlin moved that the Women's Bureau not take a position on the matter before a careful study. Her motion was of course defeated, but the conference did ask that such a study be undertaken. Thus the extremists focused attention upon themselves, forced the conference to recognize the existence of a contrary point of view on protective legislation, and secured a serious inquiry into the problem. Against this must be set the facts that the report when made was certain to endorse the social feminist position, and that the militants had confirmed their reputation as troublesome fanatics.[3]

The party was a prisoner of its own mystique. Its drive and élan came from the romantic feminists who saw its dramatic intransigence as the outward and visible sign of an inner grace. It could not behave like other women's organizations without losing its best members, yet it could not advance without becoming more like other women's organizations. The WP's dilemma was far from unique—it was hardly the first radical organization to retain its members' loyalty by fostering policies certain to inspire an overwhelming resistance—but in the unfamiliar context of the woman movement, with its cooperative tradition, the logic of the party's position is hard to grasp. Instead of focusing on the ideological and situational pressures that had brought the WP to such a pass, its enemies tended to explain away extremism as the product of mere self-interest. Florence Kelley repeatedly charged that ultra-feminism "finds substantial backing in two quarters, among powerfully organized exploiting employers of women and children, and also, among many women in the professions and the highest

3. The Women's Bureau published its report two years later, enabling the *Survey* to announce with satisfaction that "in view of the facts here soberly set down, nobody except a fanatic or a person with an ax to grind will any longer be able to urge the repeal, by blanket enactment, of all special protective laws for women on the ground that they seriously limit women's employment opportunities in general." Henry Raymond Mussey, "Law and a Living for Women," *Survey*, November 1, 1928, p. 195.

salaried ranges of business who desire complete absence of interference by the law." [4] Privately, the opposition was even more intemperate. Raymond Robins always believed that "the 'Equal Opportunity Women' . . . have been used to a finish by the intelligent members of the Property Minded interests of the country, and have been secretly financed by the Plunderbund." [5]

While there was some truth to the charge that business and professional women were especially critical of protective laws, the militant WP does not apear to have received any substantial funds from economic royalists. Many employers naturally sympathized with any group hostile to regulatory legislation, but the WP appreciated the deadly effect close relations with manufacturers might have on its position and was careful to avoid any identification with them. For the most part, social feminists and militants were the same kind of women. Both groups were largely middle class with a sprinkling of wealthy members and some working women—usually ex-working women. The chief difference between them was that most female union officers agreed with the AFL's official position favoring protective legislation for women.

One of the best evidences that the militants were not all capitalist dupes or self-seeking professionals was the strong support given the WP by Crystal Eastman. Miss Eastman was an ardent socialist, an effective and courageous peace worker, a feminist of long standing, and an authority on labor matters, having written a book on work accidents and the law for the *Pittsburgh Survey*. After the war she moved to England, but she continued her association with the WP, a relationship which dated back to 1913 when she had helped Alice Paul launch the Congressional Union. She contributed regularly to *Equal Rights* and to its opposite number in England, *Time and Tide*. In 1924 she campaigned for the WP's con-

4. In Johnsen, ed., *Special Legislation*, p. 87.
5. Raymond Robins to Mary Dreier, February 9, 1938, Robins Papers, State Historical Society of Wisconsin, Madison.

gressional candidates. Miss Eastman believed that special legislation did discriminate against working women, and that the
equal-rights amendment would force the extension of protective
laws to cover both male and female workers. Although sensitive to the fears of social feminists, she thought their cautious
approach would delay the coming of full equality for a very
long time, whereas the tactics of the WP seemed to her calculated to win a speedy victory. "The leaders of the Woman's
Party have that rare combination of zeal, fanaticism, shrewd-
ness, political judgment and executive ability that makes for
success," she told a reporter, adding that in ten years the whole
question would be resolved.[6]

Although Miss Eastman spent most of the decade abroad,
she remained in the equal-rights struggle, which became as
keen and divisive an issue in England as it was in the United
States. By 1927 English feminists had achieved roughly the
same disarray as their American sisters. Surveying the troubled
feminist scene, Miss Eastman concluded that in both countries
once the vote was won suffragists had reverted to type. Those
who were essentially reformers concentrated on the causes for
which they had thought the ballot necessary, while the "pure
feminists" continued to fight for complete equality. Crystal
Eastman was convinced that in the long run it was possible
to free women without damaging the welfare and protective
apparatus she had herself helped to erect. She deplored those
laws that protected women in ways enabling "powerful unions
to keep women out of trades for which they are manifestly
fit." [7] Miss Eastman's views made her virtually unemployable.
When she wrote Paul Kellogg, editor of the *Survey* and an old
friend, telling him that she was coming back to America and
asking his advice, he warned her that both her political radicalism and her ultra-feminist position would tell against her.

6. An interview with Elisabeth Smith in the *New York Telegram*,
October 31, 1924.
7. Crystal Eastman, "Equality or Protection," *Equal Rights*, March
15, 1924, p. 37.

Some months later, having apparently made inquiries among social feminists, Kellogg was certain that her WP connections would keep Miss Eastman from being employed by any agency concerned with women's problems.[8] This turned out to be the case. When she returned to America the only job she could find, despite her proven abilities as a social investigator, was a temporary position with the *Nation*—the only liberal journal at all sympathetic to militancy. Her tragic, all-too-early death took place soon afterward.

Few militants paid this high a price. But their acknowledged isolation from the mainstream of organized womanhood, while it evoked a certain high-spirited crisis psychology, inspired some reflection on the sources of their estrangement. Lady Rhondda, Britain's leading postwar militant, believed with Crystal Eastman that suffrage had exposed the differences between reformers and pure feminists.

> One may divide the women in the woman's movement into two groups: the Feminists and the reformers who are not in the least Feminists; who do not care tuppence about equality for itself. . . . Now, almost every women's organization recognizes that reformers are far more common than Feminists, that the passion to decide to look after your fellow-men, and especially women, to do good to them in your way is far more common than the desire to put into everyone's hand the power to look after themselves.[9]

While the heiress to a mining fortune could invoke sturdy self-reliance with fewer qualms than a social worker might, few could deny that social feminists were far more common than extremists.

Another reason why women became militants was their strong feeling that feminists had denied themselves for the sake of too many other causes. To social feminists this was a

8. Paul Kellogg to Crystal Eastman, January 20, 1927, and May 12, 1927, Survey Associates Papers, Social Welfare History Archives, University of Minnesota.

9. "Speech Made by Lady Rhondda at N.W.P. Luncheon in Paris, June 2," *Equal Rights*, June 19, 1926, p. 150.

source of pride and satisfaction. Two leading social workers pointed out before the war:

> American women would probably have got the vote long ago if they had followed the present English method of making suffrage a paramount issue first, last, and all the time. Instead of this Miss Jane Addams in Illinois, Mrs. Florence Kelley in New York, and a host of other ardent suffragists have labored with the greatest devotion and self-sacrifice to secure protective legislation for women and children.[1]

The militants believed that in doing so social feminists had made a very bad bargain. Suffrage was delayed for the sake of laws that not only handicapped women workers but were couched in humiliating terms. The majority opinion in *Muller v. Oregon*, sustaining maximum-hour laws for women, was based largely on their inferior capacities. The court ruled that

> . . . woman has always been dependent upon man. He established his control at the outset by superior physical strength, and this control in various forms, with diminishing intensity has continued to the present. As minors, though not to the same extent, she has been looked upon in the courts as needing especial care that her rights may be preserved. It is impossible to close one's eyes to the fact that she still looks to her brother and depends upon him. Even though all restrictions on political, personal, and contractual rights were taken away, and she stood as far as statutes are concerned, upon an absolutely equal plane with him, it would still be true that she is constituted that she will rest upon and look to him for protection; that her physical structure and a proper discharge of her maternal functions . . . justify legislation to protect her from the greed as well as the passion of man.[2]

From a militant point of view, protections granted in these indulgent terms were hardly worth having, even when they did

1. Edith Abbott and Sophonisba P. Breckinridge, "The Wage Earning Woman and the State" (Boston, n.d.), p. 9.
2. Johnsen, ed., *Special Legislation*, pp. 49–50.

not compromise the competitive position of working women—as ultras were convinced they did.

The WP thus demonstrated the complex interplay between the conscious and unconscious motivations of militant feminists. It was already becoming fashionable to dismiss outspoken feminists, and, indeed, ambitious women generally, as castrators and lesbians. The jargon of psychoanalysis gave the old charge that feminists were "unnatural" a more sophisticated appearance. Of course, it was also true. When society decrees that a woman's place is in the home, the woman who leaves it is by definition aberrant. Talented and ambitious women who were not neurotic to begin with could hardly escape becoming so, given the resistance they met everywhere, both before and after their formal emancipation. Nor, in a hostile society where things were largely managed by and for men, could they avoid becoming man-haters. Blacks hate whites, slaves hate their masters, and feminists hate men—although not necessarily all men all of the time. And hating men they could not help being drawn to other women, especially those who were partners in their struggle. Doubtlessly this involved lesbianism, whether physical or not, in the same way as soldiers, removed from the company of women and dependent on their comrades for life itself, sometimes become homosexual—if only for a time.[3]

Yet how far does this knowledge, inescapable in the age of Freud, take us? Is it really helpful to know that those who challenge well-established norms are abnormal? Perhaps, but it may be useful to recall the condition of women before judging their reaction to it. Feminists believed it was both unjust and irrational of society to offer women only one role to play, simply because they bore children, while men were given a thousand choices. The logic of this proposition is hard to dispute. Yet it is also true that when a position, however false or anti-social, becomes deeply entrenched it is even more irrational

3. This theme is strikingly illustrated in James Jones, *The Thin Red Line* (New York, 1962).

to contest it. Feminism had justice on its side, but psychology was against it. The real question to ask of any feminist, therefore, is not, "Was she deviant?"—how could she not be?—but rather, "Was her disorder functional?"

Carrie Chapman Catt, and even Anna Howard Shaw, had their emotions under control. For the most part their strongest feelings enabled them to accomplish what the average, well-adjusted woman would never have attempted. But with the militants this balance was tilted just enough so that their emotions got in the way of their performance. In this sense their more unusual personality traits were dysfunctional. Their anger extended to everyone who did not agree with them, male or female, feminist or not. They alienated people whose support was essential to their plans, which suggests that their role as the guerrilla fighters of the woman movement was more important to them than the equality it was supposed to secure. However irrational this might seem to be, it is characteristic of every social movement that operates under intense emotional pressures. Most of the great American causes, from anti-slavery to civil rights, have had their eccentrics. On this level the Woman's party tells us only that feminism was a great popular movement, and that like all such it encompassed a wide range of personalities and convictions.

More importantly, the WP illustrates another familiar aspect of American social history: that radicals often more correctly analyze a given situation than their adversaries, but that the very traits responsible for their insight prevent them from exploiting it successfully. The militants were quick to understand that the vote had not materially improved the condition of women. They realized that many discriminatory laws and customs remained, and that to overcome them would require the same crusading energies that had gone into the suffrage campaign. In the end, this knowledge did them little good because the passions that led them to demand a feminist revival kept them from effecting it. Their theatrical demonstrations and doctrinaire rigor antagonized most other women, leaving the Woman's party in a position of solitary grandeur. Perhaps it didn't matter really. The feminist tide was ebbing so fast in the 1920's that it probably could not have been reversed under the best of circumstances. All the same, militancy insured the defeat of those hopes it meant to advance.

This was not, of course, immediately apparent, and throughout the twenties the WP pursued an independent course. In 1928 it supported Herbert Hoover for President because, although he did not back the equal-rights amendment, he was at least vague on the matter of protective legislation, whereas Al Smith told the party: "I believe in equality, but I cannot nurse a baby"—a non sequitur that was perfectly clear to *Equal Rights.* "The entire feminist movement with its manifold victories is a challenge to this Governor Smith concept of woman. We can and do nurse babies and are proud of our role as life-givers. But we do not for that reason, as Governor Smith would make us, abrogate our equal right to determine our own destinies." [4] Hoover's election was not the party's only reason for thinking 1928 a good year. In February Doris Stevens capped an agitation among the members of the Pan-American Union by having herself made chairman of the Inter-American Commission on Women. In September she was arrested when she and other militants forced their unwelcome attentions upon the representatives of fifteen nations assembled in Paris to sign the Kellogg-Briand peace pact. The diplomats were understandably irritated at having their luncheon disrupted by the demand that they also sign an equal-rights treaty on which Miss Stevens' heart was set.

For all its symbolic triumphs, the WP had little to show at the decade's end for the nearly $800,000 it had spent since 1921. Wisconsin was still the only state with an equal-rights proviso in its constitution—the effects of which had been minimal. The party had been involved in preparing more than five hundred individual pieces of legislation across the country,

4. "Are Women a Sub-Human Species?," *Equal Rights*, October 13, 1928, p. 282.

but most of them were never made into law. It had alienated itself from the mainstream of organized womanhood and was soon to be confronted with an economic collapse that made its concentration on equal rights seem parochial if not downright cranky, and that was to dry up the supply of romantic youth which had given the organization its special force. From this point on the WP grew smaller, older, and poorer while the current of events moved ever more strongly against it.

At home, unemployment occasioned such widespread misery as to make pleas on behalf of women's special difficulties seem irrelevant, while the New Deal infused the flagging social welfare movement with new vigor. Militants experienced one shock after another. President Roosevelt personally appealed to the governors of thirteen states to sponsor minimumwage laws for women and children. The codes of the National Recovery Administration permitted employers to maintain wage differentials for men and women doing the same work. That Mr. Roosevelt also appointed the first woman cabinet member, the first woman director of the Mint, the first woman minister (to Denmark), and gave more scope to feminine talents than any previous President did not console the WP. After the Hundred Days Doris Stevens told her followers, "All about us we see attempts being made, buttressed by governmental authority, to throw women back into that morass of unlovely dependence from which they were just beginning to emerge." [5] But her call to battle went unheard. Too many terrible things, too many exciting things were happening. In the circumstances militant feminism could not retain its bold, rakish aura. Although a small band of tenacious partisans kept the party going (and it may yet see its amendment passed by Congress), the depression effectively decommissioned this

5. "Tribute to Alva Belmont," *Equal Rights*, July 15, 1933, p. 189. Miss Stevens was especially irritated by the President's economy bill which stipulated that when both husband and wife were employed by the government, one should be discharged, because that one invariably turned out to be the wife.

curious epilogue to women's fight for equality. With its eclipse after 1930, feminism as a distinctive force in the national life ceased to exist. By that time, the shape of women's lives in the postsuffrage era had already been determined, not by politics but by a combination of social and intellectual changes later to be condemned as the Feminine Mystique.

9
. . . .
toward the
feminine
mystique

*W*ell before the effects of woman suffrage were understood, it was generally admitted that the younger generation
had embraced a new code of sexual ethics. Few knew why this
had happened, or what it meant, but in the twenties most people agreed with V. F. Calverton that if the war had been a
plague, its first consequence had been not a Dance of Death
but a Dance of Priapus.

> In the flapper we find a vivid symbol of this change. This
> new girl, with all her emptiness of ideas and effusiveness
> of emotions, is a revolutionary outgrowth on the feminine
> scene. . . . Her speech, her dress, her gestures are outspoken
> evidences of the nature of her insurrection. The spread of
> her influence has been infectious.[1]

Although feminism was often blamed for this startling change,
most feminists were hardly less appalled by it than conservatives. They had, after all, labored to free women from sexual
bondage, not to promote eroticism. Indirectly, however, they
had helped to create a new type of woman by idealizing bravery
and independence, and by applauding the freedom of twen-
tieth-century girls from nineteenth-century inhibitions. But

1. Victor F. Calverton, *The Bankruptcy of Marriage* (New York,
1928), p. 12.

they never intended the modern girl to be free of as many inhibitions as she in fact became.

Of greater importance were the broad changes in American life that molded the younger generation. The working girl in her factory, store, or office, and even the college girl in her dormitory, were not subject to the same supervision and restraint as the farm girl or the home girl. It became impossible under these circumstances to maintain the elaborate protocol and careful restrictions of the Victorian age. Moreover, at the same time young women became freer in fact, they were urged by radical ideologists to go all the way and slip the bonds of conventional matrimony, too. Writers like Mona Caird, Ellen Key, and Havelock (and Edith) Ellis subjected domestic institutions to a withering fire, but unlike Charlotte Perkins Gilman, they called for a different kind of marriage rather than a different kind of home.[2] Especially after the turn of the century, contraceptives became more readily available, and literature grew progressively more candid and sexual. By the 1920's the battle for birth control had been won (although rearguard actions persist even today), and the mass media broadcast these glad tidings throughout the land. The technological advances that made lurid movies, pulp magazines, and the like readily available to all classes also solved the great problem of securing privacy, which had, until the advent of family automobiles, so gravely handicapped the art of juvenile love.

The war, the dress reform it accelerated, and the lovemaking it induced were less responsible for the new sexuality than was thought at the time. As Henry F. May has demonstrated, the old order was under attack on a great many fronts by 1912.[3] The innocent hedonism of sexual radicals like Floyd Dell was soon to be taken up by the mass media, and enthusiasms such as the dance craze of 1913–1915 prefigured that popular culture

2. For more details, see the chapters on the New Morality in my *Divorce in the Progressive Era* (New Haven, Conn., 1967).

3. Henry F. May, *The End of American Innocence* (New York, 1959).

which came of age in the twenties. Indeed, H. L. Mencken was talking about the "flapper" as early as 1915. Without the war these changes might have come more slowly, but not much. Skirts had been creeping up for years before the war offered an excuse, if any were needed, to reduce the amount of cloth in women's clothing.[4] The bobbed hair, short skirts, and bare arms of the 1920's were not more erotic than prewar styles in any case. Breasts and buttocks which, as old photographs show us, had once loomed so large, gave way to the limbs as points of interest. Fashion narrowed the gap between male and female styles. In the nineteenth century John Humphrey Noyes had pointed out, while defending the bloomer costume worn in his Oneida community, that sex distinctions were exaggerated by clothes that gave women a silhouette recognizable at great distances. By the twenties this was no longer true, and so in one sense the reform in women's dress reduced its obvious sexual purposes.

If the change in feminine sexuality was less profound than many feared, it was real enough, and startling enough, to warrant the attention it received. We know this because in the 1920's for the first time scientifically respectable attempts were made to study human sexuality. No one before Kinsey examined sexual behavior on a grand scale, but several works of value appeared which on a number of important points reinforced one another. In particular they demonstrated that the sexual lives of women born around the end of the century differed markedly from those born earlier. Dr. Gilbert Van Tassel Hamilton, a psychiatrist who studied two hundred mid-

4. Numerous changes took place after 1910 in women's dress and behavior. See James R. McGovern, "The American Woman's Pre–World War I Freedom in Manners and Morals," *Journal of American History*, LV (September 1968), 315–333. Remember, too, that while F. Scott Fitzgerald's prototypical Jazz Age novel, *This Side of Paradise*, was published in 1920, it was partially based on his college experiences which began in 1913. Fitzgerald himself ascribed the origins of the "petting party" to 1915. Arthur Mizener, *The Far Side of Paradise: A Biography of F. Scott Fitzgerald* (New York, 1960), p. 108.

dle-class married persons over a four-year period in the twenties, discovered that of fifty women born in 1890 or before, only seventeen had had either pre- or extra-marital intercourse, while of the fifty born after 1890 thirty had had illicit sex experience.[5]

A few years later Lewis M. Terman's vastly larger sample yielded a similar conclusion. Of 777 middle-class wives, he found that of those born before 1890, 86.5 per cent were virgin at marriage; of those born between 1890 and 1899, 74 per cent were virgin at marriage; between 1900 and 1909, 51 per cent; 1910 or later, 31.7 per cent.[6] Hamilton had noted a convergence in his subjects, with the women born after 1890 tending to have more premarital sexual experience and the men less. Terman secured different results. Virginity did not increase among his male subjects born after 1890, but a convergence was indeed taking place inasmuch as middle-class men were increasingly likely to have pre- or extra-marital affairs with women of their own class, rather than with the prostitutes who served the Victorian male's appetites. When the Kinsey group began interviewing their thousands of subjects they discovered that the lowest incidences of pre- and extra-marital coitus were among women born before 1900, with the rates for both sharply increasing in women born after that date.[7]

5. Gilbert V. T. Hamilton, *A Research in Marriage* (New York, 1929). Hamilton asked each of his subjects at least three hundred questions and recorded their answers verbatim. Although his subjects were few in number, he accumulated two million words of conversation from them; his study makes up in depth and perception what it lacks in breadth. Hamilton also demonstrated a humanity that has not often figured in such studies by allowing each subject "a reasonable number of clinical appointments for discussions of his case at the conclusion of his examinations. The majority of them sought such appointments, thereby giving me an opportunity to repay them, as best I could, for their kindness in acting as subjects of the research" (p. 17).

6. Lewis M. Terman, *Psychological Factors in Marital Happiness* (New York, 1938), p. 321.

7. Alfred C. Kinsey, *Sexual Behavior in the Human Female* (Philadelphia, 1953), pp. 422–423. All these studies are weighted toward white, college-educated, non-Catholic women under fifty living in the Northeast.

As important as these changes in sexual habits was the transformation in attitudes which accompanied them. After forty-seven years of practice a gynecologist observed that "in 1885 the doctor dealt with the woman who 'would rather die than be examined.' " "In the early nineties the patient instantly covered the least bare spot with the sheets; but in 1920 full exposure is taken for granted by the young." [8] In one area, however, no change seems to have taken place. Katherine Bement Davis secured 2,200 responses to a questionnaire mailed to women college graduates, which showed that half of the single women who had been out of college at least five years had had intense emotional relationships with other women, and that in slightly more than half of these cases overt physical practices were involved. Of her entire sample, about 20 per cent had had at least one homosexual experience at some point in their lives.[9] The Kinsey group also discovered that about one-fifth of its female sample had had homosexual experiences, but lesbianism was the only sexual activity that did not increase among women born after 1900. The rate of homosexuality was roughly constant for all age groups, which meant that thanks to the increase in heterosexual behavior after 1900, homosexuality became relatively less important among women.

We have already noted the sororital associations of women in the Victorian era that paved the way for their large-scale organization. One would expect these intimacies to slide over into physical expressions at times, especially among spinsters (a disproportionate number of whom were college women) and delicate wives moved by custom, training, and experience to regard heterosexual relations with distaste, if not fear and loathing. Predictably, Miss Davis found that the only professionals with a higher-than-average incidence of homosexuality were social workers. Well-educated, committed to difficult and

8. Robert Latou and Laura Bream, *A Thousand Marriages* (Baltimore, 1931), pp. 12–13.

9. Katherine B. Davis, *Factors in the Sex Life of 2,200 Women* (New York, 1929), pp. 277–278.

sometimes dangerous work, usually single by inclination or necessity, social workers needed the emotional and social supports that only their friends could give them. Although most social workers were not homosexuals, they were given to close emotional relationships which provided the warmth and security other women found in their families. Jane Addams was struck by the celibacy of her generation compared with that of young women in the twenties, but she seems not to have appreciated the extent to which her companions, like Ellen Starr and Mary Rozet Smith, were spouse surrogates who gave her the devotion and affection most women expect from their husbands. This is not to imply that Miss Addams was homosexual, but rather to suggest that as female homosexuality in the Victorian age was partially a response to middle-class women's social and sexual isolation, there was no reason for it to increase in the twentieth century as heterosexuality did, because the two originated in quite different needs. The relaxation of most sexual taboos might have been reasonably expected to increase the rate of female homosexuality. In fact, it seems not to have because the circumstances which bred the Victorian lesbian eased, while the normal channels of heterosexual activity ran wider and deeper than before and more readily handled the sexual runoff that would otherwise have found itself in stranger conduits.

Whatever the status of female homosexuality, it is quite clear—our current obsession with the "love generation" notwithstanding—that the 1920's, not the 1960's, was the time of the greatest movement toward permissive sexual behavior.[1] A generation ago Kinsey found that 80 per cent of women college students were virgin, and most recent studies suggest this figure has not been greatly reduced. Dr. Graham B. Blaine, Jr., chief of psychiatric services at Harvard, recently told the National

1. For a good analysis of this, see Erwin O. and Rita Seiden, "The Decline and Fall of the Double Standard," *Annals*, CCCLXXVI (March 1968), 7–17.

Association of College and University Chaplains that "there is no real proof of a sexual revolution on America's college campuses," because the real revolution took place almost half a century ago.[2] But there have been important developments on the love scene since 1929. A few proponents of the new morality after World War I believed that emancipated women "are the active agents in the field of sexual morality and men the passive, almost bewildered accessories to the overthrow of their long and firmly organized control of women's sexual conduct."[3] This had been the dream of prophets like Ellen Key, who in calling for motherhood without marriage deliciously reversed the Victorian stereotype by making woman the initiator and man the docile instrument of her desires. But in fact most women did not take their new freedom to such lengths. On the contrary, in a report to the American Medical Association in 1967, Dr. Robert Bell disclosed that only lately has the growth of married women's sexual pleasure caught up with their enlarged opportunities. A series of studies indicated that in the 1920's few married women seemed to want sexual relations more frequently than their husbands. By the 1940's wives more often expressed dissatisfaction with their husbands' sexual performance, while a recent study in Philadelphia discovered that one wife in four felt her husband did not meet her sexual needs. Thus only now has demand begun to outstrip supply in the sexual economy that came into being two generations ago.[4]

This development is, of course, fraught with anxious possibilities from a masculine point of view. In the nineteenth century it was believed that bestial husbands often literally violated the wives over whose bodies they exercised total power.

2. "Psychiatrist Denies Campus Sex Revolt," *New York Times*, May 14, 1967.

3. Beatrice M. Hinkel, "Women and the New Morality," *Nation*, November 19, 1924, p. 541.

4. Donald Janson, "Wives in Quest of 'The Colored Lights,'" *New York Times*, June 25, 1967.

But now the situation is reversed: wives, armored with the teachings of sexologists, analysts, and romantic novelists, are in a position to psychically violate their husbands by exposing their sexual inadequacies. Or, at the very least, having been led by a flood of polemical literature to expect more from sexual intercourse than the average husband is able to deliver, they are doomed to further disappointment. The sexualization of everyday life which has become so pronounced since the 1920's has never lived up to the expectations of its prophets. Apart from the abortions, divorces, and other such desperate acts that have taken place under the new dispensation, and because of them, there has been a continuous stream of dissatisfaction expressed by the very women who were supposed to be its principal beneficiaries. Sexual freedom had little effect on the life styles of most women.

A few proponents of the new morality continued to insist during the twenties that "today women are in a mighty struggle towards differentiation and individual direction. They have cast aside the maternal ideal as their goal and are demanding recognition as individuals first, and as wives and mothers second." [5] Still, most women went right on being wives and mothers. Even the modest proposals of Ben Lindsey gained little support. Judge Lindsey wanted to institutionalize the new pattern of youthful sexual experimentation by introducing a period of trial marriage, safeguarded by contraception, during which time either party could withdraw without penalty. As he pointed out, this was already happening, in a way, as the high divorce rate among childless young couples showed, but he thought it would do everyone good if the process could be formalized.[6] Allowing something to go on in practice and admitting it in principle were, as it turned out, quite different

5. Beatrice M. Hinkle, "Marriage in the New World," in H. A. Keyserling, ed., *The Book of Marriage* (New York, 1926), p. 232.

6. See his two books written with the help of Wainwright Evans, *The Revolt of Modern Youth* (New York, 1925), and *The Companionate Marriage* (New York, 1927).

things, and divorce as a substitute for marriage reform remained the preferred solution. Nor was the Woman's party, so daring in other respects, prepared to challenge the existing marital system. When Dr. Margaret Daniels, a professor of psychology at the Workers' College in Brookwood, New York, and a member of the WP, declared that marriage and the home were the sources of women's difficulties, and that society should be organized so "men and women could mate freely and be economically independent," the party was quick to deny her views and assert its dedication to finer homes and better marriages.[7]

Thus, while it was quite proper to acclaim Havelock Ellis as "the intellectual father of much of our present thought and social practice in the field of sex," and to applaud his having "shattered the Victorian conspiracy of silence, and brought the human body out again into a kind of Grecian sunlight," the actual effect of the new morality Ellis advocated was much slighter than his admirers supposed.[8] A survey of 252 middle-class girls between fifteen and twenty-six years of age, taken near the end of the twenties, showed that they did indeed entertain more advanced views than their mothers. Ninety-one per cent of them favored divorce as a solution to unhappy marriages. Eighty-one per cent expected to limit artificially the number of their children. Most thought extra-marital sex immoral or unwise, but only a third were prepared to say they would automatically disapprove of a friend's affair. On the other hand, few of them knew anything about the techniques of birth control, and most had learned the facts (fiction would probably be a more accurate term) of life from their peers. Most believed it wrong for married people to have social engagements with members of the opposite sex. Most striking of all, the majority expected marriage to be the principal event of

7. Margaret Whittemore, quoted in *Detroit Evening News*, June 8, 1925.

8. Leon Whipple, "He Broke the Victorian Silence," *Survey*, July 1, 1926, p. 433.

their lives. "Marriage has now become the entrance into a fuller and richer life; an opportunity for sharing joys and sorrows with a mate who will be not merely a protector or a provider but an all-round companion. . . . The modern union of man and woman is visioned as a perfect consummation of both personalities that will involve every phase of mutual living." [9]

.   .   .   .

Women who approved of this formula were sometimes disconcerted by the directness with which young women applied it. A traditional feminist who attempted to warn college girls that petting was the road to ruin, so far as their careers went, was told by them that few women of their acquaintance pursued careers after marriage, that college was the best place to find a husband, that petting was the easiest way to bring him to the altar, and that, therefore, they intended to pet.[1] Of course, the exchange of what Mrs. Gilman called "sex-capital for security" was hardly new, but the flapper initiated the transaction with a gusto her mother thought inappropriate. Nonetheless, while the flapper was more sexually knowledgeable and experienced than her mother, she was equally committed to monogamy and in some ways more romantic about marriage—she definitely expected more from sexual intercourse. In these ways she assured her future disappointment, especially since in the pursuit of domestic gratification she was inclined to give up the dream of economic independence that had appealed so strongly to earlier generations.

Although after 1920 the number of working women, and the percentage of married women who worked, continued to grow, the rate of increase declined. More important to fem-

9. Phyllis Blanchard and Carolyn Manasses, *New Girls for Old* (New York, 1937), p. 180.

1. Eleanor Wembridge, "Petting and the Campus," *Survey*, July 1, 1925, pp. 393–.

inism, however, was the relative loss of interest in careers, as opposed to mere jobs, for women. From 1910 to 1930 there was an 87 per cent increase of women in all professions as compared with an 80 per cent increase for men and women together. But most of this gain was in the first decade. From 1920 to 1930 the rate declined, the rate of increase for women being 40.6 per cent and for men 41.4 per cent. Most professions showed an absolute increase in the number of women, but by 1930 there were 6 per cent fewer women musicians and music teachers than in 1910, and 7 per cent fewer physicians.[2] During these same years the relative position of women in colleges began to decline. One Ph.D. in seven was awarded to women in 1920; by 1956 this had fallen to one in ten. While the percentage of all women who went to college increased, the proportion of women to men peaked out in 1920. In that year women made up 47.3 per cent of the enrollment of regular four-year colleges; by 1930 that figure had dropped to 43.7 per cent, and continued to fall for several decades. Since 1950 the proportion has increased but still falls far short of the 1920 high.[3] Moreover, those who secured advanced degrees have used them to less advantage. From 1900 to 1935 the percentage of women doctorates who practiced their profession for at least five years was over 75 per cent and compared favorably with the "use rate" of male doctorates. But from 1935 to 1960 the use rate of female doctorates declined to between 35 and 45 per cent—about half the male average.[4] By the same token, the percentage of women on college faculties reached a peak in the mid-twenties when over 30 per cent of the professoriat was made up of women, compared with 25 per cent in 1960. Although the twenties saw women rise to a peak of importance

2. Sophonisba P. Breckinridge, "The Activities of Women Outside the Home," in President's Research Committee on Social Trends, *Recent Social Trends in the United States* (New York, 1933), p. 723.

3. Mabel Newcomer, *A Century of Higher Education for American Women* (New York, 1959), p. 46.

4. Jean Rasmusen Droste's unpublished master's thesis, "Women at Wisconsin," (University of Wisconsin, 1967), p. 86.

in the colleges, women college teachers had already become disillusioned with their gains. A study of 844 women academicians at the end of the decade concluded:

> It would appear that the field of college teaching holds comparatively little promise for women. . . . Training represented in degrees and years of teaching experience contributes little to the advancement of women in the college teaching field. . . . The rank and file of the respondents seem to have developed a defensive attitude bordering on martyrdom, and complained, waxed bitter, and voiced resentment toward the conditions of which they were the victims.[5]

Little wonder that women students were not inspired to follow in their teachers' footsteps.

In truth, by the 1920's women had worked long enough in a sufficient number of fields so that, with the artificial distractions and excuses of the suffrage issue removed, it was possible for middle-class women to understand exactly what a career involved. Once the novelty of being business and professional women wore off, it was obvious that women were discriminated against in most fields, that their income rarely matched their qualifications, that there were ceilings above which they could not rise, and that the exhausting struggle to balance domestic against professional obligations, even when won, invariably limited their prospects. Gaining the vote had not altered women's economic status, and as this became apparent it was difficult to persuade girls that they had some kind of moral duty to engage in work, which had lost its glamour. The Blanchard survey of young women found that while 38 per cent hoped to have both a marriage and a career, only 13 per cent were willing to give up the former for the sake of the latter—though in a still un-Gilmanized society spinsterhood was the surest path to success. Observing that work was now

5. Marion O. Hawthorne, "Women as College Teachers," *Annals*, CXLIII (May 1929), 153.

obviously of secondary importance to young women, the study concluded:

> This change in attitude toward work for women is one of the first signs of disillusionment with the new freedom. Once the advocates of feminine independence may have believed that it would truly be the way to happiness. But the modern girl, who has seen the loneliness of older, unmarried friends, is beginning to discount the rewards from a material success that must be accomplished at the expense of love.[6]

Feminists were as puzzled by the new woman of the 1920's as everyone else. Having assumed that emancipated women would resemble themselves, it was difficult for them to see clearly what changes recent history had wrought in the young. One thoughtful ex-suffragist writing for the League of Women Voters, which was distressed by its difficulties in recruiting young members, pointed out that "the feministic movement isn't at all smart among the juniors. But it is interesting to observe that such rights as the old feministic movement has already won for the females of the species, the young accept as a matter of course. Especially when these rights mean personal and individual privileges." [7] Her informants used the World War, much as the young today use The Bomb, to discredit what they regarded as the moral pretensions of their elders and to demonstrate the uselessness of their advice. But at least one young woman struck closer to home when she bluntly observed that the previous generation was always putting off its own ambitions until after some job of reform had been done. "They were all going to return to their personal knitting after they had tidied up the world. Well look at the world! See how they tidied it up! Do you wonder that our generation says it will do its personal knitting first?" Indeed, this particular girl brought

6. Blanchard and Manasses, *New Girls for Old*, pp. 237–238.
7. Anne O'Hagan, "The Serious-minded Young—If Any," *The Woman's Journal* XIII (April 1928), 7.

a high degree of moral fervor to her amoral credo for she concluded:

> But we're not out to benefit society, to remold existence, to make industry safe for anyone except ourselves, to give any small peoples except ourselves their rights. We're not out for submerged tenths, we're not going to suffer over how the other half lives. We're out for Mary's job and Luella's art, and Barbara's independence and the rest of our individual careers and desires.[8]

In one sense this outburst was characteristic of the twenties, an era which insisted that the private vision took precedence over the social will, that art existed for its own sake and man (or woman) for his own sake too, that repudiated the grand causes and glorious rhetoric that seemed to have taken humanity to the brink of ruin. It was also an obvious consequence of the feminist hard line. After years of urging women to consider their own interests, feminists ought not to have been surprised when they started doing just that. The trouble was that while the educated, middle-class girl of the twenties was eager for self-fulfillment, she had almost no idea how to get it. Public service was boring, if not actually discredited; the careerist myth had been deflated; and the beliefs that had sustained previous generations of intelligent women no longer seemed adequate. What remained, as it turned out, was marriage and motherhood. The old cult of domesticity, struck down by Mrs. Gilman's wit and strength, scorned by generations of ambitious women, re-emerged in the 1920's as what Betty Friedan calls the Feminine Mystique and Andrew Sinclair the New Victorianism. Mrs. Friedan, in her lively and well-grounded polemic of the same title, dates the emergence of the feminine mystique at about the time her class graduated from college in 1942. Yet it is easy to demonstrate that the

8. *Ibid.*, p. 39.

ideas and prejudices she denounces were well established by the end of the twenties.

In essence, the feminine mystique prescribes a sexually determined role that all normal women must play. Under its terms women are at their best as wives and mothers, but these twin functions have been updated since the Victorian age by endowing them with a higher erotic charge and a greater cultural burden. Mrs. Friedan blames this on writers like Margaret Mead and Sigmund Freud who gave the mystique intellectual content and respectability, and on American industry which needs women more as consumers than producers. In order to encourage women to concentrate on their homes at a time when the old domestic pieties carried little weight, advertisers learned to key their message to the aspirations of emancipated women. The mass media wants the housewife, in the words of one advertising man, to see the home "as the expression of her creativeness. We help her think of the modern home as the artist's studio, the scientist's laboratory." [9] Women were encouraged to regard child-rearing and homemaking as complicated, lofty enterprises demanding a skilled mixture of exact science and aesthetic inspiration. This particular development was already well under way in the Progressive era. The study of home economics was stimulated by the woman movement, and Ellen Richards, who was an educator, a moderate feminist, and a founder of the Home Economics Association, was but one of many women who helped make the higher domesticity compatible with emancipation. It required little effort, therefore, in the postsuffrage era to convince bewildered young women that the home cleansed of its old imperfections by modern science, capitalism, and enlightened thought was a fit object for their attentions and a worthy challenge to their sharpened talents. The housewife was no longer a mere drudge, but a "woman administrator" or household manager, mobiliz-

9. Betty Friedan, *The Feminine Mystique* (New York, 1963), p. 217.

ing the resources of her family and her community in the interests of an efficient, democratic domestic life.[1] As most middle-class women continued to be full-time housewives, it was essential that their traditionalism be justified in modern terms, and the ethos of home economics was appropriate to the task.

This celebration of modern homemaking was, however, premature. A study released by the Department of Agriculture in 1929 showed that the average urban housewife worked fifty-one hours a week at domestic tasks, and the farm wife sixty-two hours a week. Even more striking was the discovery that almost all of this was sheer drudgery. The average housewife spent only two and a half hours purchasing, planning, and the like, while her children received only four and a half hours of her direct attention weekly. The great bulk of her time continued to be taken up with cooking, cleaning, and kindred work. In view of this, such books as Lillian Gilbreth's *The Homemaker and Her Job*, which urged women to use the techniques of scientific management in the home by making time-motion studies and drawing up process charts, had a grotesque flavor.[2] Nor did the General Federation's extensive campaign in the twenties to promote household appliances quite fill the bill. Middle-class women were already sold on the joys of mechanical housekeeping; the real problem was how to pay for it. Abraham Myerson, a non-Freudian psychiatrist, touched a deeper nerve when he argued at the outset of the New Era that neurasthenia was common among housewives precisely because the role was inadequate to their real needs.[3] Myerson pointed

1. Anne E. Richardson, "The Feminine Administrator in the Modern Home," *Annals*, CXLIII (May 1929), 21–32. The American Home Economics Association, whose views Miss Richardson expressed, was the most successful proponent of scientific homemaking and had little trouble clothing it in the business jargon of the 1920's, as this article shows.

2. Lillian Gilbreth, *The Homemaker and Her Job* (New York, 1927).

3. Abraham Myerson, *The Nervous Housewife* (Boston, 1920).

out that the average middle-class woman was still weighted down by household tasks that were inherently menial and boring, and that the housewife lacked stimulating contacts with other people. This relative isolation produced monotony, daydreaming, introspection—all conducive to neurosis. In early middle age, while their husbands were usually in a period of professional growth, housewives found their looks fading and their children slipping away.

But Myerson was rowing against the stream and his book had little effect on the popular rationalization of housewifery. Even more important (except to industry) than the glorification of homemaking was the great stream of literature that defined women anew in terms of their sexual capacities. Sigmund Freud was, as Mrs. Friedan points out, a main offender in this respect. Himself possessed of the Victorian male's characteristic chauvinism, he viewed women as passive, childlike creatures suffering from penis envy. His theories trickled down through layers of American popularizers to become firmly rooted in middle-class culture. Even without Freud the results would certainly have been the same. The radical sexual ideologists of the late nineteenth and early twentieth centuries wanted women to be freer and more responsive sexually, but few of them really desired women to act in society as men did. Grant Allen, who was considered a rabid feminist sympathizer, demonstrated this with special clarity in 1889. Speaking to the extreme English feminists—notably Mona Caird, whose attacks on marriage were widely circulated at the time—he admonished them for assaulting marriage itself, instead of the marital system which was truly at fault. He thought they wrongly idealized "the unsexed woman" when they ought to glory in their femininity. They wanted all women to be self-supporting, but in fact most women would have to continue as wives and mothers for the sake of the race. He attacked higher education for teaching women the same things as men when they needed to learn the things appropriate to their station. The goal of the woman movement, he insisted, ought not to be general celibacy and the independence of women, "but general marriage and the ample support of women by the men of the community." [4]

Allen was quite wrong in thinking that many feminists entertained extreme views on the marriage question, but his own conservative ideas about the function of women prefigured the accommodation that was to be made between marriage and the family on the one hand, and the new sexual morality on the other. Like most new moralists he favored a high degree of erotic license, but he also saw women's nature as essentially sexual, even as the Victorians did—although not in quite the same way. Thanks to him and other prophets of the new sexuality, it became possible in the 1920's to simultaneously take a radical stand on sex and a conservative one on women's social role. This development had been suggested in the writing of Ellen Key who, like Allen, urged a wider definition of feminine sexuality but did so in the context of an intense hostility to the male world. Her most radical proposal called for the regularization of unwed motherhood so as to give illegitimate children and their mothers equal social and economic status in the community. At first she was strenuously attacked as a moral corruptionist. But in time it became clear that if she was down on men in general and fathers in particular, she intended that women continue their traditional patterns of child-rearing and domesticity.

Miss Key wanted women to be the equal of men in principle, while in practice concentrating on the things that made them women, especially love and motherhood. As one of her popularizers put it, she believed that if women "descend from the peaks of enthusiasm to plod with men in the market-place of compromise, they will be only lesser men instead of full-statured women." [5] Full-statured women were easily recognized by their complete devotion to maternity. Thus, once the shock

4. Grant Allen, "Plain Words on the Woman Question," *Fortnightly Review*, XLVI (September 1889), 458.

5. Hanna Astrup Larsen, "Ellen Key: An Apostle of Life," *Forum*, XLVI (October 1911), 393. Miss Key's best-known work on this subject was *Love and Marriage* (New York, 1911).

of Ellen Key's castrating approach to sexual equality was absorbed (and most critics preferred to ignore this aspect of her thought), it was not difficult to stress, as did the *Nation* at her death, that she was "as conservative in her view of women's functions as Theodore Roosevelt—or H. L. Mencken." [6] Even the rebellious Margaret Sanger succumbed to this line of reasoning. In works like *Woman and the New Race* (1920), she called on women to seek power through their own sphere rather than man's, and to focus on their distinctively "feminine element." Thanks to the Ellen Keys, Margaret Sangers, Grant Allens, and Havelock Ellises, it was easy to be thoroughly liberated sexually while maintaining a social pattern and a domestic life much like one's unemancipated neighbors. It was possible, then, to fall away from the old feminist standards, to abandon paid employment and public service, and to lapse into familism while at the same time feeling thoroughly up to date. Femininity, not feminism, was increasingly the watchword, and by the end of the 1920's anxious moral conservatives could see that the fears they had once cherished that feminism would undermine monogamy were largely unfounded. By the end of the decade it was possible to say that women under thirty were uninterested "in fighting for causes hitherto in vogue," and unlikely to fight "for anything but the right not to fight and the privilege of just being women." [7]

The depression briefly reversed this trend. In the 1930's women renewed their interest in public affairs, but they did so as liberals, or radicals, or communists, or socialists, not as women. Although most of the old social feminist organizations survived the thirties, they did not represent the interests of active young women who, for the most part, were caught up in causes and movements that attracted young people of both sexes. In 1945 the trends initiated two decades earlier reasserted themselves. The privatization of women's lives and the

6. "Ellen Key and Feminism," *Nation*, May 5, 1926, p. 493.

7. Elizabeth Onativia, "Give Us Our Privileges," *Scribner's*, LXXXVII (June 1930), 594.

feminine mystique bloomed again more luxuriantly than ever. This development had been foreshadowed by Floyd Dell's *Love in the Machine Age*. Dell's first book, *Women as World Builders*, had supported the radical woman movement, and he had himself been a leading figure in the pre–World War I Greenwich Village bohemia which took pride in its sexual freedom. During the 1920's he became increasingly critical of radical feminism, and by the end of the decade his disenchantment was complete.

In working through a mass of historical and anthropological data that sustained his vision of the past, Dell arrived at some familiar conclusions. He spent considerable time showing that the radical feminist propositions were beside the point. Prewar feminists, he noted, believed that the home was an archaic survival which would be replaced by nurseries, apartment hotels, and the like, but the modern solution for industrial dislocations was mothers' pensions, which showed that "the actual tendency of social legislation in our machine age is toward the protection of the home, and the recognition of its services as practically irreplaceable so far as children are concerned." [8] So much for Charlotte Perkins Gilman. Others had advocated free love or its derivations as the working woman's answer to monogamy. Dell firmly declared that "useful wage-labor, enlivened by occasional secret sexual love-affairs, probably punctuated at intervals by abortions, without prospect of permanency and without hope of mutual responsible parenthood, is not a glorious or even satisfactory career for a young woman." [9] That is to say, the whole complex of radical feminist ideas like free love, free motherhood, free workers and such were simply "ideological overcompensations," which had developed to meet the needs of single women who needed to feel useful even though unmarried.

Dell's return to the old ideal of woman as wife and mother

8. Floyd Dell, *Love in the Machine Age: A Psychological Study of the Transition from Patriarchal Society* (New York, 1930), p. 120.
9. *Ibid.*, p. 142.

was of a piece with the general rejection of both the moderate feminist view of the working woman and the various radical feminist proposals for complete sexual and social emancipation. As we have seen, while social feminists had accommodated themselves to the Victorian dualism which explained men's and women's natures in entirely different terms, the essence of feminism had been its steady drive to narrow the gap between the sexes and to have women play masculine roles insofar as possible. The end of feminism came when people of advanced views conceded that women were unique after all, and thus needed to work out their special destiny. In practice this argument, once accepted, led to the conclusion that women's special destiny was sexual in character, and that their sexuality was largely geared to existing institutional arrangements. Childbirth itself, the most painful, taxing, and dangerous aspect of women's sexual role—that part of their lives about which Victorian women had the fewest illusions—came finally to be incorporated into the feminine mystique. Dora Russell, a woman of advanced views if ever there was one, signaled this development in her essay "The Poetry and Prose of Pregnancy." Thanks to medical progress and enlightened ideas, "not only may modern women actually enjoy pregnancy, stranger still they may even say that they enjoy it, without incurring the accusation of immodesty, or (I hope and believe) the scorn of short-sighted feminists who believe all preoccupation with child-bearing a return to slavery." In fact—and this was the key point when it came to enrolling educated women in the ranks of happy mothers—"vigorous women have even been known to find creative ecstasy in the pangs of birth." Although childbirth was painful and exhausting, "here as in few other practical callings is the thrill of the artist and scientist combined with the daily compulsion to work which all but the very superior being must still find necessary." [1]

1. Dora Russell, "The Poetry and Prose of Childbirth," in V. F. Calverton and S. D. Schmalhausen, eds., *Woman's Coming of Age* (New York, 1931), pp. 350–352.

The feminine mystique made such headway, then, because in the wake of a widespread postfeminist disillusionment it provided a platform on which all sorts of people could find common cause. Liberated men and women like Lady Russell and Floyd Dell could applaud the glories of marital sex and motherhood. Conservative anti-feminists, although dubious of the erotic flavoring by which the old roles were being recast in terms appropriate to the new sexual environment, could agree with most of what women were now being urged to do. After all, it was not much different from what had always been recommended to them. Both sides were united in finding that women's unique qualities demanded special treatment. Ellen Key had feared that women would merely duplicate men at the expense of their distinctive gifts, and so did anti-feminists in the 1920's. As one of them put it, "The so-called Modern Woman is only a tinsel mimic, a secondhand copy of man, and as such is neither a man nor a woman." [2] Even orthodox Marxists, like V. F. Calverton's dreary colleague Samuel D. Schmalhausen, warned that communist equality—about which Lenin had made so many fruitful observations—did not mean that women would be like men, flawed as they were by "masculine egotism," but would show the world something better than men had been able to offer.[3] With God, Freud, Marx, Nature, and a host of lesser authorities apparently agreed that woman's unique character was sexual and her destiny maternal, ambitious women eager to play out the old drama of emancipation had little working for them.

One of the few variations on this theme, which managed to be both conventional in implication and original in execution, was developed by H. L. Mencken in his entertaining book *In Defense of Women*. So far as he was concerned, women were indeed unique, but not by reason of their wombs, souls,

2. Ardeshir R. Wadia, *Ethics of Feminism* (New York, 1923), p. 100.
3. S. D. Schmalhausen, "The War of the Sexes," in Calverton and Schmalhausen, *Woman's Coming of Age*, pp. 260–297.

libidos, or whatever. They were different from, and superior to, men because their disabilities—less muscular strength and socially imposed limitations—forced them to be. Since women had found in marriage their only security, they had managed through the ages not only to marry in great numbers but to inspire man with the preposterous conviction that marriage was to his advantage. They did this by training each new generation of girls in the marital skills evolved through centuries of oppression.

> The virgin at adolescence is thus in the position of an unusually fortunate apprentice, for she is not only naturally gifted but also apprenticed to extraordinarily competent masters. While a boy at the same period is learning from his elders little more than a few empty technical tricks, a few paltry vices and a few degrading enthusiasms, his sister is under instruction in all those higher exercises of the wits that her special deficiencies make necessary to her security, and in particular in all those exercises which aim at overcoming the physical, and hence social and economic, superiority of man by attacks upon his inferior capacity for clear reasoning, uncorrupted by illusion and sentimentality.[4]

Thus, while American women had been abominably treated by boorish mankind, they had become of necessity a species of bright, clever, enterprising, and thoroughly admirable creatures. Mencken disapproved of their previous condition of servitude, but at the same time he had opposed woman suffrage and all such idiotic attempts to change it for fear of reducing women to the level of men. Now that emancipation had come, Mencken could see that even if women had lost something in the process, it was unlikely they would ever become as bombastic, muddleheaded, and disagreeable as the average man. They had never been good housekeepers, for they instinctively recognized it as a waste of time. If they could not improve their domestic performance, it could surely get no worse. Marriage might suffer a bit, for the woman who could

4. H. L. Mencken, *In Defense of Women* (Garden City, 1922), pp. 48–49.

freely choose her calling might well decide to compete economically with men.

> That is to say, she will address herself to acquiring that practical competence, that high talent for puerile and chiefly mechanical expertness, which now sets man ahead of her in the labor market of the world. To do this she will have to sacrifice some of her present intelligence; it is impossible to imagine a genuinely intelligent human being becoming a competent trial lawyer, or buttonhole worker, or newspaper sub-editor, or piano tuner, or house painter. Women, to get upon all fours with men in such stupid occupations, will have to commit a spiritual suicide, which is probably much further than they will ever actually go. Thus a shade of their present superiority to men will always remain, and with it a shade of their relative inefficiency, and so marriage will remain attractive to them, or at all events to most of them, and its overthrow will be prevented.[5]

Although no evidence suggests that any important number of women were impressed by Mencken's shrewd and good-natured defense of the old ways, his book reinforced the growing tendency among intelligent people to deprecate feminist gains and to view the traditional emphasis on femininity more favorably. Mencken's easy adjustment to the new conditions was, of course, unusual among anti-feminists. Few of them grasped the real meaning of women's changed status as Mencken did, and throughout the twenties the carping, ill-tempered, and obtuse complaints of unreconstructed antis obscured the feminine mystique's emergence.[6]

. . . . . .

The response of feminists, neo-feminists, ex-feminists, and nominal feminists to the feminine mystique was, like every-

5. *Ibid.*, pp. 193–194.
6. Typical examples of anti-feminism in the twenties are Louis E. Bisch, "Are Women Inferior or Are They Trying to Side-Track Nature?," *Century*, CXIII (April 1927), 674–681; George Jean Nathan, "Once There Was a Princess; Masculinization of Women," *American Mercury*, XIX (February 1930), 241; E. Eyre, "Woman's Influence in the Modern World," *Catholic World*, CXXV (June 1927), 387–391.

thing relating to the fading women's movement in the twenties, confused and uncertain. Mrs. Gilman, to cite only the most striking example, completely misunderstood the new sexuality. By her own admission she had been unable to adjust to the end of her age of reform, and after the war had devoted herself mainly to private matters. Disconcerted by the waning of progressivism and the collapse of feminism, she was outraged by what she called "the resurgence of phallic worship set before us in the solemn phraseology of psychoanalysis. This pitifully narrow and morbid philosophy presumes to discuss sex from observation of humanity only. It is confronted with our excessive development and assumes it to be normal." In fact, Mrs. Gilman continued, the human race was oversexed because of the long enslavement and exploitation of women by men. "The women of today, emerging from long repression, finding themselves overcharged with sex-energy and warmly urged to use it, in the justification of this highly masculine philosophy, seem quite largely to have adopted the theory that the purpose of sex is recreation." [7] Mrs. Gilman's personal difficulties, and her distrust of sexual relations, prevented her from seeing that while popular Freudianism and the new sex ethic were certainly masculine in character, their purpose was not to divert women from marriage and motherhood but to repopularize these institutions, to make them intellectually respectable, as it were.

Other attempts to explain what was going on tended to promote, rather than discourage, the subtle undermining of feminist morale. One analyst named Dorothy Bromley declared that " 'feminism' has become a term of opprobrium to the modern younger woman" because "the word suggests either the old school of fighting feminists who wore flat heels and had very little feminine charm, or the current species who antagonize men with their constant clamor about maiden names, equal rights, woman's place in the world and many

7. Charlotte Perkins Gilman, "Parasitism and Civilized Vice," in Calverton and Schmalhausen, *Woman's Coming of Age*, p. 125.

another cause." [8] She went on to describe a new feminism unblemished by these defects. Apart from demonstrating how the old anti-feminist stereotypes had been accepted by emancipated youth, what was most arresting about Miss Bromley's essay was the code she ascribed to new-style feminists. It was comprised of ten points and included the following precepts: The young woman wants a career as well as a home and children, but she will not make unreasonable sacrifices for its sake and consequently does not expect to achieve professional greatness. The young woman feels no loyalty to other women as such, for they are mainly vapid and silly, while their leaders are noisy, strident, and domineering. She believes free love is impractical rather than immoral. She wants home, children, an ideal marriage notable for its freedom and honesty, and self-fulfillment through interesting work. In short, the new feminist was no feminist at all but a privatized young woman who wanted to have her cake and eat it too. That so isolated a creature could be called feminist, of whatever style, demonstrated how meaningless the term was rapidly becoming.

One of the first large-scale efforts to evaluate the feminine scene after 1920 was Beatrice Hale's *What's Wrong with Our Girls?* Although Mrs. Hale was a declared feminist, and proved it by employing the movement's more shopworn phrases, her book clearly illustrated the retrograde nature of postwar feminist thought. She began by admitting that the old woman movement came to an end with the World War, and that the future of women depended upon a younger generation unaffected by the prevailing disillusionment. The main concern of feminists ought to be directed, therefore, at properly educating young women to their responsibilities. She recognized that her generation ought to approach this great task with some humility. "If we give our youth no better understanding of the world's real needs than we were given a generation since; if we train it to meet the shock of a disintegrating society no better than

8. Dorothy D. Bromley, "Feminist, New Style," *Harper's*, CLV (October 1927), 552.

we were trained, we may well despair." [9] But Mrs. Hale, cheerful feminist that she was, did not despair, for she knew that the women of the world were bound together by The Mother Force, which properly understood held the key to feminine success.

The first thing to be done, she felt, was to distinguish between the two modern schools of feminist thought. One tendency, which she called the School of Self-Expression, argued that the woman movement was no longer needed: nothing remained but individual achievement in competition with men. The hearts of its members swelled with pride whenever a woman broke into a closed occupation or swam across a large body of water. They were, of course, in the wrong. Right thinkers were not interested in competition with men but in the development of women as a whole. "Those of us who belong to the second group would rather enlarge upon the difference than the likeness of men and women." [1] This group understood that "the whole field of struggle and competition is essentially masculine, the field of growth and cooperation essentially feminine." Yet men had not done such a perfect job of organizing the world that they could do without the help of "women's complementary instincts." At the time Mrs. Hale wrote, these instincts were best employed in training young women in a "wider spiritual maternity." The balance of her argument was devoted to the means by which this could be accomplished (religion, sensible clothing, a spartan physical regime, vocational instruction, education for maternity). Of course, this was nothing more than social feminism warmed over, with its specific reforms eliminated, its feminist component reduced to the vanishing point, and with special emphasis placed on the fuzziest, most sentimental banalities of the old women movement.

9. Beatrice Forbes-Robertson Hale, *What's Wrong with Our Girls: The Environment, Training and Future of American Girls* (New York, 1923), p. xvii.
1. *Ibid.*, p. x.

Despite the tide of opinion, the feminine mystique did not go unchallenged, nor women's real problems undefined, during the twenties. The old attack on domesticity was modified and brought up to date by Lorine Pruette, Ph.D., who if she could not fill Mrs. Gilman's boots at least managed to walk in her footsteps. Dr. Pruette's major contribution to the postwar discussion was a book, *Women and Leisure*, built around a survey of teen-age aspirations.[2] Her thesis, dressed up in an elaborate sociological treatise, was simply that women needed more outside work. Mrs. Gilman had already said this about as well as anyone could, so Dr. Pruette apparently hoped to advance the argument by filling in the factual details that were beneath Mrs. Gilman's notice. Thus she spent much space proving the obvious before addressing the problem of how girls viewed their roles. Her questionnaire was filled out by 347 girls in New York City and Chattanooga. While confusing, repetitious, and often irrelevant, it did confirm certain feminist fears. Although presented with a list of 238 specific careers, 149 girls wanted none, and most said that if forced to choose they would put marriage ahead of a career. These were perfectly conventional sentiments, of course, but other questions were more illustrative of the true state of affairs. Of those who aspired to careers, 46 per cent hoped for artistic occupations. Only fifteen listed social work as their first choice, and only thirty-five expected to be teachers. When the girls were asked to name four heroines from either history or fiction, Jane Addams was cited once, Frances Willard twice, and Madame Curie three times, whereas Cleopatra got forty votes and Joan of Arc a staggering one hundred. In short, few of these young girls had realistic goals. They spurned occupations like teaching and social work, in which most professional women were actually employed, in favor of the arts, where few women could hope to succeed. Their heroines were romantic and

2. Lorine Pruette, *Women and Leisure* (New York, 1924).

sentimental figures, quite unlike the great women of their own time.

Dr. Pruette continued to worry about the problems thus exposed. In an article for the *Annals'* important study of American women in 1929, she declared boldly: "The worst thing that can be said for the American home is that it ruins so many of its members. It is a disheartening and disillusioning business to survey the middle-aged married women of the country. They have been permanently damaged as persons by the disintegrating influences of the modern home and family life." And again: "It is only the rare woman who can pass without deterioration through many years of uninterrupted domesticity." [3] What could be done? The only thing Dr. Pruette could think of was to try to create more part-time jobs which mothers could fill. This marked something of a retreat from the earlier feminist emphasis on achievement. Obviously, part-time work was not going to produce a high level of feminine accomplishment. Her argument was practical in that it could be effected within the contemporary socio-economic context. Unfortunately, while it was practical it was not realistic, as Dr. Pruette herself suspected. It was possible to create a myriad of part-time jobs, but it was not likely to happen because large employers had nothing to gain by expanding their work force with no corresponding increase in productivity. As long as hiring practices were dictated by narrowly economic rather than largely social motives, women could expect little outside help.

A more astute and successful effort to accommodate Gilmanism to the New Era while avoiding the difficulties posed by part-time work was Alice Beal Parsons' *Woman's Dilemma*. Mrs. Parsons was thoroughly alert to the regressive implications of the argument for feminine uniqueness. She saw that Mrs. Gilman had failed to grasp the ways in which uniqueness could

3. Lorine Pruette, "The Married Woman and the Part-Time Job," *Annals*, CXLIII (May 1929), 302.

be interpreted to support the New Victorianism, and she was especially conscious of the threatening implications of teachings like those advanced by Ellen Key and Havelock Ellis. She pointed out that if it was once believed that woman's place was determined by her intrinsic limitations, the New Moralists achieved the same effect by declaring that it was woman's glorious destiny to exploit fully her biological capacities. In either case women ended up in the home, but the more refined, sexually adventurous and seemingly modern teachings of Ellis and company were harder to combat than the old pejorative arguments. Ellis thought women's happiness and well-being depended on a satisfactory sex life, so other forms of feminine emancipation appeared relatively unimportant to him. This seemed unfair to Mrs. Parsons because modern psychologists, while insisting that men needed a healthy sex life, did not carry this to the point of suggesting it as a substitute for economic and social independence. Mrs. Parsons believed, on the other hand, that the capacity of women for important and productive work was much the same as men's, but that historically childbearing and child-rearing had been such exhausting and time-consuming enterprises that women had fallen behind men and were only just beginning to catch up.

A large part of her book was made up of material demonstrating that women were capable of functioning in the world on an equal basis with men, and refuting contentions like Ellis' that women were biologically more childlike than men and therefore constitutionally ordained to rear as well as bear children. It was naturally flattering for women to have their special faculties glorified in the manner of an Ellis or an Ellen Key—even though their writings offered a scientific basis for discrimination. This fallacy Mrs. Parsons proposed to refute chapter and verse. While in the 1920's when medical science had not gone so far as it has today in proving that—save only in muscular power—the female organism in many ways is superior to the male, it was not hard to show that whatever was biologically unique about women hardly disqualified them for serious employment.[4] The real difficulty was in attacking the social, intellectual, and economic conditions that kept women in the home. Thus Mrs. Parsons found herself covering the old familiar ground that had been so well plowed by generations of feminist ideologists.[5]

It would be wrong to conclude from this that the critical tradition exemplified by Charlotte Perkins Gilman had gone bankrupt, or that Mrs. Parsons was simply parroting old formulas. Her refutation of the emerging feminine mystique was perceptive, and her suggestions mainly to the point. The trouble with Mrs. Parsons and the other neo-Gilmanites of this period was not merely that they were following a well-blazed trail, but that an audience for their message no longer existed. Mrs. Gilman had not only been more radical and pungent than they, but her principal books were written at a time when the prospects for effective change seemed very good. It was reasonable to suppose in 1900 that the truth would make women free. A quarter of a century later it was evident that middle-class women were singing quite different tunes, and that feminists who wanted their attention would have to start writing another kind of song. Yet the difficulties involved were so formidable, and the chances of undermining the higher domesticity so slight, that the quality of feminist thought probably made little difference in the long run.

The hopelessness of the situation from a feminist point of view was probably best demonstrated by Suzanne La Follette, the most original feminist writer of the 1920's, and the only one whose work compared favorably with Mrs. Gilman's. Although her book, *Concerning Women*, was eccentric in places, it reflected a deep understanding of the feminine condition and an intellectual adventurousness that was rare among

4. The physical and intellectual differences between the sexes are far more numerous than feminists used to think, but the significance of these differences is still not clear. See Eleanor E. Maccoby, ed., *The Development of Sex Differences* (Stanford, 1966).

5. Alice Beal Parsons, *Woman's Dilemma* (New York, 1926), p. 146.

feminist writers. She was, moreover, infinitely more radical than her peers, a kind of throwback to the era of Frances Wright and the young Elizabeth Cady Stanton. Her radicalism was not confined to the woman question, nor was it particularly Marxist. Instead she combined an anarchical distrust of government with a hostility to monopoly and unregulated enterprise, and a belief in socialized solutions to social problems. She was, in short, what might be called an anarcho-single-taxer of a type more common in the nineteenth than the twentieth century. Her basic proposition was the unexceptional thesis that woman's inferiority was rooted in an economic system that treated her as a form of property. Marriage was the principal means by which this was accomplished. It operated, particularly for the poor, to keep women chained to the home and men chained to their jobs.

After beginning with a typical feminist complaint, Miss La Follette moved quickly to an advanced position by attacking the institution of marriage, and then beyond it to challenge the most sacred tenet of social feminism, that emancipation was needed to improve motherhood. Liberty, she insisted, was its own justification. To say that women needed to be freed for motherhood was rather as if the colonists had told King George they required independence in order to become better husbands and fathers. That whole argument reflected the traditional assumption that marriage and motherhood are woman's special province, and that the individual exists for the sake of the species. The old feminist movement had also erred, she believed, in placing so much weight on eliminating legal and political restrictions. This was a desirable first step, but it led only to the situation where "women would enjoy precisely that degree of freedom which men now enjoy—that is to say, very little." [6] By a special irony of history, women had struggled to gain political rights in a period when they were worth less than at any time since the eighteenth century. In Europe,

6. Suzanne La Follette, *Concerning Women* (New York, 1926), p. 266.

parliamentary government was breaking down altogether, and in the United States it could hardly survive given "the cynical disregard of both law and principle which government in America regularly exhibits."

While the movement was struggling for legal rights of little value, it largely ignored the humiliating effects of marriage laws and actively promoted protective legislation which handicapped working women. In a fit of misplaced enthusiasm, feminists had promoted laws that enabled employers to discriminate against women with impunity and reduce their freedom to secure congenial work. Protective legislation miscarried because "the tendency of modern welfare-legislation is to make a complete sacrifice of individual rights not to the rights but to the hypothetical interests of others, and for every individual who happens to benefit by the sacrifice, there is another who suffers by it." [7] Thus women workers continued to earn less money than their male counterparts, and when single to contribute more to the support of their families. In this manner the age-old custom of sacrificing women for the supposed good of society had been adjusted to industrial conditions.

In the largest sense, Miss La Follette wrote, although women suffered from peculiar injustices, the core of their problem was the inequitable economic system which pressed down on most Americans, male and female alike. Repealing the laws that purported to defend working women, or at least making them apply equally to both sexes, and making marriage a genuinely free relationship would help, but real freedom awaited a wholesale reconstruction of the economic order. This could most easily be accomplished by dissolving "the private monopoly of natural resources." Marxists, she thought, were wrong in wanting to transfer private property to the state, because that would simply create another and more odious monopoly. Miss La Follette called herself a physiocrat, but her proposal was really an expanded version of Henry George's

7. *Ibid.*, p. 177.

single tax. She believed natural resources were the source of all wealth, and if everyone had equal access to them poverty and inequity would be abolished, crime eliminated, ignorance banished, and vice destroyed.

On one level Miss La Follette's thesis was absurd, her ignorance of economics astounding, and her grasp of history and sociology shaky in the extreme. Yet she did face up to certain unhappy realities which most feminists preferred to avoid. She understood, as hard-core feminists did not, that the woman problem was, for all women's unique disadvantages, a part of the larger social question. She also saw, as few social feminists did, that a little patching up here and there was not enough to make the system workable, much less admirable. The United States, she declared, was engaged in a vast experiment

> . . . to prove that human beings can live a generally satisfactory life without the exercise of the reflective intellect, without ideas, without ideals, and in a proper use of the word without emotions, so long as they may see the prospect of a moderate well-being, and so long as they are kept powerfully under the spell of a great number of mechanical devices for the enhancement of comfort, convenience and pleasure.[8]

In pursuit of this ignoble vision, America had joined with other Western governments in "carrying on imperialist activities abroad and persecuting dissenters at home."

If this were the case (and of course it was), if even the modest plans of social feminists had gone awry, what reason had Miss La Follette to think that her own more ambitious hopes had a chance? Surprisingly enough, there were quite a few hopeful signs even before the Great Depression. The masses had become cynical about government thanks to Prohibition and the scandals of the Harding administration. The old faith in political liberalism had been destroyed by its misconduct during the war, when it showed itself to be little more

8. *Ibid.*, p. 270.

than Toryism plus hypocrisy. The growth of a farm bloc in Congress based solely on economic interest pointed the way to an effective coalition of the disadvantaged while undermining the meaningless party system. The cooperative movement was also gaining ground. Feminists ought, therefore, to merge themselves with this groundswell, she argued, so that when the struggle for economic freedom began they would be in a position to make women an important part of the new order. In many respects this was a sound analysis. She had identified some of the elements that would go into the Roosevelt coalition—wets, farmers, the underemployed. Where she erred was in thinking that liberalism had been permanently discredited by the war. She thought the coming struggle would see liberals pitted against true advocates of social and economic justice, whereas in actuality the contest was to be between liberalism and a motley alliance of bigots, reactionaries, businessmen, unreconstructed Progressives, isolationists, and what all.

Partly because utopian eccentricity was out of fashion, mostly as a result of the feminist moral collapse and the emerging feminine mystique, Miss La Follette never got the attention she deserved. She had freed herself from the conventional wisdom of the woman movement and established a new point of departure from which, if they wished, feminists could begin to rethink their position. Unfortunately, feminists were in no shape to reconsider their strategy at this late date. By the end of the decade it was apparent to thoughtful women that their movement's difficulties were not simply local and temporary, as had been thought in the immediate postwar period, but part of a fundamental malaise. Even this understanding was not enough to provoke the radical changes that alone could make feminism relevant to the coming generation. One of the most astute of the older feminists in these years was Ethel Puffer Howes, who argued in 1929 that the woman movement was facing in two directions, and that a choice between them must soon be made. One choice would be to continue the traditional emphasis on work. The problem here was that relatively few educated women continued their careers after marriage, and working women did so only when necessity forced them. Neither educators nor those public agencies like the Women's Bureau that were supposed to concern themselves with such problems would admit this. Vocational counseling and training continued in the old ways, even though women continued to lose faith in their prospects and possibilities.

At the same time another point of view was gaining ground which threatened to eliminate women's public roles altogether. This was the logical consequence of the argument advanced by Ellen Key and Havelock Ellis that women should concentrate on developing their own sphere of life. As an immediate effect of this, educators were more inclined to "deprecate all systematic training except that for family living and to identify this with 'training for life.'" [9] Dr. Howes was hopeful this tendency would be short-lived, for if it continued the average woman would find her vocation as mother ending "just at that time when the woman herself is at the zenith of her powers. Result, either a frantic attempt to hold on to her vocation (with the 'fixation' and 'mother-in-law' evils of which modern mental hygiene has too fully shown us); or, resolute self-withdrawal, with the torture of twenty or more remaining years of futilities, social and cultural." "No," she continued, "the romantic program is a glorious picture of the possibilities of the wife and mother *relation,* but is not the solution of the ultimate destiny of the woman who has a mind, talents, energy, and a long life to be lived in a world of creative doings." [1]

Dr. Puffer appreciated that the woman movement's dilemma was largely of its own making. Since Mary Wollstonecraft, it had thought in terms of removing woman's disabilities but had given little attention to the necessity for a positive set of goals. Without clear objectives there could be no permanent

9. Ethel Puffer Howes, "The Meaning of Progress in the Woman Movement," *Annals,* CXLIII (May 1929), 17.
1. *Ibid.,* pp. 18–19.

achievements. The basic problem, then, was that "the 'woman question' has never had an answer." For herself, Dr. Puffer answered the question in much the same way as Mrs. Gilman. "The man demands of life that he have love, home, fatherhood and the special work which his particular brain combination fits. Shall the woman demand less?" Their emancipation had been delayed because "women as a class have been too humble, too timid, to claim an ultimate principle of life for themselves, what every man has without asking"—that is to say, the integration of work and life. But Dr. Puffer went Mrs. Gilman and similar ideologists one better, for she not only defined the problem but provided the means for its solution. At Smith College, where she had graduated in 1891, she presided over the Institute for the Coordination of Women's Interests, which attempted to apply Gilmanesque solutions to the career-versus-marriage conflict. It sponsored programs like a cooperative nursery to show how women could free themselves for outside work, and produced instructive pamphlets with titles like "Cooked Food Supply Experiments in America" and "A Community Home Assistants' Experiment."

Gilmanism had never been carried to such lengths before, but to genuine radicals like Suzanne La Follette the Smith Institute was itself a subtle capitulation to male prejudice. Noting that President Neilson of Smith described the institute as an effort to reconcile marriage with women's educational interests, Miss La Follette remarked: "Here again is the tacit assumption that marriage is the special concern of woman, and one whose claims must take precedence over her other interests . . . that marriage and motherhood constitute her normal life, and her other interests something extra-normal." [2] No, this was just another way of making woman's reproductive capacity an excuse for confining her in the home (or trapping her in a part-time job with no future, since the institute

2. La Follette, *Concerning Women*, p. 195.

expected that its suggestions would be most helpful to part-time workers). The real answer was public day nurseries, free marriage, and the equal sharing of domestic work between husbands and wives. No one would expect a radical like Miss La Follette to be satisfied with half a loaf, but, despite her vision, the mass of educated married women no longer believed that paid employment was worth the trouble. Why should they exhaust themselves with complicated alternatives to their usual routines when it was so easy to stay at home and cultivate that higher domesticity which, it was now understood, had been the real purpose of the woman movement all along?

The depression and the Second World War only aggravated these feelings. The insecurities of life in the thirties and early forties made a stable, traditional family life seem all the more desirable. Women continued to work in large numbers, especially during the war, but with the advent of peace they plunged into domesticity with unprecedented vigor and intensity, aided by well-deserved veterans' benefits that—with a general prosperity—made early marriage and large families more feasible than at almost any time since the eighteenth century. The long trend toward later marriages and fewer children was sharply reversed, for a time, and the great baby boom got under way. In one sense this was a normal response to the long period of deprivation that began in the depression and lasted through the war. After fifteen years of hardship and denial, during which people were compelled to put off getting married and having children for one reason or another, it was natural that when conditions permitted they would make up for lost time. Nor was it surprising that in an unsettled and dangerous world, where to defer a pleasure might mean losing it altogether when the balloon next went up, there was little disposition to approach marriage with the caution of previous generations. Even so, the postwar orgy of domesticity was of such dimensions and went on for so long as to suggest that something else was at work. That something else was probably the feminine mystique which, having sprouted during the twenties and been nourished by depression and war, was now in full flower.

.   .   .   .

Professor Joseph Folsom, a sociologist of the family whose position on the faculty of an Eastern woman's college put him in close touch with the trend-setting element of the female population, saw the wave coming before it actually broke. Writing under the influence of that short-lived democratic enthusiasm born of World War II, he was still troubled by tendencies which threatened the future of sexual egalitarianism. Not only were young women increasingly disenchanted with outside work and more attracted to domestic life, but a flood of polemical literature was urging them homeward. In fiction the old duality between marriage and career was manifesting itself again, with marriage as the approved choice. "The ominous feature is that this neo-familism, cultivated by the schools and colleges, can be used through upper-class prestige and adroit publicity to bring into disrepute the movement for equal opportunity and thus prepare the way for a resubjection of women."[3] This, of course, is exactly what happened. Women did not lose the political and legal rights so painfully acquired, but in a relative sense the postwar era saw middle-class women abandon the attitudes and aspirations that had marked their century of struggle and accept a more limited definition of their social roles than anyone would have thought possible fifty years earlier.

One could understand the conservative ideology accelerating this retreat without being able to affect it in the slightest. Thus, Viola Klein's astute dissection of the psychoanalytic and literary components of the feminine mystique was over-

3. Joseph Kirk Folsom, *The Family and Democratic Society* (New York, 1943), p. 623.

shadowed by the far more popular writings of people like Ferdinand Lundberg and Marynia F. Farnham. Dr. Klein's *The Feminine Character: History of an Ideology* grew out of her dissertation for London University's sociology department and was first published in 1946. The book evaluated the chief contributions to the modern definition of femininity with an eye toward determining both their intrinsic value and general effects. Dr. Klein was able to show that the feminist critics of the twenties had been entirely justified in distrusting Freud and the new moralists like Havelock Ellis. Ellis had a lively sense of justice and believed in the equality—more properly the "equivalence"—of the sexes, but his mystical approach to feminine nature had unfortunate consequences. Since he saw all life as made up of opposites, contradictions, and polarities, he naturally believed the sexes to be profoundly unlike, although not unequal. To Ellis, "the question of the superiority of either sex cannot arise, just as it does not arise between mind and matter, or hydrogen and oxygen. However different they may be, the two sexes are designed for each other and complementary to each other." [4] But in fact Ellis' analysis did point back toward a prefeminist view of woman's nature and was compatible in most respects with woman's traditional role. He saw women as more plastic than men, more irritable, more practical, given to muddling through rather than thinking through situations, and closer to nature. These attributes, plus their childlike qualities which made them pre-eminently suited for child-rearing, were all consistent with the domestic vision of his day, even though more flattering to women than the usual expositions.

In recent years, however, Freud had come to be the chief authority on woman's nature. Ironically, his ideas, which had done more than any other man's to break down Victorian morality, had been themselves so heavily colored by Victorian prejudice as to perpetuate many of the period's most unfor-

4. Viola Klein, *The Feminine Character: History of an Ideology* (New York, 1949), p. 45.

tunate concepts. According to Freud, woman's central feature is that she has no penis. Man develops the social virtues because his super-ego is strengthened by overcoming the Oedipal complex through fear of castration. Woman has no such fear, consequently her growth is arrested. She never entirely frees herself of the Oedipal complex and thus is prone to envy, jealousy, social injustice, narcissism, and has a weaker capacity for sublimation—in other words, cultural activity—than man. Penis envy is the crucial aspect of her emotional life. Hence woman's sense of inferiority is constitutional and not acquired. She is inferior to man in most respects, and her best chance for healthy living is to accept the procreative function as her principal reason for being and leave the big, complex world of affairs to the men who are so well-suited to manage it.[5] Of course, it was possible to stand Freud's thesis on its head and argue, as Karen Horney did, that man's creative achievements were produced by his inability to bear children, that he was driven to do in the alien world what woman does effortlessly and naturally at home. It was possible to look at the matter in this way, but by the 1940's few people did.[6]

From a feminist standpoint, the worst effects of psychoanalytic theory were not Freud's own writings, bad as they were, but the work of his popularizers who carried Freud's ideas to absurd lengths. The chief offender in this regard, according to Betty Friedan, was Lundberg and Farnham's *Modern Woman: The Lost Sex*, which first appeared during World War II but reached its largest audience later in a paperback edition. At the very moment when Viola Klein and Karen Horney were exposing the masculine bias of orthodox psychoanalytic thought, American women were overwhelmed by a flood of literature bringing them Freud's ideas secondhand in

5. For a superb critique along the same lines, see Raymond V. Sampson, *The Psychology of Power* (New York, 1966).
6. Dr. Horney's views on the subject are conveniently available in *Feminine Psychology* (New York, 1967). See especially her essay "The Dread of Women," pp. 133–146.

books like *Modern Woman: The Lost Sex,* and thirdhand in novels, short stories, and women's magazines that popularized Freud's popularizers. Lundberg and Farnham's thesis was marvelously simple: practically everyone in the modern world was neurotic and miserable, but women were especially so because the industrial revolution had destroyed their essential functions. By breaking up the family and putting most of its members in outside institutions like schools and factories, and by destroying the home as a productive unit, modern life had abolished the value of children. Instead of being economic assets they became liabilities, and so the birthrate had been falling steadily since 1810. Children were nevertheless women's power in the world. Women without children were like men without penises. Thus modern life had deeply wounded women's libidinal organization and made them ever more neurotic. The principal manifestation of this neurosis was feminism, which attempted to convert their tragedy into a triumph by saying that modern conditions had freed women from the burdens of child-rearing.

Lundberg and Farnham conceded that feminists had some reason to be discontented in the past, but the burden of their argument was that feminism was a destructive compensation for women's mutilated procreational capacity. Beginning with a vicious attack on Mary Wollstonecraft, whose unhappy life afforded the authors numerous opportunities for invective— man-hater, power-driven, puritanical, anti-sex, classic case of penis envy—they went on to explore exhaustively the psychopathology of feminism. Deriving its ideology from Mary Wollstonecraft's neurotic effusions, and its emotional drive from thwarted motherhood, feminism culminated in the Russian Revolution, which put into effect its most monstrous precepts. The Soviets, however, discovered it to be virtually unworkable, and now discouraged it at home while promulgating it abroad to the confusion of their enemies. In America, although feminism still had great prestige, it had been a demonstrable failure in two ways. First, "the social and political program failed because it is not in the capacity of the female organism to attain feelings of well-being by the route of male achievement. . . . It was the error of the feminists that they attempted to put women on the essentially male road of exploit, off the female road of nurture." [7] So much for women's century of struggle and the thousands who wore out their lives in its service. Secondly, "the ideology of hatred directed against the men failed . . . because it rested on a faulty analysis of what the fundamental trouble for women was." Extreme feminists called for sex freedom when what they needed was the freedom to have babies. Thus, "the more they attained outward 'sex freedom,' the less successful were they in achieving inner sexual gratification."

Feminism had, therefore, only aggravated the condition of women which it was intended to improve. What was needed to arrest the plunging birthrate and redirect women to their proper biological and psychic destiny was a national program of psychiatric care, a mighty campaign to make domesticity popular, and devices to encourage propagation and discourage contraception. All bachelors over thirty years of age should be required to see a therapist, and tax penalties ought to be laid against them. Mothers should be encouraged to teach in the public schools, and spinsters forbidden by law from teaching, not only as an inducement to motherhood but to save the children from their perverted ministrations. At this point, having done all that bad taste and insensitivity could do, the authors rested their case.

One does not have to be a feminist to grasp the shortcomings of the Lundberg and Farnham argument. For one thing, since the declining birthrate was the pivot on which their entire analysis swung, the population explosion that was visibly underway in 1947 when their paperback edition came out destroyed their case. If women were neurotic because they had too few babies, when their output shot up they were either cured, or, more likely, the whole argument was nonsense to

7. Ferdinand Lundberg and Marynia F. Farnham, *Modern Woman: The Lost Sex* (New York, 1947), pp. 173–174.

begin with. Yet if this type of Freudianizing was unprovable when not demonstrably false, the message was still potent at a time when millions of women were plunging headlong down the road to domesticity. It gave them reasons for eschewing competition with men in school or office, it discredited the achievements of public women, and it depressed the level of feminine aspiration. With Dr. Farnham the wheel had turned full circle: the social sciences which had once stood with emancipated women against the conventional wisdom were now pressed into its service. The worst features of traditional anti-feminism—bigotry, meanness, a brutal contempt for the dreams of others—were combined with the most meretricious aspects of popular psychology, sociology, and anthropology to form a rationale for women's retreat from greatness, if not actually their resubjugation.

Throughout the forties and fifties, then, middle-class American women gave themselves over to the higher domesticity. This was not simply a matter of rhetoric and ideology, of the feminine mystique's domination of the social sciences and mass media, but, as we have already seen, a matter of actual fact. Women married earlier and had more children than in the 1920's. The percentage of employed women who were professional workers declined from 15 per cent in 1930 to less than 11 per cent in 1960, even though this was a growing sector of the work force.[8] More women went to college, but they were a smaller part of the total enrollment. And so it went. Most striking of all, perhaps, was the inability of the female population to produce truly great women on the order of Elizabeth Cady Stanton, Carrie Chapman Catt, Florence Kelley, and Jane Addams. With the death of Eleanor Roosevelt, an entire generation of splendid public women had passed away leaving no heirs. Not that individual women failed to distinguish themselves in this period, but not one of them achieved

8. Ethel J. Alpenfels, "Women in the Professional World," in Beverly Benner Cassara, ed., *American Women: The Changing Image* (Boston, 1962), pp. 73–89.

the stature of that brilliant galaxy who made the American woman the envy of her sisters before World War I. In part, of course, the comparatively mediocre attainments of American women in the Truman-Eisenhower era reflected the general drabness of those years. At a time when novelists and social scientists were describing the typical middle-class American as a security-obsessed conformist (*The Man in the Gray Flannel Suit*, *The Organization Man*, *The Lonely Crowd*), celebrating *The End of Ideology*, and characterizing college students as *The Silent Generation*, it was hardly to be expected that women would display contrasting attributes. Educated women were expected to be young, attractive, sexually agile, fertile, bright, but not too bright, and most of them struggled gallantly to live up (or down) to these ideals.

. . . .

The consequences of their docility were not nearly so agreeable as might have been supposed. When the postwar era drew to a close, the position of American women became again the subject of critical attention. In part this was a reaction to the unnatural repression of feminine ambitions—which could not be forever endured. It also was stimulated by the country's renewed interest in quality and achievement—excellence was the preferred term—occasioned by the Soviet Union's unexpected triumphs in space. Americans became aware again of a vast, untapped reservoir of feminine ability—a point underlined by the Soviets, who in putting not only the first man but the first woman in space reminded us that a society that neglects the talents of half its population does so at its own peril. It was becoming evident that despite the national emphasis on security and happiness, the folkways of the fifties had produced neither, especially among the women whose life styles had been most affected by the postwar climate of opinion.

The initial shots in the second war for feminine independence (if that is not too strong a term for what is still a modest affair) went virtually unnoticed. In 1959 Eleanor Flexner's *Century of Struggle,* the first professional history of the woman's rights movement, with its implicit call to arms, received little attention except from scholars. In the same year Mabel Newcomer published her *A Century of Higher Education for American Women,* which avoided the usual self-congratulations and firmly declared that while women had done well in the past, their relative position in the academic world was in decline and that nothing was being done—especially by the women's colleges—about it. Also in the same year Robert Smuts's excellent study, *Women and Work in America,* drew attention to the fact that "the picture of women's occupations outside the home has changed since 1890 in only a few essentials." [9] Subsequent research has demonstrated that even in the matter of sex discrimination this is literally the case. Professor Edward Gross recently discovered that the degree of sexual segregation is almost the same today as it was at the turn of the century, for once women infiltrate an occupation in substantial numbers men usually leave it.[1] In 1961 David Potter, the distinguished social historian, in a series of lectures at Stetson University explored the reasons behind what he clearly saw as woman's present discontent. He began by describing the crucial transformation in woman's condition when they found work outside the home. "Once a woman possessed access to such earning power, whether she used it or not, the historic basis for her traditional subordination had been swept away." [2]

The machine, by compensating for the deficiency in muscular strength that was woman's principal organic handicap in competition with men, had in fact equalized their condition.

9. Robert Smuts, *Women and Work in America* (New York, 1959), p. 35.

1. Edward Gross, *"Plus Ca Change* . . . The Sexual Structure of Occupations over Time," a paper delivered at the American Sociological Association meeting in 1967.

2. David Potter, "American Women and the American Character," *Stetson University Bulletin,* LXII (January 1962), 5.

But its leveling effects had not been as great in practice as in theory they should have been. The demise of subsistence farming, which had transformed men from producers to wage-earners, had only changed women from processors to consumers. While this was in some respects advantageous to them, the advertising industry and its allies treated the consumer as an object of flattery, as a target for bullying, and as anything but a mature adult. Thus her increased purchasing power involved an actual loss of dignity and self-respect. The woman who was once exploited as a female was now exploited as a consumer.

> The essential strength of her position has increased, but the combined effect of the manipulation by the media and the emphasis upon monetary earning as a standard for the valuation of work has threatened her with a new kind of subordination, imposed by the system of values which she herself accepts, rather than by masculine values imposed upon her against her will.[3]

It seemed to Potter, therefore, that the actual improvement of women's status had not been matched by a corresponding improvement in their morale because of conflicts between "the principle of equality, which denies a difference, and the practice of wifehood and motherhood which recognizes a difference in the roles of men and women." The tension between these two produced the current discontent. A little later the psychologist Bruno Bettelheim described the position of women in this way: "Our educational system has ostensibly prepared them for a kind of liberated marital and occupational life that in fact rarely exists in our society; at the same time it celebrates the values of an antiquated form of marriage inherited from a time when wives were prepared for little else." A girl was educated in the same way as a boy, "but the girl is made to feel that she must undergo precisely the same training only because she may need it if she is a failure—an unfortunate

3. *Ibid.*, p. 19.

who somehow cannot gain admission to the haven of marriage and motherhood where she properly belongs." [4]

In 1961 President Kennedy formed a Commission on the Status of Women. Many states followed his example, the implication being that the status of women was somehow dubious. The growing sense that the woman question, which presumably had been answered in the postwar era, was still alive was quickened by the emergence of a new generation of young activists. Large numbers of women participated in the civil rights movement, joined the Peace Corps, marched, demonstrated, sat in, sat down, and generally woke up. Much of this went beyond the traditional social-feminist-nurture complex and involved genuine heroism. True, young women did not join in their generation's great adventure as women; the feminist stirrings in this collective impulse were barely noticeable. But their enthusiasm demonstrated the conventional wisdom's inadequacies precisely because in the freedom movement there was no special role for women. They voted with their feet, as it were, demonstrating in practice that they were prepared to run the same risks and fight for the same ends as men. The argument for feminine uniqueness was therefore dealt a mighty blow even though, or rather because, the point rarely came up.

Thus, by 1963 conditions were ripe for Betty Friedan's splendid polemic, *The Feminine Mystique*. If there is to be a new feminism, Mrs. Friedan has to be its Mary Wollstonecraft. Her central point is similar to David Potter's, that women are unhappy because the opportunities provided by their emancipation have been frustrated by an anti-feminist and reactionary ideology. Mrs. Friedan differs from Professor Potter in seeing this, as a good agitator must, as the product of conspiratorial forces. Potter emphasized that domestic pressure is generated to a great extent by women themselves, that it is not an alien doctrine imposed for reasons of masculine self-interest. Mrs. Friedan is inclined to see the whole thing as a plot concocted

4. Bruno Bettelheim, "Growing Up Female," *Harper's*, CCXXV (October 1962), 121.

by greedy advertisers, sex-directed educators, and the like. This gives her a strident tone which many find offensive, and, to the extent that she is in thrall to the conspiratorial vision, her book suffers. But matters of tone and style aside, Mrs. Friedan's case is well documented, strongly argued, and, while anything but dispassionate or judicial, very persuasive. Great social and intellectual changes rarely come about by design, as she implies, but her facts speak for themselves. That Mrs. Friedan was unhappy, or that her classmates were, does not of itself prove anything—happiness being a relative matter. But the comparative position of women in the whole society had deteriorated considerably by the time she wrote her tract, the feminine mystique did exist, and the growing sense of unease to which she spoke needed only something like her book to crystallize.

The controversy Mrs. Friedan provoked still continues, demonstrating that the problems she discussed trouble many more people than had been guessed. There is more interest today in the history of women than at any time since the feminist movement decayed. Television programs investigate the subject in one way or another, and an abundant post-Friedan literature, of which the *Daedalus* special issue on women is an outstanding example, now exists.[5] In a practical way, a great many centers or institutes for the continuing education of women have been established, usually in connection with colleges or universities, to meet the growing demand of older women for a second chance at careers interrupted by marriage and child-rearing.

Not all of the response to the new feminism has been favorable, but much of the critical work has itself tended to support rather than refute it. A good example is the book *Life Styles of Educated Women* by Eli Ginzberg, *et al.* This study grew out of an earlier attempt to investigate talented people; it had to be divided when it was discovered that talented men

5. Published in book form as Robert Jay Lifton, ed., *The Woman in America* (Boston, 1967).

and women had such different lives as to require separate treatment. What finally emerged purported to be a value-free analysis of the way extremely gifted women live. The basic data came from an extensive questionnaire filled out by women who had been high-achievers in the graduate school of Columbia University during the years 1946–1951. An elite group to begin with, drawn mainly from the white, Protestant, upper middle class, most of them were married to equally high-status males. Fifty-five per cent of them had at least one graduate degree, and three-quarters of their husbands were similarly blessed.

The first thing the book pointed out was that the career pattern of men "followed a relatively simple and straightforward pattern compared with the much more complex career and life patterns characteristic of the majority of our women." [6] Whereas men followed a smooth track through college and into careers, women got off the track. On graduating from college they had more choices to make than the simple one of which career to choose, and thereafter they had to balance contradictory demands in ways men were rarely required to do. This was, of course, what women had been complaining about for generations, but to Ginzberg and his associates it was no problem at all. The whole thing was a matter of incorrect terminology. The poor and the disadvantaged had problems, while educated women faced "options." They could have careers, or they could marry and have careers, or they could get married, have children, and still pursue careers—if they were resourceful enough. Their multiple choices posed difficulties, of course, but not problems.

With this out of the way it was possible to show how women chose among their options, and the many things that happened to them as a result. A few clear facts emerged from this inquiry. A great many of the women never married—28 per cent of the group were spinsters, four and a half times the

6. Eli Ginzberg, *et al.*, *Life Styles of Educated Women* (New York, 1966), pp. 4–5.

national average—which resolved that particular difficulty. While 70 per cent of the women worked at least half of their adult lives, only about 50 per cent had successful careers, mainly because they did not spend enough time at it. Fortunately, their happiness rating ("schema of satisfaction") was very good. Less than one out of ten were dissatisfied with all aspects of their lives, while three out of four were satisfied with their lives as a whole. Ninety per cent were satisfied with at least one area of their lives. Thus, "there is little in our analysis to support the widespread belief that most educated women are trapped in situations which create frustration and disappointment and that it is the rare woman indeed who is able to fulfill her potentiality. The opposite is much closer to the truth." [7] But since the authors had already shown that relatively few of these gifted women enjoyed the professional success of their male peers, they had clearly fulfilled other sorts of potentialities than those which had distinguished them as graduate students—which was simply another way of expressing the feminine mystique. Even given the self-fulfilling character of this study, it did not really support its own conclusions. And, if one wanted to play the happiness game, what was to be made of the study conducted by Dr. Genevieve Knupfer, a psychiatrist at the Mental Research Institute in Berkeley, of 785 adults?

> On the basis of intensive interviews she discovered that when it came to happiness, high spirits, and job satisfaction, married and single women scored the same, while married men were the happiest of all.[8]

Happiness apart, Ginzberg *et al.* did show that the social return from their subjects' education was unimpressive. This becomes even more evident if one looks at the next level down from Ginzberg's intellectual elite: the graduates of prominent women's colleges. Once seedbeds of feminism, they had begun

7. *Ibid.*, p. 142.
8. "No Tears, Married Men—You're Happy!," *Boulder Daily Camera*, March 27, 1966, p. 1.

to harvest a different kind of crop in the thirties. The *New York Times Magazine* made a survey of the class of 1934 from seven leading women's colleges fifteen years after graduation.[9] It discovered that only 12 per cent of the women had been regularly employed since graduation. They earned $3,790 a year on the average. The 82 per cent of the class which married, however, had husbands earning $9,800 a year. From a financial point of view alone, marriage was clearly more rewarding than spinsterhood. The *Times* study as a whole failed to indicate any other way in which college had been of permanent value to these graduates. They read more than uneducated women—thirty-nine books a year, mainly novels and the like. They subscribed to five magazines, with *Time*, the *New Yorker*, and the *Reader's Digest* preferred. Seventy per cent of the graduates thought that college had increased their political awareness, but only about 20 per cent participated in any kind of political activity—usually with the League of Women Voters. Although these figures vary greatly depending on the institution whose graduates are questioned, the length of time since graduation, and so forth, similar studies have produced roughly similar results. Perhaps the most sobering of them all was the University of Michigan's Survey Research Center's discovery that the average college-trained housewife devoted but twelve minutes a day more to educational activities than the uneducated housewife.[1]

There is no escaping the fact, therefore, that society's return on its heavy investment in higher education for women has diminished over the years. A similar decline is apparent in the job market, where more and more women are employed to less and less effect. As Mary D. Keyserling points out, the percentage of workers who are women is steadily increasing. It is

9. John Willig, "Class of '34 (Female) Fifteen Years Later," *New York Times Magazine*, June 12, 1949, pp. 10–.

1. Daryl J. Bem and Sandra L. Bem, "Training the Woman to Know Her Place," an unpublished paper delivered at the Delaware Governor's Conference on the Status of Women, April 8, 1967.

estimated that by 1970 the female sector of the work force will have increased by 17 per cent as compared with a projected 9 per cent increase in the number of working men. But this increase in women workers is weighted in the direction of unskilled or semi-skilled jobs. The percentage of professional, technical, and other skilled jobs which women hold has been declining since 1947, while the percentage of service workers who are women has increased from 44 to 54 per cent, and the percentage of clerical workers from 60 to 70 per cent.[2] This despite the fact that the percentage of women with college degrees in the female work force has been increasing of late, and it is estimated that by 1980, 75 per cent of all women college graduates will be employed. In consequence of their low occupational status, the dollar gap between male and female workers, which has been widening for twenty-five years, continues to grow. In 1963 the income of working women was only 59 per cent of the average male income, even though the woman worker who retires at age sixty-two has typically been employed for thirty-three years, only four less than the male.

Such facts cannot be blurred over with schemas of satisfaction and the like. Whether they know it or not, American women are an exploited sector of the work force; they contribute in measurable terms far less to society than their education warrants; and their objective position is generally inferior to that of women in other developed countries. The failure of feminism has had immense repercussions in this respect. Whatever else is responsible for educated woman's dilemma today, the collapse of the feminist movement and the ideology, imperfect as it was, that supported it, has had a greater impact than anyone would have dared guess fifty years ago. Perhaps this will continue to be the case. Women are stirring today as they have not for generations. There seems to be a renewed interest in achievement on their part, and articulate spokesmen

2. Mary Dublin Keyserling, "Facing the Facts About Women's Lives Today," in *New Approaches to Counseling Girls in the 1960's* (Washington, D.C., 1966), pp. 2–10.

like Mrs. Friedan and her National Organization for Women have begun to make themselves heard. But if this new feminism, if such it be, is to fare better than the old, it will have to take a much closer look at the feminine experience in this country than it now shows any sign of doing. It might be helpful, therefore, to review what the evidence of this book seems to indicate.

10

. . . .
*an end
and a
beginning*

Only a few years ago this effort to explain the failure of American feminism would have seemed absurd, if not actually perverse. Everyone knew that the feminist movement had dissolved because its purposes had been accomplished. Women had won the vote, gained access to virtually all the important occupational categories, and had secured everything—perhaps more than everything—a reasonable sex could desire. As the preceding chapter demonstrated, this line of reasoning is much the same as the homily that socialism prevails in America because of social security and medicare. In both cases certain planks have been taken for the whole platform. Equal suffrage did not make women equal to men in fact, any more than social security produced a welfare state. We have only to compare American women with their counterparts in advanced European countries to appreciate how far behind they have fallen. It is not just in socialist Russia that women comprise a large part of the professions and hold high public offices, nor only in social democracies like Sweden; even in fairly traditional countries like England women make a more important contribution to the public welfare than in America.[1] Yet not too long ago conditions were just the opposite, and American women with their great organizations, high level of education, and enterprising spirit were the envy of feminists the world over.

In trying to account for this change I have concentrated on the woman's rights movement, on certain organizations that appealed to emancipated women, and on the body of assumptions, ideas, prejudices, and hopes upon which these groups rested. The woman movement in its broadest sense originated in what Jane Addams called "subjective necessity." Women first came together in local societies, church groups, and the like because of their own needs. But almost immediately they started elaborating on the "objective necessity" that had called their organizations into being: those social ills that women could best remedy. The men who supported feminist activities often did so because they believed it was good for women, because it would make them better persons, or better mothers, or, as Floyd Dell put it, better companions. The emancipated woman "became like us, like what the world we worked in had made us, for good or ill—more interested in ideas, more honest, and less finicking."[2] Of course, the fickle male was often unhappy with the results. Dell learned that emancipated women were not interested in becoming the "glorious play-fellows" that he and his friends desired.

> They wanted Happiness—the happiness that comes from being a freely expressive and largely active personality. And they did not find it in the outside world into which they had so confidently burst—not at college, nor in the professions, nor on the stage, nor in settlement work. We had not

1. A curious exception to this general rule is their performance as artists since the late 1950's, when what had always been a male monopoly was broken by a remarkable group of women. The ambiguous consequences of this event are explored in Bernard Rosenberg and Norris Fliegel, *The Vanguard Artist: Portrait and Self-Portrait* (Chicago, 1965).

2. Floyd Dell, *Intellectual Vagabondage: An Apology for the Intelligentsia* (New York, 1926), pp. 138–139.

expected that they would. We thought they would be content with the joy of struggle. But they needed the joy of achievement.[3]

Randolph Bourne, who like Dell had been an enthusiastic admirer of the New Woman, came to much the same conclusions. Christopher Lasch tells us that by the end of Bourne's life "his disillusionment with feminism seems to have become complete." Certainly this is the burden of his essay on "Karen," in which the feminist is shown to be self-absorbed and anti-masculine to an extraordinary degree.[4]

Although these qualities may have distinguished extreme feminists, the striking thing about organized women was the degree to which they upheld the traditional womanly concern for altruism and benevolence, to the point where almost everything they did was justified in these terms. Men easily came together in labor unions, trade and professional associations, and political groups which frankly appealed to the members' desire for power, profit, or protection, and no one thought the less of them for it. Women were rarely able to organize on such a casual basis. Society discouraged them from pursuing their own advantage, and few of them wished to in any case. Thus the double standard of morals did not mean simply that men enjoyed sexual advantages denied to women, but also that masculine activities were self-justifying while women had always to identify themselves with the highest moral and social good to excuse even relatively modest enterprises. In order to break with the Victorian definition of appropriate female behavior, they had to invoke it. If woman's nature was understood to be spiritual, self-denying, and supportive, then to be acceptable her public activities had to partake of, or embody, these characteristics. In some ways this had admirable results. Organized women in the nineteenth century were quite correct

3. *Ibid.*, p. 139.
4. Christopher Lasch, *The New Radicalism in America, 1889–1963* (New York, 1965), p. 95. "Karen, a Portrait," *New Republic*, September 23, 1916, pp. 187–188.

in thinking they sustained a higher ethical standard than men. The national well-being was immeasurably strengthened by their contributions as teachers, social workers, reformers, clubwomen, and philanthropists. But ultimately social feminism had a fatal effect on the woman movement for two important reasons. In the first place, by driving extreme feminists underground it prevented women from coming to grips with the conditions that made their emancipation necessary, that is, with the domestic system itself. Radical feminism of the Stanton-Anthony type was important not because it embraced a variety of causes, although it did, but because it was ruthlessly self-centered and potentially capable of grappling with the essential sources of women's disadvantaged state.

These women demonstrated their ruthlessness by refusing to admit that the Negroes' needs were greater than their own. They proved their radicalism by challenging briefly the marital and domestic institutions that insured their practical inferiority. The failure of radical feminism was, perhaps, the decisive event in the history of American women. It meant the development of feminism as a vaguely reformist influence. Susan B. Anthony had properly called her periodical the *Revolution*, for she and her friends wanted to revolutionize the American domestic system. Not only did they propose to get at the roots of woman's oppressed condition, but they also had that narrow dedication to the interests of one's own group, and that willingness to sacrifice the interests of others, that distinguishes revolutionary leaders.

After Reconstruction, and after the Woodhull affair, social feminism displaced radical feminism, and while social feminism had its virtues it was incapable of coping with those customs and institutions that prevented women from securing the advantages and opportunities enjoyed by men as a matter of course. This was not just because social feminists were reasonable and fair-minded women eager to avoid discord and reconcile conflicting interests, aware of the needs of others, responsible and moderate in their demands, but because their entire rationale precluded the attainment of genuine equality. By justifying their activities on the grounds that society was an extension of the home and woman's work in it merely an enlargement of her maternal powers, social feminists froze the domestic status quo. In effect they declared that it was not marriage and the family that needed to be changed, only certain social malformations that were inconsistent with the domestic ideal. Yet because it was the obligations imposed on women by their marital and familial roles that prevented them from achieving full equality, social feminism was far more social than feministic. In fact, it sacrificed full emancipation to the social reforms that public-spirited, middle-class women thought most important. In reality, then, the cause of women's rights and that broad, amorphous impulse which contemporaries called the woman movement were quite distinct, and in some respects, incompatible phenomena. As we have seen, when equal suffrage no longer served to bind them together, their contradictions became manifest. It was quite true, as Dr. Howes pointed out in 1929, that the woman question had never been answered, for the simple reason that the great majority of women were afraid, unconsciously at least, to ask it. The Stanton-Anthony group had raised it with results so frightening that generations of women labored to prevent the event from ever recurring.

The second way that social feminism worked against the long-range interests of the woman movement concerned the expectations it encouraged. Extreme feminists had promised that the vote would secure desirable results, but the heart of their case was that, as a matter of justice, women were entitled to the same rights that men enjoyed, all apart from whatever useful consequences emancipation might produce. When women's rights were justified in terms of the good they would do, however, they became conditional rather than absolute. Social feminists wedded their interests as women to their concerns as reformers, little realizing that this made the one contingent upon the other. Of course, in the late nineteenth century this strategy seemed the most obvious kind of common sense. Feminists did not think there was any risk involved in predicting the great social advances they were certain would follow women's emancipation. Since they failed to appreciate how difficult it would be to advance even the smallest welfare programs, it was hardly to be expected that they would appreciate the effect of unsuccessful reforms upon themselves. It was only after the movement was disintegrating that some feminists apprehended the deadly relationship between social reform and women's rights, and by then, as the experience of the Woman's party demonstrated, it was too late. Social feminism put the case for emancipation in pragmatic terms—women ought to be liberated because they would then accomplish great reforms. Unfortunately, pragmatism cuts both ways. If the results by which a thing is to be judged are inadequate, then the thing itself is at fault. Social feminists in the postwar era were victims of their own logic. Having failed to deliver the goods as promised, they were in no position to demand that young women rally round a program that was, if not discredited, at least eminently discardable.

There is a special irony, therefore, in the fact that the most admired (and most admirable) aspects of the woman movement were precisely those that contributed to its downfall. This is true even though the subjective consequences of social feminism were very good indeed. Whatever else emerges from a close examination of organizations like the Federation of Settlements and the GFWC, it is indisputable that the women themselves were better for having worked in them. Even if these groups had not reached a single one of their goals—and this was far from being the case—millions of women were stimulated, enriched, and sensitized by them in a variety of ways, and this was of itself sufficient reason for their existence. But organized women aimed much higher than this, and the greater their aspirations the more disappointing their performance. It was not by accident that the organizations which flourished in the postsuffrage era were either narrowly directed at realizable goals, like the AAUW, or capable of generating enough internal satisfactions to compensate for programmatic failures, as was the General Federation.

In this sense, then, the privatized young women of the twenties drew the appropriate conclusions from their mothers' experience. They learned from the AAUW and, for a time, from the Woman's party that to help others you must first help yourself. From the suffragists and pacifists and social workers they learned to guard against disappointment by not embarking on those great crusades that recent history had shown to be so heartbreakingly difficult. Since feminism had been most successful in knocking down obstacles and opening doors to individual opportunity, the postsuffrage generation believed that conditions had never been better for self-fulfillment and never worse for collective action. This was indeed the case, and while the Woman's party repeatedly drew attention to the many laws and customs that made an equal-rights amendment necessary, it was clear that the lack of one did not prevent women of talent and energy from realizing their ambitions to a considerable degree—especially since these ambitions were becoming more modest. We can see now that the postsuffrage generation misjudged the extent to which real equality had been secured. Still, their position was sounder than that of the old feminists who could do nothing more than repeat the irrelevant propositions of a bankrupt tradition. Even the Woman's party, which more than any other group appreciated the work that needed to be done and understood that the struggle for social justice had been, from a feminist point of view, diversionary and unproductive, was dominated by the same narrow legalism that had led feminists to overinvest so heavily in equal suffrage. What was needed was a fundamental re-evaluation of women's role in American life, and no organization was then capable of such an effort. The young women of the twenties took the only road open to them, never thinking that this marked the beginning of a retreat which was to continue down to our time.

And yet, no one who has studied the feminists for any

length of time can end on this dim note. While feminism did fail to achieve real equality for American women, who are likely to enjoy an inferior status until either our domestic institutions are radically reconstructed, or until a genuine social democracy that will give women truly equal opportunities is built, the woman movement itself wrote a bright passage in our history. It produced magnificent individuals like Elizabeth Cady Stanton and Carrie Chapman Catt and drew out brave deeds and bold thoughts from women who would otherwise never have known what they were capable of. If the achievement of social feminists fell short of their dreams, if the good society managed to elude them, they still left the country a better place than they found it. The bills they passed, the lives they saved, the social wounds they helped to heal speak for them more eloquently than any words can. From Jane Addams down to the most obscure clubwoman, they gave themselves to causes whose intrinsic value no man can question. If, as I have suggested, they did so at considerable expense to their interests as women, this is all the more impressive.

It might be argued that the feminism of a Florence Kelley or a Lillian Wald was not what enabled these women to advance the public welfare. The fact is, however, that these great women were feminists, and that since the collapse of feminism no women have enjoyed such commanding positions. Eleanor Roosevelt appears to have been the last representative of the heroic tradition. This is not to denigrate the accomplishments of women since 1930. Dozens of examples readily come to mind of individuals and groups that have contributed to our well-being. Yet no group of women has since had the impact that settlement workers and suffragists made on their time, and no single woman has achieved the stature of the great line of women with whom this book has been concerned. There is no doubt in my mind that the feminist context was crucial to their greatness. They did not function as isolated individuals in the way exceptional women now seem to do, but as a part of a movement that, however loose or indistinct or contradictory it may have been, enriched and gave depth and meaning to their activities. This is what women have lost with the movement's passing, and it is hard to see that they have gained in consequence anything of equal value.

All the same, the prospects of American women appear a little brighter now than they have been for a generation or more. Not only has the literature on women's past and present status grown rapidly in the last few years, but in Betty Friedan's National Organization for Women (NOW) the NAWSA has found an heir. Equally interesting has been the emergence of a women's liberation movement to the left of NOW. Groups of militant feminists reminiscent of the Woman's party in its youth have appeared in New York City, Berkeley, and Madison, Wisconsin. They sent pickets to Atlantic City, New Jersey, in 1968 to protest against the false image of American womanhood presented by the Miss America Pageant. Women students from Barnard and Sarah Lawrence colleges joined the men of Columbia University in occupying campus buildings during the great demonstrations of that year. When they were assigned as kitchen police while the men got on with the revolution's grimmer business, they rose up crying, "Liberated women do not cook," and forced an equal division of housekeeping chores in the occupied buildings.[5]

These events may only fortify the maxim that history always repeats itself, first as tragedy and then as farce, or it may signal a feminist renaissance. Other indications suggest a turn for the better in women's fortunes. The birthrate has declined of late and the average age at marriage risen. The pro-

5. An excellent account is Martha Weinman Lear, "The Second Feminist Wave," *New York Times Magazine*, March 10, 1968, pp. 24–. On the Women's Liberation Movement, see Peter Babcox, "Meet the Women of the Revolution, 1969," *New York Times Magazine*, February 9, 1969, pp. 24–. The radical student movement in Germany, where the position of women is even worse than in the United States, has also produced a left-feminism critical of masculine chauvinism within the movement as well as in the larger society. David Binder, "West German Women Protest Curbs," *New York Times*, September 15, 1968, p. 3.

portion of female graduate students has grown slightly. The University of Pennsylvania's placement service reports that for the first time in 1968, starting salaries for women graduates increased over the previous year at a greater rate than men's.[6] Whether or not these signs foreshadow another feminist springtime depends partially, of course, on those great social, demographic, and historical movements over which no one exercises any control. But it also depends to a degree on the decisions which people who believe in sexual equality make. I am not at all certain that the study of history contributes greatly to policy-making in this sense. For what it is worth, however, the history recorded in this volume suggests to me that at least three basic conditions must be satisfied if women are to become genuinely equal. (In all honesty, of course, it should also be admitted that the lesson of history so far is that women cannot gain equality regardless of the methods used to obtain it.) First, an efficient welfare state which compensates mothers for their service to society. Secondly, an ideology or animating ethos that will inspire women to exploit the opportunities thus secured. And, most importantly of all I suspect, if women are to be free they must engage in the kind of radical and profound analysis of themselves, their social context, and their possibilities which has been so conspicuously absent up to this point.

Sexual parity, not simply reforms within the existing system along Swedish lines but a genuinely functional equality, would mean revolutionizing our domestic life. Perhaps we do not want it, do not need it, and should not have it. Nonetheless, such a revolution is what equality presupposes. As we have seen, feminist thought on this question has been generally weak and evasive. If this feminist new wave continues to mistake rhetoric for theory in the traditional manner, it is not

6. Up 9.9 per cent as against 2.2 per cent for men. This may only reflect the large draft call of 1968; but other placement services have testified to a growing interest in women graduates on the part of many corporations even before the war in Vietnam was escalated. "Women's Salary Gains Held More Than Men's," *New York Times*, August 4, 1968, Sec. 3, p. 15.

likely to improve on its predecessors' example. On the other hand, if it produces someone who can do for the sexual struggle what Marx did for the class struggle, then the experience of the woman movement will not have been wasted. In that event, women would be no longer bound by their past but liberated from it with unimaginable consequences for the future of mankind.

afterword

. . . .

i first became interested in the history of women in 1963 as an outgrowth of my earlier work on the history of divorce. The study of feminism was then mainly an academic concern, and still was in 1967 when I completed my research. It was only when I started the second draft of my manuscript in 1968 that feminism began showing signs of life again. This was just in time for me to take account of that fact, but the book went to press before women's liberation was far enough advanced to generalize about. It is still a young movement, hardly four years old, but enough has happened since 1969 to make a few more remarks in order.

As a historian, what I first notice about feminism today is the extent to which it resembles the original movement. Mrs. Friedan's NOW is a true heir of the NAWSA. It is largely made up of educated, middle-class, white women of comparatively moderate views. Like the NAWSA, it is strongly political and interested chiefly in legal and insitutional reforms. But, also like the NAWSA, it is capable of embracing a broad spectrum of issues, personalities, and interests. If feminism develops real power, NOW will almost certainly deserve much of the credit. Where the NAWSA concentrated on votes for women, NOW has lately given high priority to the equal-rights amendment. As in the 1920's, however, this is proving divisive. Congress is more friendly to the amendment than before, but organized labor and some radical feminists still think it will deny working women legal protections without giving them new opportunities of comparable value. On the other hand, NOW has had some success in getting existing legislation enforced more vigorously. And certain employers, notably universities, are being told to equalize opportunities for women faculty and staff if they wish to retain federally funded contracts.

As before, a number of smaller women's organizations have moved left. Some radical feminists are entirely concerned with women's rights, some with the oppressions women share with others—the poor and black especially. Pure feminists have taken extreme steps—learning karate, abstaining from any but the most formal relations with men, and so on—far beyond what the Woman's party advocated. In spirit, though, militants of both eras have much in common. Some radical women resemble social feminists in putting the interests of other disadvantaged people ahead of their own, or at least on the same plane. Women of generous sympathies are still likely to assign themselves a lower priority in the hierarchy of social need. Some even deny that women have any problems to speak of compared with the truly poor and disadvantaged. This has produced the usual diffusion of effort and raised fears that in attempting again to do everything, radical women will succeed at nothing.

All these patterns are familiar enough. Like circumstances produce like reactions. Since the condition of women is much as it was fifty or sixty years ago, contemporary responses resemble past ones. There is bound to be confusion and uncertainty. Women will disagree on what, if anything, has to be done, and will divide along lines of interest and ideology. Those who think their problems a consequence of the capitalist system will become revolutionaries, those who feel male chauvinism is at fault will turn against men and rely more on one another—sometimes to the point of celibacy, or even homosexuality. And, as always, women will seek models appropriate to their convictions. The Woman's party copied English suffragettes. Radical feminists now look to groups like the Weathermen and the Black Panthers for inspiration. When these models are unsuitable, which they mostly are, only failure can result.

If this were all there was to contemporary feminism, we might expect little from it. But liberated women have shown strength in certain areas where the old feminism was weakest. Laws, customs, and prejudices keep women down, yet even when they don't women still find equality hard to get. There are many reasons for this, but chief among them are the sexual relationships and roles that make women responsible for domestic life. As we saw, some feminists have always known this. Elizabeth Cady Stanton and her associates raised the marriage question, but with such results that leading feminists never again dared confront the issue openly. Celibacy, lesbianism, childless marriages, and the delay of careers until middle age were the most common solutions feminists arrived at. These were all personal accommodations, however, and did not help women as a whole. And each required sacrifice. Though inadequate, they were probably the best women could do at a time when spinsterhood and monogamy were the only practical alternatives.

Affluence and more relaxed sexual norms have created new opportunities of late, and some liberated women have taken advantage of them. Free love and lesbianism have gotten the most publicity, but they are neither very new nor, probably, very important. Common-law marriages pose nearly all the problems that legal marriages do, and though participants may feel freer, in practice most might just as well be married. Lesbianism is helpful now, as in the past, to certain women. But the most useful aspect of it is not so much the practice as the acceptance of female homosexuality. Few women are likely to find lesbianism the solution to their problems. Yet by erasing the stigma associated with it, women may more easily work together and cultivate the sisterly affections on which feminism depends. And by sanctioning lesbianism, feminists disarm one kind of enemy. When liberated women first appeared a few years ago they were often called lesbians, to their dismay. Experience has shown that the best response to such a charge is to claim that being homosexual makes no difference. This protects women from being divided according to sexual tastes. It helps straight women keep their poise under fire. A few prominent feminists recently acknowledged their homosexuality, or at least bisexuality, which was a step forward. But more vital have been the expressions of solidarity made by their straight sisters. Perhaps this will eliminate lesbianism as an issue and clear minds for larger tasks.

Chief among these is the reform of domestic life. Most women are not going to abandon marriage and motherhood for the sake of work. In a just society they would not have to. Sweden and other advanced countries have shown that welfare-state methods solve some problems, but not all of them. Women need equal pay for equal work, paid maternity leaves, child-care centers, and the like. But some also need more flexible domestic arrangements. There are sharp limits to what married couples can accomplish in this respect. A frequent demand is for husbands to do more work around the house. But husbands who already work full time will rarely find this an agreeable solution. A few couples have solved the problem by having each partner hold a part-time job. Still, only creative people, professionals, and a few other specialized types can manage this feat. In the long run what will be needed is an economy that defines jobs not only by skills and income but according to human satisfactions. This would mean making work itself more interesting, as well as creating more part-time jobs for both men and women. But in the short run other kinds of domestic arrangements may be needed. Communal living is one popular experiment. It is too early to say whether current efforts along these lines will turn out better than past ones. More modest solutions involve the sharing of domestic facilities without going so far as collective ownership, still less group marriage. One reason why Charlotte Perkins Gilman's ideas were never implemented is that they required too large a capital investment. It may turn out that groups of families can achieve the same results in more homely ways.

Apart from these ventures, another encouraging sign has

been the decline of career ambitions among many young people. It has always been true that great achievements are purchased at a great price. Successful women always had to give up many domestic pleasures, but so did successful men. Where career expectations are lower, however, it should be possible to have one's cake and eat it too. This is not said pejoratively. Feminists used to argue that emancipated women would infuse society with what are always thought to be feminine virtues—pacifism, nurture, cooperation, life-centeredness. This hope was blighted, partly because women didn't quite know how to launch the process, mostly because men were so unresponsive. Now many young men have declared themselves believers in these qualities, hence making possible domestic arrangements based on them. One can dimly sense the advent of a different style of life based not simply on feminist aspirations but on the desires of men also. This is a crucial point, for if what is wanted is a life-centered, pacific culture oriented toward personal development, then, as Alice Rossi puts it, "the real task of re-socialization that lies ahead may involve more change in the socialization of the American male than of the female." [1] If this is to be our new world, then clearly women are already better suited to it than men.

Only fools think such an outcome certain. Biology is still destiny for most women. Science has not yet made any of us better persons. There is no guarantee that the hopes raised by genetic engineering and similar fields will produce happier results than have scientific advances in the past. Values too have changed before without arresting the drift toward extinction so many think we are trapped in now. Even if these fears are overdrawn, it is obvious that a society which cannot presently even find work, however sterile, for all who want it is very far from reorganizing labor patterns to make them humanly rewarding. Yet that is the first requisite for a social order such as feminists envision. All the same, feminism must of necessity be utopian.

1. Alice S. Rossi, "Feminist Ideology and Politics," an unpublished paper given at the 1970 meeting of the American Historical Association.

If their history tells us nothing else it is that women will not be moved to great enterprises purely for gain. The old woman movement derived its strength not from the few who wanted an equal share in the present but from the many who dreamed of a better future. This is not to denigrate the militant feminists who were concerned solely with equal rights. Self-interest is always the prime mover of change. In the end, though, women want more than mere equality. Altruism, as we have seen, can be a source of weakness when it leads feminists to spread themselves too thinly over too many causes. Still, the hope of a richer life for everyone is, justice apart, feminism's best claim on the attention of mankind.

All this is, of course, for later. For the present women are mainly looking after themselves, and rightly so. Equal pay for equal work remains exceptional. Women are discriminated against in most desirable occupations. They remain too passive in the face of inequity. The most original device modern feminists have devised to make women sensible of being wronged, and to nerve them to protest, is the "consciousness-raising" or "rap" group. As we saw, women have been assembling for mutual support and to redress grievances for a long time. What distinguishes the consciousness-raising group is that it accomplishes by design what earlier was done by accident.

Women, more than men, have to work at maintaining close relations with each other. They compete for husbands. Marriage isolates them. They are conditioned to be unreservedly loyal to spouses and children. The difference here between men and women may be instinctual. Desmond Morris suggests that man was first a hunting animal.[2] As they hunted in packs, males could not allow competitiveness to impair teamwork. Male camaraderie functioned, then, as the lubricant which enabled men who were rivals in love to be colleagues at work. Females, on the other hand, were chiefly occupied with children. Pair-bonding had to be extra effective with them since their mates were frequently ab-

2. Desmond Morris, *The Naked Ape* (New York, 1967).

sent. Promiscuity was intolerable because it threatened ties on which the survival of the species depended. So, to a lesser extent, were relations with other females, and for the same reasons. But, as so often happens, drives persist even after the need for them has vanished. Child-rearing is not now a full-time job. Social changes have long since eroded the sharp distinction between hunting males and nurturing females. More androgynous sex roles are not only possible but perhaps even essential. The old tradition—instinct perhaps—of pair-bonding and female exclusiveness must give way if these new possibilities are to be realized.

This is why the consciousness-raising group has been devised. It begins with catharsis. Modern women have many grievances that need airing. Men are appalled, and women often astonished, to find so much rage struggling for expression. But as women have long been conceded in theory what they rarely obtain in practice, it would be surprising if they weren't full of anger and in need of expressing it. The next function of the group is to build those sororital ties on which the organization of women depends. Consciousness-raising groups have already accomplished both these objectives on a small scale. What remains to be seen is how broadly the process can be extended, and whether or not the energies thus mobilized can be turned to larger purposes.

Nor is it clear that the invidious patterns that afflicted women the last time around can be broken. However many reasons women have to be angry, and however much they need to bring that suppressed rage to the surface, it remains true that beyond certain limits hostility is self-defeating. As with the ballot, what women want are things that men must be made to give. This cannot be done simply by issuing manifestos and demands. Coercion is necessary at points, but so is persuasion. Name-calling (male chauvinist pig, and so forth) has little value. It has not helped the Black Panthers and will not do much for liberated women either.

A more serious problem is the tendency for feminists to find the work they do liberating of itself. Everyone is familiar with the successful career woman who, having solved her own problem, cannot understand why others complain. Less obvious is the successful activist who finds fulfillment in the movement and so takes the means for the end. The purpose of feminism, however, is not just to struggle but to win. When the fight itself becomes too satisfying, the chances of winning decline.

But so far feminists have done themselves more good than harm. It was thought silly of them to attack women's magazines. Yet two (*Ladies' Home Journal* and *Cosmopolitan*) have given them space to address millions of readers directly. Feminists have not had so large an audience since the old movement was at its peak, and perhaps not even then. Television has conceded less. Liberated women have appeared on many talk shows with mixed results. David Susskind invites feminists on his program to insult them. The more popular Dick Cavett still sees women's liberation as a comic subject, though told by Gloria Steinem, a writer and probably the most beautiful and fluent woman in the movement, that injustice is never funny. Men take the point where Negroes and other disadvantaged groups are concerned, but women's feelings are not yet regarded so seriously.

When levity fails to keep women down, stronger language is used. Men deny that women have a just claim. Some even argue, all evidence to the contrary, that women have more advantages than men. Nonetheless, feminists have made real gains. When Betty Friedan called for a day of demonstrations in August 1970 to draw attention to women's needs, many thousands responded. This was the strongest showing women have made on their own behalf since the suffrage was won. In many books and articles during the last few years, no feminist has reached the level of a Charlotte Perkins Gilman, still less a Simone de Beauvoir, but the level of quality is impressively high. Academicians have responded too. When *Everyone Was Brave* came out, the professional histories of women could be counted on the fingers of one hand. Now there are dozens of scholars, and graduate students who will soon be scholars, at work on them. Many universities offer courses in female studies, though none did only a few years ago. Some even hire women to teach them. 1970–1971 was the first academic year in memory when colleges actively sought women for faculty appointments.

While in one sense everything remains to be done, since most men are still hostile and suspicious and most women still unconverted, feminists have made remarkable progress. Two years ago the new woman movement was scarcely more than a promise. Now it is a reality. But it remains to be seen if feminists can escape from history. Organizing women will be nearly as hard in the future as it has been in the past. Even if middle-class women are galvanized, feminists will still need to reach working-class women, who were largely untouched by the original movement. And organization is only the first step. Beyond that is the need for reforms that will give women functional equality with men where they desire it. And after that is the greater challenge of building not simply a just society but a rewarding one in which all may share. The struggle will be a long one. Women may find, as blacks have, that once the easy, symbolic concessions are made, further advances come harder. That is no reason for despair. All great reforms require one to dare a lot to win a little. Human relations change slowly, but they do change. The first feminist wave produced a finer woman. The second one may form a better man. The chances of gain are so much brighter than a few years ago that only a cynic would foreclose any possibilities now, however unlikely they might seem. This book was originally sub-titled "The Rise and Fall of Feminism in America," a judgment that events have already voided. How many others are yet to be repealed?

index

· · · · · · · · · · · ·

73